"This theologically rich, warm, and personal look at a rare servant of the Lord is masterful. The range of R. C.'s vast interest and contribution, along with the irresistible charm of his personality, require a biographer who is a church historian, theologian, and very close friend. Stephen Nichols is the best choice, as this account demonstrates. He has brought to the pages a story truly revealing R. C.—an account that lives and breathes the man we loved as our teacher and friend. There will be other biographies of R. C., but I cannot imagine any that would come close to this one."

John MacArthur, Pastor, Grace Community Church, Sun Valley, California; Chancellor Emeritus, The Master's University and Seminary

"This book is worth your time because it celebrates a man worth remembering. R. C. was a masterful theologian who could so easily squeeze sweetness from what others considered dry doctrine. His sermons and books beautifully adorned the gospel, but so did his life. It's what I love about Stephen Nichols's remarkable work. He takes us behind the scenes to reveal the true makings of this great saint of the twentieth century, why his words endure, and why we are inexorably drawn to his live-large character. I've always admired R. C. Sproul for his razor-sharp mind; now, with this biography, he's printed on my heart. Thank you, Stephen Nichols, for helping the reader fall in love with this lion of a man, my friend, the good Doctor Sproul."

Joni Eareckson Tada, Founder, Joni and Friends International Disability Center

"I couldn't put this book down, for it doesn't just tell the fascinating story of a life well lived; it takes you on R. C.'s own journey. Through it you see where the fire came from. Through it you get the thrill of soaking up his passion for the gospel of Christ, for biblical truth, and for the beauty of God in his holiness. But my hope for this book is not that it might provide a nice reunion for those of us who knew and loved R. C.; my prayer is that the Lord might use it to inspire more faithful Reformers, more God-fearing defenders and proclaimers of the faith, more like R. C. Sproul."

Michael Reeves, President and Professor of Theology, Union School of Theology, UK

"I remember once hearing R. C. Sproul preach on Psalm 51, and I asked him afterward how long it had taken him to prepare his lecture that day. He smiled and said, 'About five minutes . . . and thirty years.' I have no doubt that future generations will benefit from R. C.'s prolific ministry two hundred years from now, should the Lord tarry. Stephen Nichols has given us a gift in this book. Anyone whose life was marked, as mine has been, by R. C.'s life and ministry will treasure getting to know him better through these pages."

Bob Lepine, Cohost, *FamilyLife Today*; Teaching Pastor, Redeemer Community Church, Little Rock, Arkansas

"I am thankful for this accessible biography of R. C. Sproul by Stephen Nichols. His clear and simple way of writing is certainly appropriate in his biography of a man who always sought to communicate the glorious theology of Scripture in a clear and simple way."

Burk Parsons, Senior Pastor, Saint Andrew's Chapel, Sanford, Florida; Editor, *Tabletalk*

"Stephen Nichols has written a fantastic biography about one of the greatest minds and finest teachers of our time. This book highlights the theology, biblical integrity, courage, character, and intellectual prowess of one the late giants of the modern-day church—a man who fought the good fight and had the honor of finishing well the race set before him by his Lord, whom he loved, revered, and worshiped all his life. R. C. immediately recognized when the gospel was at stake, and he applied his keen mind in defense of it, sometimes at great cost. It was a privilege and a delight to read about R. C. Sproul, one of the three men who have most influenced my thinking concerning the character of God in general and his piercing holiness in particular. I am indebted to him in so many ways."

Miguel Núñez, Senior Pastor, International Baptist Church, Santo Domingo, Dominican Republic; Founding President, Wisdom and Integrity Ministries

"Even though R. C. Sproul's name will stand in the annals of church history as one of its great theologians in the twentieth and twenty-first centuries, few people know about his life, career, struggles, victories, and ministries. This book will give you the historical and spiritual context around R. C.'s greatest series, books, and sermons. You will be able to understand the power of God's grace in R. C.'s life, R. C.'s dominion of all areas in systematic theology, and his ability to understand and teach biblical text in a simple and clear way. Knowing the man helps you better understand the preacher. Stephen Nichols has helped me get to know better the man that God has used to bless my ministry."

Augustus Nicodemus Lopes, Assistant Pastor, First Presbyterian Church, Recife, Brazil; Vice President, Supreme Council, Presbyterian Church of Brazil

"This book is about a man from a small town outside Pittsburgh who was chosen by God to teach, preach, and communicate the gospel to millions of people around the world. The Lord used this disciple of Jesus Christ in a mighty way. His ability to convey the word of God in simple yet powerful ways and his love and kindness toward his fellow man were evident throughout his life. His teaching ministry, books, and lessons have taught so many the truth and holiness of God. We miss him, but he fought the good fight, he finished the race, and he kept the faith as a servant to our holy God."

Robert M. Wohleber, Retired CFO, Kerr-McGee

"Stephen Nichols, an extraordinary scholar and exhaustive researcher, does an outstanding job portraying a man of intelligence, communicative ability, and love who devoted his life to Jesus Christ by teaching and preaching the inspiration and inerrancy of Scripture, the holiness of God, and the *solas*. R. C. was devoted to keeping the gospel pure, logical, and understandable for the laymen. The Holy Spirit, using R. C.'s time, patience, wit, and logic, without ever compromising biblical doctrine, led this 'heathen' lawyer and countless others to Jesus Christ. As Nichols so clearly illustrates in this biography of the life of a titan of the Christian faith, R. C.'s ministry will continue to 'count forever' for many as they live *coram Deo*."

Guy T. Rizzo, attorney

"Stephen Nichols is thorough, well-balanced, and theologically alert in this biography of R. C. Sproul. He writes the way R. C. lived and taught. Readers of R. C. and Reformation lovers will appreciate this story of the leader of Reformed revival for a new generation."

Russ Pulliam, Columnist, *Indianapolis Star*

R. C. SPROUL

Other Crossway books by Stephen J. Nichols

Ancient Word, Changing Worlds: The Doctrine of Scripture in a Modern Age, 2009 (coauthor)

Bible History ABCs: God's Story from A to Z, 2019

Bonhoeffer on the Christian Life: From the Cross, for the World, 2013

The Church History ABCs: Augustine and 25 Other Heroes of the Faith, 2010 (coauthor)

For Us and for Our Salvation: The Doctrine of Christ in the Early Church, 2007

Heaven on Earth: Capturing Jonathan Edwards's Vision of Living in Between, 2006

The Reformation: How a Monk and a Mallet Changed the World, 2007

Reformation ABCs: The People, Places, and Things of the Reformation—from A to Z, 2017

Welcome to the Story: Reading, Loving, and Living God's Word, 2011

R. C. SPROUL

A Life

STEPHEN J. NICHOLS

WHEATON, ILLINOIS

Library of Congress Cataloging-in-Publication Data

Names: Nichols, Stephen J., 1970- author.
Title: R.C. Sproul : a life / Stephen J. Nichols.
Description: Wheaton, Illinois : Crossway, [2021] | Includes bibliographical references and index.
Identifiers: LCCN 2020020318 (print) | LCCN 2020020319 (ebook) | ISBN 9781433544774 (hardcover) | ISBN 9781433544781 (pdf) | ISBN 9781433544798 (mobi) | ISBN 9781433544804 (epub)
Subjects: LCSH: Sproul, R. C. (Robert Charles), 1939–2017. | Presbyterian Church—United States—Clergy—Biography. | Theologians—United States—Biography.
Classification: LCC BX9225.S718 N53 2021 (print) | LCC BX9225.S718 (ebook) | DDC 285/.1092 [B]—dc23
LC record available at https://lccn.loc.gov/2020020318
LC ebook record available at https://lccn.loc.gov/2020020319

Crossway is a publishing ministry of Good News Publishers.

SH		30	29	28	27	26	25	24	23	22	21
15	14	13	12	11	10	9	8	7	6	5	4	3	2	1

For Vesta
Since the first and second grade,
it has been R. C. and Vesta.

CONTENTS

PROLOGUE

The Great Escape

R. C. SPROUL PACED AND ROARED when he preached. But by the end of his life he needed to sit on a stool. He relied on his portable oxygen, which went with him everywhere. He struggled with the effects of COPD. He had long ago sacrificed his knees to the athletic field. The years, but especially the miles, had caught up with him. At age seventy-eight, however, he still showed up for work. When he stepped into the pulpit, the athlete that he was burst forth. With passion his game face was on. The stool swiveled. He would clutch the edges of the pulpit, pull himself forward, and lean toward his congregation. He somehow managed still to pace while he preached. Somehow his voice would find strength. He still roared. For thirty minutes he was the sandlot quarterback again, making plays. He was on the back nine, golf balls at his mercy.

His wit—where did it come from?—liberally dispensed wisdom and humor. It's what people, over the years, had come so accustomed to hear from him. He made it look so easy. Effortless. With no notes he could preach a sermon on any text or give a lecture on the epistemological views of the modern philosophers. Whether it was before a crowd of thousands or around a dinner table, you simply wanted to listen to him. You wanted to see his smile, mischievous, as wide as the sky. You wanted to hear what he had to say.

They say that old-school Cambridge University runners were never seen training. They did not show up early to a meet and go through all the stretching and warm-up rituals like everyone else. They were casual. They just walked into the stadium, stepped to the line, and waited for the sound of the starter pistol. Then they were off, pure beauty in motion. They made it appear all so effortless. It's like the concert violinist taking her place on an empty stage. Calm, serene as she places the violin, readies the bow, and proceeds. Perfection. And it all looks so effortless. But the athlete, the musician, the preacher—they all know what lies behind the appearance. The work, the discipline, the constant honing of the skill. It is craftsmanship.

R. C. was a communicator. He not only knew what to say; he knew how to say it. Precision, passion, power. On this particular Sunday, his text was Hebrews 2:1–4. He called the sermon "A Great Salvation."[1] He could have called it "The Great Escape."

R. C. had always told his homiletics students, "Find the drama in the text. Then preach the drama." He found the drama in Hebrews 2:1–4. "How shall we escape?" When we think of escape, R. C. said we think of imprisonment; we think of a jailbreak. R. C. transported the congregation of Saint Andrew's Chapel to "the most dreadful of all French prisons, the Château d'If," and into the pages of his second-greatest, most favorite novel, *The Count of Monte Cristo*, the harrowing tale of Edmond Dantes, framed and falsely thrown into the dreaded prison. Edmond Dantes had done the impossible. He had escaped from the inescapable prison.

But there is a far more dreadful prison than the Château d'If. "You can't dig under it. You can't climb over it. No guard can be bribed. The sentence cannot be ameliorated or commuted." There is no escape from hell—except from salvation, a great salvation in Christ. R. C. echoed the plea of the author of Hebrews: "Do not neglect such a great salvation" (see 2:3).

---

1 R. C. Sproul, "A Great Salvation," sermon on Heb. 2:1–4, Saint Andrew's Chapel, Sanford, FL, November 26, 2017. A full, edited transcript of this sermon may be found in the back of the book, pages 317–23.

He once said it's what kept him up at night, that there might be professing but not possessing Christians in the congregation of Saint Andrew's. The zeal to proclaim the holiness of God and the gospel of Christ propelled him to devote his life to teaching, to preaching, to traveling, to writing. It kept him going even into his late seventies and despite the toll all the miles had taken. He prayed and labored for an awakening.

By the end of the sermon, R. C. had swept the congregation along with him in a fervent moment. It was sacred time. There was no humor or lightheartedness as this particular sermon came to a close. It was zeal, passion. R. C. was communicating the most important truth, the truth of the gospel. He was pleading that no one under the sound of his voice would neglect so great a salvation. It was palpable.

As he finished the sermon, this was his very last sentence: "So I pray with all my heart that God will awaken each one of us today to the sweetness, the loveliness, the glory of the gospel declared by Christ."

This very last sentence of his very last sermon reveals his heart, his passion. *Sweetness* is a word that he had learned from Jonathan Edwards, who in turn had learned it from Calvin, who in turn had learned it from Augustine, who in turn had learned it from the psalmist. You can read about how sweet honey is. You can hear of the experience of others who have tasted honey. Or you can taste it for yourself. Sweetness is the apprehension of truth.

Loveliness is that oftentimes forgotten category of beauty. R. C. often noted that while we contend for truth and fight for goodness, we far too often neglect beauty. God is a God of beauty. The word, *beauty*, overflows the pages of Scripture. That was enough for R. C. to want to pursue it, to desire it.

Glory is that elusive word that represents the transcendent, sheer luminosity. It belongs to the orbit of words that you heard so often from R. C., the words *holiness, splendor, majesty, refulgence*.

Sweetness, loveliness, glory—these are the words that describe God, Christ, the gospel. These words have transformative power. These words are what a renewed mind meditates upon. There is also, in this last sentence of his sermon, the word *awaken*. Before the mind can be renewed, it must be awakened. We are dead; a fallen, rotting tree lying in the forest. We need a "divine and supernatural light," as Edwards would put it. Or as Jesus said to Peter, "flesh and blood has not revealed this to you." No, no, it was "My Father who is in heaven" (Matt. 16:17 NKJV). Jesus pronounced Peter blessed. The stunning truth that Jesus Himself would say to someone, "Blessed are you," sent true joy to the core of R. C.'s being. He wanted everyone to experience it. How R. C. longed for an awakening. It was the last sentence of his sermon on Hebrews 2:1–4.

After he delivered that last sentence, R. C. offered a short, earnest prayer, and then an audible sigh. He slid off the stool, steadied his feet, and, with help, started to descend from the pulpit.

R. C. Sproul preached this sermon on November 26, 2017. By Tuesday he had a cold, which daily grew worse. By Saturday he had such difficulty breathing that he was taken to the hospital. There he remained. On December 14, 2017, as Vesta and family were gathered in the hospital room, R. C. went into the sweet, lovely, and glorious presence of the Lord.

Final sermon: "A Great Salvation." Final sentence: "So I pray with all my heart that God will awaken each one of us today to the sweetness, the loveliness, the glory of the gospel declared by Christ." Then exit stage left. And it was in the year of the five hundredth anniversary of the Reformation. It was all pure poetry.

The story of R. C.'s life ends in 2017 in central Florida. It had been his home, or home base, for thirty-three years. The story begins in Pittsburgh in 1939. The world was about to go to war.

PITTSBURGH

*You can take the man out of Pittsburgh, but you
can't take Pittsburgh out of the man.*

R. C. SPROUL

THE ALLEGHENY RIVER RUNS in from the north. The Monongahela
runs in from the east. At their confluence, the Ohio River begins. Three
rivers converge to form a point. Nearby, in 1754 the French built Fort
Duquesne, a key post during the Seven Years' War. The British marched
on it in November of 1758. The French knew they were greatly outnumbered. They gathered their supplies, blew up the fort, and retreated
across the Ohio River. When the place where the fort had stood was
taken, a new fort was built and named Fort Pitt, after William Pitt the
Elder. Over the next centuries, a city, Pittsburgh, would eventually grow
upon this triangular plateau with its gentle westward slope and surrounding steep and rolling hills, part of the Allegheny Mountains of the vast
Appalachian Range. This was not a river valley plateau for farming but
a place for industry.

Among the many immigrants who settled in Pittsburgh over the centuries were the Sprouls, from County Donegal in Ireland, who emigrated
in 1849. They made their home to the south, across the Monongahela
on Mount Washington. Cable cars now ascend the steep slope. Another

immigrant family, the Yardis family from Croatia, settled on the north side of the city near Troy Hill and German Hill. English-speaking Scotch-Irish to the south. Immigrants from the European continent to the north. White-collar management to the south. Blue-collar labor to the north.

The Sprouls were management, eventually establishing R. C. Sproul and Sons, an accounting firm specializing in bankruptcy. Pittsburgh has seen several cycles, several reinventions of the city—enough to keep an accounting firm specializing in bankruptcy busy and prosperous.

The Yardises were labor. Mayre Ann Yardis began her working life as a teenager and as a secretary. She learned her trade at the Sarah Heinz House, established by the son of German immigrants, H. J. Heinz. Eventually she took a job at the R. C. Sproul and Sons accounting firm.

The R. C. Sproul in the accounting firm was Robert C. Sproul (1872–1945), R. C.'s grandfather. The "Sons" were Robert Cecil Sproul (1903–1956), R. C.'s father; and his brother Charles Sproul, R. C.'s uncle. The offices were located on Grant Street in the heart of downtown. Mayre worked for Robert Cecil Sproul as a secretary. They married. Pittsburgh management married Pittsburgh labor.[1]

Number Five

Robert Cecil and Mayre Sproul settled on McClellan Drive in the borough of Pleasant Hills, to the south of the city. On February 13, 1939, Marye Ann Sproul gave birth to the second of their two children, Robert Charles Sproul. The family was full of R. C.s, Roberts, and Bobs. There were even a number of Robertas. R. C.'s older sister, born in 1936, was one of the Robertas. From the day R. C. came home from the hospital, he was named "Sonny." Newspapers would write of his sports exploits during his junior and senior high school years. In those columns he was always referred to as "Sonny" Sproul.

With a little pride, R. C. would say that he was actually the first baby

1 "Sproul Memoirs," session 1, recorded November 2010, Ligonier Ministries, Sanford, Florida.

born of Pleasant Hills. Incorporated as a borough in 1939, R. C.'s birth made him the first resident born into that newly minted community of Pleasant Hills. Before it was Pleasant Hills, it was known as Number Five, short for Curry Number Five Mine of the vast Pittsburgh Coalfield.[2]

In the late nineteenth century and through most of the twentieth, Pittsburgh by far led the nation in coal and coke production, which along with iron ore and manpower are the necessary ingredients for the steel industry. The United States dominated the world steel market, and Pittsburgh played the leading role. Andrew Carnegie pioneered the steel industry in that region. Eventually his company consolidated with others to form United States Steel, which would at one time produce fully 30 percent of the world's steel. Pittsburgh was the Steel City. Its steel bridges crisscrossing the rivers show off its hometown product. Pittsburgh, even all of western Pennsylvania, has a toughness to match the product it shipped around the world. Both Pittsburgh labor and Pittsburgh management have that toughness.

All of that coal and coke excavation also meant Pittsburgh and surrounding towns sit upon a web of subterranean tunnels and mines, like Number Five. Above ground, Number Five was home to about four thousand white-collar residents in the 1940s.

R. C.'s first memories of living in Pleasant Hills orbit his father. One is of his dad coming home one day carrying a cardboard box. He set the box in the den, which was two steps down from the rest of the first floor of the house. Inside the box was a dachshund puppy. His dad had named it Soldier. The second memory is walking hand in hand with his dad to the bus stop, his dad wearing an officer's uniform. As a pillar of the community, Robert Cecil Sproul served as the head of the draft board. One day he came home wearing an Army Air Force officer's uniform. He told his wife he could no longer send busloads of young men to war and remain at home. While thirty-nine years of age and well past the

2 Stephen Nichols with R. C. Sproul, personal interview, March 24, 2017.

draft age, he nevertheless felt duty bound to go himself. His dad was headed for training at Westover Field, now Westover Air Reserve Base, just outside of Springfield, Massachusetts. The puppy was to keep R. C. company while his dad was gone.

Two-Gun Charlie

R. C.'s dad entered the service as a captain. After his training, he arrived in Casablanca on Christmas Eve 1942. The Allied forces had, just the month before, driven the German forces out of Casablanca. It was a turning point in the North African theater that portended the continued push of the Germans, and the Axis Powers, into containment and eventual defeat three long years later.

In the war, Robert Cecil Sproul served as an accountant, mirroring his civilian occupation. He would later tell people, "I flew a desk in the war." He was in Casablanca, then Algiers, on to Sicily, and then through Italy. As the advanced guard moved forward, his unit followed, ensuring that they had all they needed and that all was accounted for and in order. He was promoted to the rank of major.

Back home, the war dominated every aspect of life. Families tuned their Philco and RCA radios to hear the casualty reports and updates, hoping and praying. Soap, sugar, butter, gas—nearly every product was rationed. Seemingly ubiquitous "Do with less, so they'll have enough" and "Buy War Bonds" posters reminded all on the homefront to do their part for the war effort. Factories converted their assembly lines to make whatever was needed for the war effort. Pittsburgh's steel mills ran 24 hours a day, producing a staggering ninety-five million tons of steel.

The war dominated everything in R. C.'s childhood too. He missed his father. As a four-year-old he ran away, making it to the end of the street or perhaps the next street until he met up with one of the neighbors. When questioned, R. C. said he was on his way to Italy to see his dad.

Before Pittsburgh International Airport opened, the Allegheny County Airport served that region. The flight path went directly over the Sproul home. Planes flew sometimes not more than forty or fifty feet above the house. R. C. lacked a sense of geography at this time, as already established. As a young boy he was terrified when those planes flew over during a blackout. He thought he was in the middle of a bombing raid, like the ones he heard about on the radio.

The war was an ever-present reality by night and by day. R. C. helped his mother and sister in the victory garden in the backyard. He scraped labels off cans, crushed them flat, and turned them in for reclamation. A flag hung from the front window of their home on McClellan Drive, signaling that it was the home of a soldier. Similar flags could be seen up and down the street and around the neighborhood. The Sprouls, like everyone else, had installed black curtains that were pulled across the windows when the air raid sirens were sounded.

Around the corner and on the next street stood a drugstore. Rows of pictures of uniformed men of Pleasant Hills serving in the war lined the windows. R. C. would scan the photos until he locked onto his father's face.

His mother took on extra responsibilities at the accounting firm to supplement the reduced salary his father received from the AAF. Before he left for the war, his father wanted to make sure that his family had a man living in the house, so he arranged for his wife's sister, her German husband, and their daughter to live in the home on McClellan Drive.

And R. C. would sit on his mother's lap and help her type V-mail letters to her husband. This is one of the earliest memories that R. C. has of his mom. V-mail letters were a one-sided form provided to families by the military. Once the family wrote or typed the letter onto the form, the letters went first to Washington, DC, where they were reviewed by censors, and then transferred to 16-mm film. The film would be flown overseas, the individual letters would be printed from the film, and the hand-size letters from home would be delivered to soldiers. Of the more than 550 million V-letters crossing between soldiers and their families, Mayre Ann and Robert Cecil accounted for hundreds of them. Robert Cecil handwrote his. She typed hers.

She had a rather sophisticated (for its time) electric typewriter. R. C. would sit on her lap as she typed. When she finished, it was R. C.'s turn. He would fill the bottom line with X's and O's. It was the first time he ever typed.

Robert Cecil wrote often to R. C. The letters are playful and warm, full of humor and kindness. He would remind R. C. to be a dutiful son in taking care of his mother, his older sister, and Soldier, the dog. He would address him as "Sonny" or as "Two-Gun Charlie" or with playful names like "Tootlebug." He would tell him how he missed him, and he would tell him he'd be home soon. Here's one letter sent from Sicily, June 1945, a few months before the war ended and as R. C. received his kindergarten diploma:

> My Great Big Boy,
> I got your letter on June 18 and sure glad to hear that you are being such a good boy getting a lot of sun and drinking your milk and buttermilk. I'm glad you are having a good time in your play yard, and I hope the old war ends real soon so I can come play with you. I am real proud that you are getting a diploma and will send you a nice present. I sure would love to see your G-I haircut. Be good to Soldier and take care of Mommy and Bobby Anne.
> Love,
> Daddy

R. C.'s earliest memories of his older sister, Roberta "Bobby" Anne, were also from the war years. He remembered that she had a dollhouse. Their father would send her dolls from Europe. Any time he moved along with the army, he would look for dolls that he could send home to her. R. C. also remembers getting a hand-me-down tricycle from Roberta. Much too big for him, it had enormous, oversized tires. R. C. described it as a three-wheel bicycle, adult-sized. He likely needed another year or two to even remotely fit it. But it was the only mode of transportation afforded to him. He chose mobility, despite the awkwardness. He wrangled that tricycle up and down the hills of his community, many times his feet entirely unable to keep up with or reach the rapid rotation of the pedals. It was a sight for all to see.

In 1945 Mayre Ann got her husband back, and R. C. got his dad back. Having given so much to the war effort "over there," it was now time to tend to matters close to home. Like the rest of the country, the Sprouls were ready to get back to the normal routines of life.

R. C. + V. V.

As R. C. entered his elementary school years, his world consisted of a few-mile radius. Just off McClellan Drive was the aforementioned drugstore, complete with a soda fountain and soda jerks. R. C.'s favorite was always the milkshake. There was the shoe repair shop and the radio and television repair shop. On a corner lot stood the elementary school, with its playground. Up and down a few hills and a few streets away was the park, perched on top of a hill and home to a newly christened ball field. R. C. played in the opening game.

Draw a straight line from R. C.'s home 9 miles to the northwest, and you arrive at the accounting office of R. C. Sproul and Sons on Grant Street. Not far from there was Forbes Field. (Today the Pittsburgh Pirates play at PNC Park, and the Steelers play on Heinz Field. Before that, they both shared Three Rivers Stadium. And before that they played at Forbes Field.) R. C. never missed a Pittsburgh Pirates' opening day. He would skip school, hitchhike, and watch a game—all with his parents' blessing. He could remember, play by play, the first game he ever saw. Pirates 5, Reds 3. R. C. was in the stands of Forbes Field when Roberto Clemente wore his number-13 jersey in the season opener of 1955. And he saw Clemente hit his first home run. The 1940s and 50s were not the best decades to be a Pirates fan. In sum, they lost as many games as they won. That did not stop R. C. from being a devoted fan. At any time during those years, were you to stop and ask him what he wanted to be when he grew up, he would have said a ballplayer. And there was no other uniform he'd rather wear than the black and gold of the Bucs.

R. C.'s mother and father went to the office every day. R. C. realized how unusual that was. Few mothers worked outside the home in those days. R. C. loved the days when he could go along with his parents to work. He would sit at the window and watch the bustling activity of the city. He would play with his cars and toys under a desk somewhere in the offices. He especially loved the Christmas season. All the department store windows had amazing displays that captivated R. C. Wide-eyed, he would just stand and stare.

The offices provided the best seat in the house for the parades that went by. Pittsburgh was in full throttle in the post-war years, and R. C. had a view to it all, both at a distance, perched from his home up in the south hills, and also up close from the windows of the office on Grant Street.

Years later, when the firm dissolved, the building was sold and torn down. On the very site rose the sixty-four-story United States Steel building, known as the US Steel Tower. For years, the sixty-second floor housed a restaurant dubbed "Top of the Triangle." R. C. had occasional business lunches and dinners there. As he did, the memories would come back as he thought of himself as a little kid at play and his parents at work some 800 feet below.

In 1945 a new structure went up near R. C.'s home on McClellan Drive. Next to the elementary school, Pleasant Hills Community Church, a United Presbyterian Church, opened its doors.

R. C.'s dad had been a longstanding member of the Mount Washington Methodist Church. In fact, R. C.'s grandfather had been one of the founding members. R. C.'s dad was a lay minister at times and regularly taught Sunday school. R. C. was baptized as an infant in that Methodist church. During the war years, every Sunday his family headed off to the Methodist church. But when Pleasant Hills Community Church opened, the family became Presbyterian. It was, by R. C.'s reckoning, a liberal church—very liberal. But it left an indelible impression on him through its high liturgy, which R. C. said was quite nearly Episcopalian. His pastor was committed to a formal service, to a well-crafted, even dramatic, homily. The original building was a small structure, which now houses the church offices. A much larger sanctuary was built later. The floor was brick for acoustical purposes. The exterior was colonial revival–style red brick with white columns and a towering spire. The interior was the traditional Presbyterian rectangle, with the pulpit prominently placed on the short side and the long nave. The cornerstone outside bore a Latin inscription.

The move to a Presbyterian church would have everything to do with R. C.'s future. He would eventually attend a Presbyterian college and seminary. He would be ordained Presbyterian. He would champion the Westminster Standards—the doctrinal confession of the Presbyterian church. The move to Presbyterianism also provided a rather important link to his past. R. C. liked to regale listeners with the story of the first minister ordained by the Scottish Reformer John Knox.

The Sprouls had emigrated from County Donegal, Ireland. Sproul, however, is not an Irish name. It's lowland Scots. And here the Reformation and John Knox enter the story. Knox, a Scottish priest who found himself at odds with his church and crown, first endured a sentence on a galley ship and then a time of exile. Knox ended up in Calvin's Geneva while Bloody Mary reigned during the 1550s. Inspired by all that Geneva accomplished under Calvin's leadership, by God's grace Knox returned to his native Scotland determined to reform the entire country. "Give me Scotland or I die," he pleaded with God.

The first step to reform was to establish a new church, given the depth of corruption of the current church. This new church would be the Church of Scotland, the Kirk. The very first minister ordained by Knox in this new church was a lowlands Scot named Robert Campbell Sproul. Knox then dispatched Rev. Sproul to Ireland. One of his descendants, named John, presumably after John Knox, served as a ruling elder and a commissioner at Raphoe Presbyterian Church in County Donegal, Ireland, during the years 1672 to 1700.[3]

R. C.'s great-grandfather came to America from this very place during the great potato famine in the middle of the nineteenth century. R. C. wrote this of his great-grandfather:

> During the nineteenth-century potato famine in Ireland, my great-grandfather Charles Sproul, fled his native land to seek refuge in America. He left his thatched roof and mud floor cottage in a northern Ireland village and made his way barefoot to Dublin—to the wharf from which he sailed to New York. After registering as an immigrant at Ellis Island, he made his way west to Pittsburgh, where a large colony of Scots-Irish people had settled. They were drawn to that site by the industrial steel mills led by the Scot Andrew Carnegie.[4]

This Irish immigrant fought for the Union on the SS Grampas. One of his sons, R. C.'s grandfather, took the family into the Methodist church on Mount Washington. When Robert Cecil Sproul, R. C.'s father, moved his membership from the Methodist church to the Presbyterian church in 1945, he was bringing his family home.

In 1946 the Voorhis family moved into the neighborhood a few houses down from the church. They had a daughter. The family moved in sometime in May from New Castle, Pennsylvania. Mr. William Voorhis worked as a national buyer for G. C. Murphy Co., one of the five-and-dime chain stores. He spent one week every month in New York City meeting with manufacturers and wholesalers.

At this time R. C. was in the first grade at Pleasant Hills Elementary School. Vesta Voorhis was in the second grade. R. C. vividly remembers seeing her for the first time, and when he did, with clarity, he knew he would marry her. Apparently, it was all one-sided. Vesta was busy with

---

3 William M. Mervine, "Scottish Settlers in Raphoe, County Donegal, Ireland: A Contribution to Pennsylvania Genealogy," *Pennsylvania Magazine of History and Biography*, vol. 36, no. 3 (1912), 272.

4 R. C. Sproul, "All Truth Is God's Truth," *Tabletalk*, July 1, 2008.

her new friends on the playground. Boys on the ball field. Girls on the playground. A few weeks of school went by and then it was summer break. R. C. would later say that during his elementary and junior high years he was all about one thing: sports. It was likely two: sports and Vesta. If you were to look on most trees lining old Clairton Road and McClellan Drive, you'd see four initials carved: "R. C. + V. V." After that first encounter, a few more years passed before R. C. and Vesta became on-again, off-again boyfriend and girlfriend. Ultimately, the story of R. C. would be that of R. C. and Vesta.

The aunt, the uncle, and the cousin stayed in the home for another six or seven years after the war. It was always busy, always full of family. The extended family often came together for gatherings at the home on McClellan Drive. R. C. recalled, "I loved it. I used to stand at the top of the street waiting for the cars to come to bring our relatives to these gatherings. Our family was everything. I was big into family. Always was, still am."[5]

Most evenings R. C. would lie on the floor with Soldier and listen to the Philco radio. The airwaves during the day were filled with soap operas, but at night the adventure shows came on. *The Falcon, Suspense, Escape*, and, his favorite, *The Lone Ranger*—these were the shows that captivated the imagination of R. C. On Saturdays and most Sundays after church, R. C. went to the movies to catch the double feature. The Frankenstein and Dracula movies with Lon Cheney and Bela Lugosi were his favorites on the silver screen.

R. C., like most kids, dreamed of school letting out for the freedom of the summer months. Family vacations included trips far north to Muskoka Lake in Ontario, Canada. It was a popular spot for celebrities in the summer cottages and for Toronto Maple Leaf hockey players. The Sprouls stayed next to an enclave of them. The players took to R. C., teaching him dives from a diving board on a dock and giving him all sorts

5 "Sproul Memoirs," session 1.

of hockey tips and techniques. As a ten-year-old, he was likely having the best vacation ever. The players gave him a fine leather jacket with a big embroidered emblem. It was adult-size small, sleeves dangling long past the end of R. C.'s fingertips. He posed wearing it proudly and happily along the shore of Muskoka Lake.

In between summer vacations, R. C. had Christmas to look forward to. Christmas season was especially, according to R. C., "extraordinary." During the war years, R. C.'s uncle started a tradition they called the "Christmas platform." This was an elaborate display, constructed in the den, of papier-mâché mountains with skiers dotting the slopes and a ski jump, cars moving along on a conveyer belt through a main street, a merry-go-round, and train sets.

The Christmas of 1950 proved rather memorable for R. C. Pittsburgh sat buried under three feet of snow that year. It was perfect timing for the gift he received, a toboggan. The next day R. C. along with two buddies set out for the maiden voyage. They went to the largest hill in town. At the bottom of the hill was a creek, with a rock wall bordering the banks. The first time down, the trio stopped short of the creek in an amazing ride. For trek number two, the boys plied all of their engineering skills, biggest kid in the front. The first ride had also packed the snow, so the second time, they zoomed down, slamming right into the rock wall. R. C. hurt his back. One boy broke his toe. And the third had shattered his leg. They managed to get him secure on the toboggan, which R. C. then, by himself, dragged through the snow to the first home they came to, about a half mile away. For the rest of the school year, R. C. went to visit him at his home as he sat propped up and recovering. For both of them, it was their last toboggan ride.

Other Christmas memories were much more joyous. R. C. especially remembered Christmas Eve candlelight services, starting at 11:00 p.m. and ending as the clock struck midnight. They sang "O Holy Night" a capella. And then there was the Christmas Eve of 1952. This was the year that R. C. and Vesta began going steady—mostly. Before the candlelight church service, R. C. was at Vesta's home for Christmas Eve.

R. C. and Vesta were in the choir together at school and at church, both run by the same director. The church paid both an organist and a choir director. As mentioned, the church also had a formal liturgy. All that taken together means that the children's choir was all business. Robes, starched collars—they looked like a proper cathedral boys' choir. And R. C. loved it. He would speak of how the church's preaching was devoid of any good theology or biblical content, but they sang classical anthems and hymns. R. C. would later say, "Most of the knowledge I had of any of the content of Christianity came from the music that we were singing."[6]

R. C. also remembered the sacrament of the Lord's Supper. The pastor, Dr. Paul Hudson, trained the elders to come forward, after the elements had been distributed, in perfectly synchronized lockstep formation. Footfalls rhythmically struck the brick floor, echoing through the sanctuary.

But when it came to theology, there was no such precision. The pastor would catechize the children; however, rather than follow the Westminster Shorter Catechism, the confessional standard of the Presbyterian church, he wrote his own questions that he had the children focus on:

Question: Who is the greatest Christian who ever lived?
Answer: Albert Schweitzer.

Albert Schweitzer might have been a great humanitarian and was truly a genius, having taken doctorates in theology, philosophy, music, and medicine. But he was patently liberal. He was a key figure in the so-called quest for the historical Jesus, the efforts by German scholars to find the kernel of historical truth shrouded in the husks of the four Gospels.

Dr. Hudson applied to his sermon what he had learned from the higher-critical scholars. The miracle of the feeding of the five thousand was a miracle of the selfless example of the little boy. The folks in the

---

6 Stephen Nichols with R. C. Sproul, personal interview, April 17, 2017.

crowd brought food with them, but they didn't want to admit it in case they would be forced to share. When the little boy freely gave of what he had, this inspired the crowd to pull their lunch bags from the folds of their robes. A miracle. Every Easter, R. C. was taught that the resurrection of Jesus Christ meant that each day he, too, could rise again in newness to meet afresh the challenges of the day.

R. C. did not learn his theology from Pleasant Hills Community Church. He did not learn his biblical studies there either. These fields, which would become his profession later in life, were of little to no interest to him in his young years.

Sonny Sproul at Bat

Sports were far more interesting to the young R. C. He played baseball, basketball, and football. He was likely best at baseball but competitive at all three. The sport he actually enjoyed most was hockey, though by his own account he was the least proficient at it. R. C. and his friends flooded the field at Mowry Park and created a rink, and they also played at a quarry. They had their own version of a Zamboni. They had augers and drilled five or six holes through the ice. Overnight the water seeped out to form a perfectly smooth glaze for them to play on.

In addition to sports, writing was a part of R. C.'s early life. R. C. had a teacher named Miss Graham, until she married another teacher and became Mrs. Gregg. She taught English, and R. C. had her as a teacher in elementary school and again later in junior high. The elementary art teachers would periodically post the best student art prominently on a display board. R. C. remembered always wanting but never seeing his artwork getting the pride of place. But one time, Mrs. Gregg put R. C.'s descriptive essay on the art display board. It was a work of art. Later, when R. C. was in the eighth grade, she told him, and he never forgot it, "Don't let anyone tell you you can't write."

In the sixth grade R. C. played baseball for a sponsored team in a neighborhood league. Players were mostly in high school, some even in their early twenties. There was R. C., punching above his weight as a sixth grader. He was a starter. He was traded. The announcement even made the local paper. He was traded for three players—all of them older than he. The paper said the three were traded for the "slick-fielding infielder, Sonny Sproul . . . who lacked a potential bat."

That was enough to inspire R. C. In the next game, he faced a twenty-one-year-old pitcher. The first time at bat, R. C. hit a sharp single. The second time he knocked it over the fence for a home run. Sonny Sproul indeed had a bat.

R. C. loved his junior high years. He excelled at sports. He was loved by his classmates. He was captain of the basketball team, president of the student council, and had earned the number two rank of all students academically. All of that stands in contrast to his high school years. While R. C. was in the ninth grade, his dad had a stroke, followed by a few more.

R. C. idolized his dad, who always wore a crisp white shirt and tie. R. C. remembers only a handful of times seeing him in casual clothes. As an accountant, his dad also enjoyed studying and discussing economics. His dad was not handy but he, too, had been an athlete. He was accepted at Princeton, but he never went. Instead, his father, R. C.'s grandfather, thrust him right into the family business. He self-studied for the CPA exam and passed. He also served as the president of the accounting firm. He had the competencies and skills, and he could lead and manage. That first stroke left him mostly debilitated; R. C.'s dad could work no longer.

Robert Cecil Sproul's speech was slurred, his vision hampered; he could no longer walk on his own. He spent most days sitting in the chair in the den. R. C. remembers him reading his Bible with a magnifying glass. In the evening R. C. would help him up out of the chair, grasp his hands around his neck and drag him to the dinner table. From the time he was a child, R. C. remembered his dad always at the dinner table with white starched shirt and tie. That didn't change after the stroke. After dinner, R. C. dragged his dad to bed.

This took its toll on the family. R. C.'s mom loved his dad. He was Prince Charming to her Cinderella. R. C. simply said, "My mother adored my father."[7]

Just before the stroke, R. C.'s dad counseled R. C. to give up football and focus on basketball and baseball. He did, much to the football coach's displeasure. That coach pressured the basketball coach to bench R. C.—who had been the team's highest scorer. R. C. had a finely tuned sense of justice and fair play. None of that set well with him. It was also the exact opposite of his prior experience with coaches. His pony league and junior high coaches were true mentors, who influenced him greatly at the time and continued to have an impact on his life decades later.

This experience did not entirely detract from his competitive spirit. R. C. could put his game face on. He continued playing in community leagues and even played on a semi-pro football team for a time. All of this caught the attention of college athletic department scouts.

But high school remained a wearisome season. R. C. was bused to Clairton High School. He had always loved his teachers at Pleasant Hills Elementary and Junior High. He spoke of how he knew his teachers were for him. That was not the case at Clairton. R. C. felt a little lost in this new environment.

With his father's illness, he took on a part-time job at the neighborhood TV repair shop up the street and around the corner from his home. He once knew nearly everything one needed to know about television tubes (when televisions actually had tubes). He slept little and simply slogged through his high school years. In his novel, R. C. writes of Scooter, the main character, as one who "mastered the art of sleeping in the back of the classroom with a book propped up in front him."[8] Most of that novel is fiction. Some sentences are straight autobiography.

There were bright spots in those years. One was, of course, Vesta. The other was R. C.'s best friend, Johnny Coles. Johnny would be a major

---

7   "Sproul Memoirs," session 1.

8   R. C. Sproul, *Thy Brother's Keeper: A Novel* (Brentwood, TN: Wolgemuth & Hyatt, 1988), 39.

character in the later novel. Those were two bright spots. A third one involved a car.

When he first learned to drive, R. C. used the family car, a big boat of an Oldsmobile. Before his senior year of high school, he got his own car. Not just any car. A black and red Ford Fairlane 500 hardtop convertible with two four-barrel carburetors, dual exhaust, and lots of chrome. Yes, a muscle car. In the 1950s, Detroit knew how to make a car. This was one of them.

Just before Vesta left for college—she was one year older—the relationship ceased to be on and off. From then on, until the time of R. C.'s death, it would be R. C. and Vesta. They were steady, and nothing ever came between. From the family phone in the den, R. C. called Vesta every night while he was in his senior year of high school and she was in her freshman year at Wooster College in Ohio. R. C. would later say he had no idea why she stuck with him through that miserable time, but she did.

One night as R. C. was dragging his father from the dinner table to bed, his dad asked R. C. to stop for a moment and set him down on the couch. He had something he wanted to tell him. Through slurred speech, he said, "I have fought the good fight of the faith, I have run the race, I've finished the course, I've kept the faith." R. C., unaware that he was quoting Scripture, said to him, "Don't say that, Dad." He then dragged his father to his room and put him in bed. A little later, R. C. heard a thump. He found his dad on the floor. He slipped into a coma. For the next day and a half, R. C. sat with him. Then his dad suddenly lifted up in bed, then lay back down, and died. He was fifty-three years old. R. C. was seventeen.

R. C., like his mother, adored his father. He never heard his father complain during his illness. He only knew his father to be a kind and gracious man. He knew him to be a man of honor. And now he was gone. Decades later, R. C. recalled the whole incident in his 1983 book *The Hunger for Significance*. His extended words follow:

I remember my father's final words—how can I forget them? But what haunts me are my last words to him.

Death often leaves a burden of guilt to the survivors who are plagued by memories of things left unsaid or undone or of hurts imposed on the deceased. My guilt resides in the insensitive, nay, the stupid words I said to my father. I said the wrong thing, the juvenile thing for which death gave me no opportunity to say, "I'm sorry."

I long for the chance to replay the scene, but it is too late. I must trust the power of heaven to heal the wound. What is done can be forgiven—it can be augmented, diminished and, in some cases, repaired. But it cannot be undone.

Certain things cannot be recalled: the speeding bullet from the gun, the arrow released from the bow, the word that escapes our lips. We can pray that the bullet misses or that the arrow falls harmlessly to the ground, but we cannot command them to return in midflight.

What did I say that makes me curse my tongue? They were not words of rebellion or shouts of temper; they were words of denial—a refusal to accept my father's final statement. I simply said, "Don't say that, Dad."

In his final moments my father tried to leave me with a legacy to live by. He sought to overcome his own agony by encouraging me. He was heroic; I shrank from his words in cowardice. I could not face what he had to face.

I pled ignorance as I only understood enough of his words to recoil from them. He said, "Son, I have fought the good fight, I have finished the race, I have kept the faith."

He was quoting the apostle Paul's closing words to his beloved disciple Timothy. But I failed to recognize that fact. I had never read the Bible—I had no faith to keep, no race to finish.

My father was speaking from a posture of victory. He knew who he was and where he was going. But all I could hear in those words was that he was going to die.

What impertinence for me to reply, "Don't say that!" I rebuked my father in the most valiant moment of his life. I tramped on his soul with my own unbelief.

Nothing more was said between us—ever. I put his paralyzed arms around my neck, hoisting his useless body partially off the ground, supporting him on my back and shoulders, and dragged him to his bed. I left his room and shifted my thought to my homework assignments.

An hour later my studies were interrupted by the sound of a crash from a distant part of the house. I hastened to investigate the sound. I found my father sprawled in a heap on the floor with blood trickling from his ear and nose.

He lingered a day and a half in a coma before the rattle of death signaled the end. When his labored breathing stopped, I leaned over and kissed his forehead.

I did not cry. I played the man, being outwardly calm through the following days of funeral home visitations and burial in the grave. But inside, I was devastated.

How much value did my father have to me then? I would have done anything I could, given everything I had, to bring him back. I had never tasted defeat so final or lost anything so precious.[9]

R. C. had no such faith, at that time, to see him through.

As he approached high school graduation, R. C. had three options. He was invited to try out for one of the farm teams that fed the Pittsburgh Pirates. He was offered a baseball scholarship to the University of Pittsburgh. And he was offered an athletic scholarship, for basketball and football, to Westminster College in New Wilmington, Pennsylvania, about an hour's drive north of Pittsburgh.

By his own account, it was an easy choice. He never applied to Pittsburgh, and never applied to any other college. "I fell in love with that college," R. C. testified.[10] That fall he was in New Wilmington.

---

9 R. C. Sproul, *In Search of Dignity* (Ventura, CA: Regal, 1983), 91–92. Republished as *The Hunger for Significance*, new ed. (Phillipsburg, NJ: P&R, 2020). Used with permission from P&R Publishing Co., PO Box 817, Phillipsburg, NJ 08865.

10 Stephen Nichols with R. C. Sproul, personal interview, April 7, 2017.

Place and Time

Many decades later, after R. C. had been living for some time in central Florida, he was invited to speak at an anniversary for the pastorate of an old friend, and former Ligonier Valley Study Center colleague, back in Pittsburgh. He couldn't attend, but he wrote some words to be read for the occasion. In his typical cursive script on yellow paper, which was then typed up by his secretary, he wrote:

> You can take the man out of Pittsburgh, but you cannot take Pittsburgh out of the man. My roots are in Pittsburgh and to this day, I love every tree, every blade of grass, and every pothole in the Burgh.

One has to have firsthand experience of Pittsburgh's streets to fully appreciate the comment on potholes. Pittsburgh was the place. World War II and the 1950s was the time. Both this place and this time formed R. C. Sproul. On the radio or at a conference, that distinct western PA accent gave away how significantly this particular place had shaped him.

Pittsburgh remained an important place in his life, especially up until the move to central Florida in the mid 1980s. Robert Carro, author of the (yet) unfinished monumental biography of Lyndon Baynes Johnson, has noted, "The importance of a sense of place is commonly accepted in the world of fiction. I wish that were also true about biography and history."[11] No doubt, the life of R. C. Sproul is better understood against the setting of this place and time.

While Pittsburgh was the place of his early years, World War II was the significant and determining factor of the time. His father's absence in the service was by R. C.'s own account "very formative." His father was of that "Greatest Generation," being, in fact, one of the older members of that storied generation. The unpredictable nature of the war gave way to an ordered post-war society: neighborhood drugstore, neighborhood grocer, and neighborhood repairman. This age provided the solidity and

---

11 Robert A. Carro, *Working: Researching, Interviewing, Writing* (New York: Knopf, 2019), 141.

security of life within a walking circumference: school, church, playground, ball field, girlfriend's home. There were rhythms: school, play, sports, a movie. R. C.'s father's illness disrupted the rhythms. Being bused to high school broke the circumference. But this space and time were filling in the backdrop of the portrait that would become R. C. Sproul.

In the opening pages of *Classical Apologetics*, R. C., writing of the growing secularism, draws attention to two Latin words: *saeculum* and *mundum*, translated as time and place.[12] The Latin words *chronos* and *tempus* also mean time. The distinctive nuance of *saeculum* in this word group entails the connotation of "age." There is the 1940s, then there is the age of World War II. There is the 1950s, then there is the "golden age of television." It's not just about the moment, but the texture and the particularity of the moment, the ethos around the moment.

So it is with *mundum*. *Topos* also means place, as in a spot on a map. But *mundum*, which entails topography and geography, also captures all of the granular detail of a place, the ethos around the spot on a map. So it is with Pittsburgh. The ethos is a toughness equal to the moniker "Steel City." The ethos is management on the South Hills, labor in the North Hills—all neighborhoods of immigrants. There are rivers that separate and bridges that connect. Coal and coke mines below the surface, steel mills above. This was a one-time frontier outpost. No one plays defense quite like the Steelers. There are mountains. There are potholes.

In 1957, R. C. headed north for Westminster College, but he didn't go too far from Pittsburgh. In one sense, he never did.

---

12 R. C. Sproul, *Classical Apologetics* (Grand Rapids, MI: Zondervan, 1984), 6.

2

ECCLESIASTES 11:3

*I think I am the only person in church history
who was converted by that verse.*

R. C. SPROUL

IT TOOK R. C. ABOUT an hour to drive directly north from his home
in Pittsburgh to Westminster College, New Wilmington, Pennsylvania.
Founded by Presbyterians in 1852, Westminster still had markers of
its identity when R. C. arrived at Westminster a century and five years
later. There was a Bible department. Freshman were required to take
Bible survey courses in their fall and spring semesters. They had chapel
services. But it certainly did not wear its religious identity on its sleeve.
Neither did the vestiges of religion that had remained reflect theological
conservatism or biblical fidelity. The Presbyterian confessionalism of
Westminster's roots no longer ran deep and wide. But R. C. did not go
to Westminster to get religion. Or so he thought.

R. C. was in fact terrified of the prospects of college. On autopilot
through high school, he did not feel equipped for the academic challenge that lay ahead. It did not help that at orientation the president
instructed each of the incoming students to look to the person to their
right. Then he said, "One of you won't make it past your first semester."
R. C. started as a history major, and he started in the athletic training

camps in preparation for the seasons to come. First up would be football, then the long basketball season straddling the semesters, then baseball. R. C. had an athletic scholarship, but that did not secure him a place on any of these teams. He calculated his chances were high for football, not likely for basketball as a freshman—Westminster boasted championship teams—and baseball was too far off to consider. All that to say, whether it was academics or athletics, R. C. knew he had much work ahead.

But what he did not expect was what would happen on a weekend in September early in his college tenure.

R. C.'s roommate was his childhood friend Johnny. Johnny's father was a bit of a legend at Westminster, a four-sport letterman who would go on to be a successful businessman. Johnny got in as a legacy student, not on the merits of his grades. He, like R. C., trembled at the task ahead. But it was the weekend.

A Funny Thing Happened on the Way to Youngstown

R. C. and Johnny were intending to head west across the Allegheny River to Youngstown, Ohio. A tough-as-nails city, Youngstown was notorious for its bars—all with a reputation for not checking IDs at the door, making it a favorite haunt for the underage undergrads of Westminster. As they got in the car, both Johnny and R. C. realized they were out of cigarettes. They hopped out and went back into the lobby of their dorm to get a pack of Lucky Strikes from the cigarette vending machine. R. C.'s quarter dropped in the slot and the pack fell. As R. C. bent down to retrieve it, he saw two guys sitting at a table. They motioned for R. C. and Johnny to come join them. R. C. recognized them instantly, one of them being the star of the football team. Of course, R. C. and Johnny obeyed the summons immediately. The two upperclassmen were hunched over a book.

"What are you two doing?" the football star asked. "Nothing," R. C. demurred—not about to confess their plans. So Johnny and R. C. were invited to sit and join them. The bars of Youngstown would have to wait.

The two upperclassmen were engaged in a Bible study. R. C. had seen his dad read his Bible daily, but this was the first time R. C. ever witnessed a Bible study. The two upperclassmen talked about Christianity and the things of God and the Bible for well over an hour—all new territory for R. C. Then one of them turned the open Bible in R. C.'s direction, and he instructed R. C. to look. It was Ecclesiastes 11:3. The second part of that verse reads:

> If a tree falls to the south or to the north,
>   in the place where the tree falls, there it will lie.

It cut R. C. in two. He saw himself as that tree. He saw himself in a state of torpid paralysis, fallen, rotting, and decaying. He left the table and returned to his dorm room. When he entered, he didn't turn on the light. He just knelt down beside his bed, praying to God, asking God to forgive his sins.

R. C. never made it to Youngstown, Ohio, that Friday night. God had other plans for his life.

Ecclesiastes 11:3 is not the first verse one typically thinks of for evangelism. R. C. would say, "I think I'm probably the only person in church history who was converted to Christ by that verse."[1] I think it's safe to remove the "probably" from his assessment. While it's not typical, or even thought of, as an evangelistic verse, it nevertheless fits rather well. The verse has texture, imagery, a hint of drama. Even though R. C. would not consider himself a Calvinist or embrace Calvinism for a few years yet, the verse is also Calvinistic. Better, one could say the verse is Pauline.

God used that verse to show R. C. the true state of his own soul and life. R. C. had felt dead. Now he knew that his true spiritual condition was death. He had considered himself a Christian. He went to church, after all. Now he knew what Christianity was truly about.

---

1   R. C. Sproul, "R. C. Sproul's Awakening to the Christian Faith," September 13, 2017, https://www .ligonier.org/blog/rc-sprouls-awakening-christian-faith/.

Sixty years later in September of 2017, in what would be R. C.'s final months, Ligonier Ministries recorded R. C.'s recollection of his conversion:

> I'm coming up on the 60th anniversary of my conversion to the Christian faith. It was in September of 1957. And I will never forget, I think I'm the only person in the history of the church to be converted by a particular verse that God used to open up my heart and my eyes to the truth of Christ. It came from the book of Ecclesiastes, where the author of Ecclesiastes describes, in metaphorical terms, a tree that falls in the forest and where it falls, there it stays. And God awakened my soul by considering that passage, as I saw myself as a tree falling, and rotting, and decaying. And that was the description of my life. That's where I was. Nobody had to tell me that I was a sinner, I knew that. It was abundantly clear to me.
>
> But as I went to my bedroom that night and got on my knees, my experience was one of transcendent forgiveness. And I was overwhelmed by the tender mercy of God, the sweetness of His grace, and the awakening He gave me for my life. And I pray that any of you who have not yet experienced an awakening to the reality of Christ would have that experience in your life. That you would look carefully at the Scriptures and the Word of God, and that that Word may be used in power to quicken your soul and your spirit that you too may be awakened to the fullness of glory, and peace, and joy that is ours in Christ.[2]

Johnny was also affected by that conversation with the two upperclassmen. That night, he too prayed for forgiveness.

The next morning, on Saturday, R. C. awoke a changed man. He was eager to talk to Johnny about what happened and what would come next. Johnny, on the other hand, seemed not even to remember much of what had happened. He didn't want to talk about it. He just rolled

2 Sproul, "R. C. Sproul's Awakening."

on like it never happened. All Johnny wanted to do was to make it to Youngstown that night. But R. C. truly had been turned from his sin and was turned toward God.

R. C. had never read the Bible. Now he read it through in a couple of weeks. He devoured it. He devoted so much attention to reading the Bible and exploring all that he could of Christianity that he had little time for anything else. He became obsessed.

He had entered college as a history major. In his freshman history course he realized he had no framework for understanding history. The class began exploring the great civilizations. R. C. had no geographical or chronological grid on which to put them. It was time to change his major.

In keeping with his newfound faith, the only subject that interested him was the Bible. At the registrar's office, he switched to a major in religion.

R. C.'s conversion had a significant immediate impact. It also had long-term, even lifelong, impacts. At least three lifelong impacts stem from R. C.'s conversion. First, R. C. would later say, "I owe every human being I know to do everything I can to communicate the gospel to them." That dedication led R. C. to devote his life to teaching. Second, as mentioned, R. C. devoured the Bible in those first few weeks after his conversion. He would continue that intense biblical study throughout his life, eventually undertaking the production of a study Bible. When the revised edition of the Reformation Study Bible was produced in 2015, R. C. said, "We call this the Reformation Study Bible, but we really hope that it causes a Bible study Reformation." It's not enough to read the Bible, he would often say; we are called to study it. The third lifelong impact has to do with R. C.'s understanding of the author of the Bible. He testified how his original, virginal reading of the Bible left him with one overwhelming realization: the God of the Bible is a God who plays for keeps. It's worth noting that R. C. began in the Old Testament, read it through, and then moved on to the New. He called the Old Testament "the personal autobiography of God."[3]

3   Stephen Nichols with R. C. Sproul, personal interview, October 20, 2017.

R. C.'s life may be characterized by earnestness, even dogged determination. He certainly accomplished a great deal between his conversion in 1957 and his death in 2017. That drive stemmed from his desire, his deep-seated passion, to know God and to make God known. The seed for that was sewn in September of 1957.

Those are the lifelong impacts of R. C.'s conversion. There were also more immediate impacts. R. C. had to tell his steady girlfriend, Vesta. Several months after his conversion, and Vesta knowing about it full well, Vesta visited R. C. at Westminster College from her college, Wooster, in Ohio. That was unusual. He usually made the four-hour trek to see her. But this time, R. C. had invited her to come to see him. She took the bus and arrived on campus. He was then going to drive her home. He asked, however, if she wouldn't mind going to a prayer meeting before they left for Pleasant Hills. At that prayer meeting in February, Vesta, convicted of her own sin and need of a savior, became a Christian. She recalls now that she thought it was nice for R. C. that he had become a Christian. Coming off his challenging years of high school and his father's death, she thought his becoming a Christian would be a good thing for him. She was glad to go along to this prayer meeting.

They had a short devotional; then they began to pray. Vesta thought, "If my friends at college could see me now, they would die laughing." But during that time of prayer, Vesta had a sudden and distinct impression "like an electric current." She knew then that the Holy Spirit is real, that the Spirit converts, and that the Spirit works in people's lives. Vesta said, "Now I know who the Holy Spirit is."[4] R. C. added, "Of course, she had attended church for years. She had heard the Holy Spirit mentioned. . . . In her conversion, she made a transition from understanding Christianity in an abstract sense to understanding it as a personal relationship with God."[5] The Holy Spirit worked in her life that night in February. As they left, she told R. C. she had been converted. He was excited. R. C. and

---

4 Vesta Sproul, cited in R. C. Sproul, *Who Is the Holy Spirit?* (Sanford, FL: Reformation Trust, 2012), 3.
5 Sproul, Who Is the Holy Spirit?, 5.

Vesta, already with so many shared memories, places, and times, had one new significant place and memory in common. They were both converted on the campus of Westminster College.

The Blessing of Great Teachers

The strangest and most unlikely response to R. C.'s conversion came from his pastor. R. C. was so excited to tell him. So he did. After hearing R. C.'s testimony of his conversion, his pastor said to him, "If you believe in the physical resurrection of Christ, you're a damn fool."[6] R. C. had been surrounded by liberalism all his life. Now, on the other side of his conversion and knowing the reality and truth of Christianity, he saw liberalism for the insidious force that it is.

Having quickly realized that his pastor would not be the one mentoring him, R. C. soon met one who would be such a mentor, Dr. Thomas Gregory. The number of freshmen at Westminster College necessitated fifteen sections of the required Bible survey course. This was more than the Bible department could fill. Each year they relied on a professor from the philosophy department, Thomas Gregory, to take one of the sections. After earning his undergraduate degree at Temple University, Dr. Gregory received his MDiv from Westminster Theological Seminary in Philadelphia. There he studied under Ned Stonehouse, E. J. Young, John Murray, and Cornelius Van Til. After Westminster Seminary, Dr. Gregory received an MA and a PhD in philosophy from the University of Pennsylvania. He was a scholar, and he was a thoroughgoing theological conservative. He taught philosophy at Westminster College. Students were assigned faculty members for their Bible survey course. They did not choose. Of all the faculty teaching the Bible survey sections, Dr. Gregory was the only theological conservative, the only one committed to a high view of the authority of Scripture. R. C. was assigned to Dr. Gregory's section.

6 "Sproul Memoirs," session 3, recorded January 2011, Ligonier Ministries, Sanford, Florida.

R. C. assiduously applied himself to the Bible survey course. He had a reputation on campus as a Christian. After his conversion early in the semester, he told anyone who stood still long enough to listen to him about Christ and about the Bible. Consequently, R. C. had this self-imposed commitment to knowing everything he could know about the Bible. He did not want to appear as though he didn't know something. No biblical detail escaped him. This was a man who had nearly every statistic imaginable for the Pirates, from the inception of the team, at his fingertips. He was skilled in mastering details, and he plied that skill to mastering Holy Writ. He was ready for any question, any quiz, any test. All the while, R. C. sat under the tutelage of Dr. Gregory.

R. C. Sproul preached his first sermon as a freshman in college and within a year of his conversion. He entitled it "With Child-Like Faith" and delivered it at a Christian and Missionary Alliance church not far from the campus of Westminster. The second sermon came that same year. It was delivered at the New Castle Rescue Mission. R. C. was part of a gospel team. There was music, a sermon, an altar call. R. C. had been converted; it changed his entire outlook and gave his life new direction.

As for sports while in college, R. C. had his setbacks. His multisport junior and high school life had taken a toll on his knees. R. C. was the kind of athlete that left it all out on the field, dragging himself home after nearly every game. He had fluid drained regularly and some kind of liquid injected into his knees by an orthopedic surgeon in Pittsburgh. After these visits, R. C. recalled that he could hear fluid squishing in his knees as he walked. While playing basketball in a pickup game at home over the weekend, he was on the receiving end of a thrown elbow to his temple. He drove back to college, 60 miles north. Not feeling well, he visited the infirmary. The campus doctor sent him right back to a downtown Pittsburgh hospital. R. C. drove another sixty miles south. A neurologist examined R. C. Since R. C. was alone, the neurologist asked him how he got to the hospital. R. C. said he drove. The neurologist replied, "That's not possible." R. C. had suffered a severe concussion.

He had driven not only once but twice—and for a total of 120 miles at that. He was ordered to stay home for several weeks, during which he was significantly distressed and in pain.[7]

Westminster had a policy at that time that if you were admitted on an athletic scholarship and then injured, you retained the scholarship during your tenure. R. C. never wore a Westminster uniform in a single game. Westminster also had a policy that if you were on an athletic scholarship, you received an A in physical education. That, along with his A in his Bible survey courses, kept R. C. from flunking out his first year in college.

One irony from his freshman year concerned his speech course. R. C. was elected from all the freshman speech sections to give the address to the whole college—a big deal. On the one hand, this comes as no surprise. R. C. was known as a consummate orator. On the other hand—and here's the irony—his grade in speech was a D.

Second Conversion

For his sophomore year in college, R. C. was determined to learn under Dr. Gregory again. This time it was an introduction to philosophy class. You might recall that R. C. was not hearing edifying sermons from the pulpit of Pleasant Hills Community United Presbyterian Church. As a substitute, R. C. acquired a number of small printed booklets of Billy Graham sermons. You might also recall that in high school R. C. had mastered the skill of holding up a book in front of him while he slept in class. In college he modified that skill. He sat through most of his classes with the course's text open in front of him, only as cover while he read those Billy Graham sermons.

But he was excited about Dr. Gregory's class. The first day, the lecture was on David Hume's *An Enquiry Concerning Human Understanding*. Boring, thought R. C. "So much nonsense." And it was back to a Billy Graham sermon. Then one day Dr. Gregory started lecturing on

7 Stephen Nichols with R. C. Sproul, personal interview, April 7, 2017.

Augustine's concept of creation *ex nihilo*, that God created all things out of nothing. Augustine had coined this term, creation *ex nihilo*, and it spoke to the very nature and essence of God. R. C. would later testify, "My understanding of the nature of God had exploded." It was, actually, only the beginning of the explosion.

The first thing R. C. did after that lecture was to go to the registrar's office again, to change his major again. He had changed from history to religion. Now he changed his major from religion to philosophy. There would be no more changes. He would graduate from Westminster College as a philosophy major. Vesta once commented on that change of major in his sophomore year at college, observing that it had made all the difference in R. C.'s future teaching, writing, and ministry.[8]

Changing his major was the first thing R. C. did. The second thing he did was to take his midnight walk to the chapel on the campus of Westminster College. The way R. C. tells it, however, it was not something he did. It was something he was compelled to do. He writes of this moment, what he called his second conversion, in the opening pages of *The Holiness of God*. He also tells the story in the very first episode of *Renewing Your Mind*, aired on October 3, 1994. R. C. recalls the nighttime trek:

> If you think back over your life, you will be able to identify, I'm sure, a handful of crisis experiences, crisis moments that forever afterwards changed the course of your life. When I think over my own life, I always go back to a moment in the year 1958, that took place in the dead of winter during my years in college.
>
> I was lying in bed one night and my body was tired, but I couldn't get to sleep. My mind was racing. I had this overwhelming urge to get up out of bed. I was compelled to leave the room. A deep, undeniable summons called me. I swung my legs out over the bed and I got into my clothes and I went out into the night. It was a bitter cold night.

8 Nichols with Sproul, personal interview, April 7, 2017.

I remember it vividly. It had snowed the entire day and long into the evening. But by now, nearing midnight, the skies had cleared. There was a full moon. The stars were bright in the heavens. It was one of those ghostly moments in a country rural setting after a fresh snowfall where the night was silent and still, and there was a beautiful blanket of snow across the fields and hanging from the limbs of the trees.

I began to make my way across the campus. No one else was out. There was this eerie silence. I could hear the ice crunching under my feet as I was walking up the street. I made my way deliberately to the college chapel, which was adjacent to the chief administration building of the college. It was called Old Main. And Old Main was adorned with this huge tower, and in the tower there was this large clock like Big Ben. It was always my custom to listen to the chimes and count them every time to make sure that the clock was correct. In the silence of the night, I could hear the gears of the clock as they began to grind and as they clunked into place. Then came four musical chimes to signal the full hour, followed by the strikes. This night, this moment, I counted the striking of the chimes to the number twelve. Midnight. And then I opened the front door of the chapel. It was a huge oak door under a gothic arch leading into the narthex and beyond that, the chapel, a mini-cathedral. I opened the creaking door, feeling its heaviness. Every single sound was accentuated by the silence. The door closed behind me. I had to stand in the narthex to allow my eyes to adjust to the darkness. The only light came from the reflected rays from the moon as they seeped through the stained glass windows.

I began to walk down the center aisle of the chapel and my footsteps sounded like hobnail boots of German soldiers marching up cobblestone streets. I could hear them reverberating throughout the chapel. Finally, I reached the chancel. I knelt at that place and had a sensation of a foreboding loneliness. I sensed that I was absolutely alone. And then almost in an instant, I was overcome by the sense of another presence. It was almost tactile. It was like I could reach out and touch the massive presence of God. I just knelt there and basked in this sensation of being in the presence of God.

I had an inner conflict of two emotions colliding in my heart. On the one hand I had this dreadful fear. I had the sensation, this chill that began at the base of my spine and ran all the way up my back into my fingers, and I had goose bumps on my flesh. I was clearly frightened by a sense of the presence of God, and yet at the same time I felt drawn to luxuriate, to bask in that moment. I sensed an overwhelming flood of peace come into my soul. It was one of those experiences that I wanted to continue forever. I didn't want to move.

I had been a Christian for a little over a year, and my conversion to Christ was, up until this evening, obviously the most dramatic changing point in my life. I had fallen in love with Jesus, and my life turned upside down. My friends thought I had lost my mind. They couldn't get over this transformation and concern that had marked my personality. I was obsessed with learning the Bible in that first year. But that night in the chapel, I had a sudden epiphany of the grandeur, of the otherness, of the majesty of God. What happened was almost like a second conversion experience for me. I had gone through this conversion to Christ. I had fallen in love with Jesus, the Second Person of the Trinity. But on this occasion, I suddenly had a whole new understanding of the character of God the Father. I knew in that hour that I had tasted of the holy grail. Within me was born a new thirst that could never be fully satisfied in this world.

I know that God is not isolated to the confines of a church building, but there is something about a sanctuary that is holy ground. There's something about the front door to a church that marks a threshold from the profane to the sacred, from the secular to the holy. Even in Israel in the tabernacle and the temple there was a place within that sanctuary that was called the holy place, and even the holy place was separated by this massive veil from the inner sanctum that was called the *sanctus sanctorum*—the holy of holies, where only the high priest could go, and that only after elaborate rituals of ceremonial cleansing and then only once a year. I was looking for a place like that. That's why I had to answer that summons and get out of bed. And that's why I had to walk through the cold and through the snow to go to that chapel. I found a refuge, a haven, a sanctuary where I could be still and know that He was God. A holy God.[9]

This moment marked R. C.'s lifelong pursuit of the holiness of God. R. C. summarized it in one sentence: "I had an awakening to the biblical concept of God that changed my whole life after that."[10]

John Calvin opened his magisterial *Institutes of the Christian Religion* with this sentence: "Nearly all the wisdom that we possess, that is sound and true wisdom, consists of two parts: the knowledge of God and the knowledge of ourselves."[11] R. C.'s first and second conversions illustrate this nearly precisely. His first conversion testifies to the knowledge that R. C. had of himself as a dead tree. Powerless. Unable. Rotting. Dead and decaying. His second conversion testifies to who God is in his transcendent being. Alive. Eternal. All-powerful. Holy.

These two poles, who God is and who we are, introduced a third key theological theme, that of the necessity of a substitute. As R. C.'s theology developed—and as his teaching ministry began—three themes emerged that may be put into simple, direct propositions:

1. God is holy.
2. We are not.
3. We need a substitute.

These three propositions came to serve as the foundation for his teaching and for his major contributions to the Christian tradition and to

---

9 R. C. Sproul, "The Otherness of God," *Renewing Your Mind*, October 3, 1994, edited transcript. See also his account in *The Holiness of God* (1985; repr., Carol Stream, IL: Tyndale, 1998), 3–7.

10 Nichols with Sproul, personal interview, October 20, 2017.

11 John Calvin, *Institutes of the Christian Religion*, ed. John T. McNeill, trans. Ford Lewis Battles (Philadelphia: Westminster Press, 1960), 1.1.1.

twentieth- and twenty-first-century evangelical and Reformed thought and life. What is important to see at this juncture in R. C.'s life is the building of the foundation for these emphases and contributions. That foundation consisted of the following: assiduous biblical study, especially engaging the Old Testament; deep theological reflection, especially of the Reformed classical tradition; and attention to the history and consequences of ideas, especially the history of philosophy. On top of this, R. C. had considerable communication skills. The words of his elementary teacher, "Don't let anyone tell you you can't write," echoed more and more strongly as he made his way through his college courses. We could add to a young R. C., "Never let anyone tell you you can't speak."

Outselling the Fuller Brush Man

During college, R. C. lived in a Civil War–era apartment building on the second floor. Fastidious from the time he was young, he liked to keep the apartment clean. During one such cleaning time, he realized he needed a mop. There was a hardware store across the street. It was raining outside, so he put on a coat and his boots and had just reached for the door that led to the landing of the external stairs, when he heard a knock on the door. It was a Fuller Brush salesman. He asked R. C. if he needed anything. R. C. said, "I could use a mop."

While R. C. was taking off his coat and boots and staying dry, the Fuller Brush salesman was outside in the rain going down the steps to retrieve a mop from his car, then back up the steps to R. C.'s apartment. They started talking, and R. C. mentioned that he too was a salesman for a publishing company, which was Samuel Craig's Presbyterian & Reformed Publishing Company out of, at that time, Philadelphia, Pennsylvania. Presbyterian & Reformed, shortened in 1992 to just P&R, published hefty texts from the Reformed stalwarts of the late nineteenth and early twentieth centuries. They published the writings of B. B. Warfield, Oswald T. Allis, Cornelius Van Til, Marcellus Kik, and Geerhardus Vos. Presbyterian & Reformed enlisted students across campuses to sell books for them. This student salesforce received a personal copy of the publisher's entire list and made a percentage from every book sold. R. C. started sharing the virtues of the publisher's books with the Fuller Brush man. By the time R. C. was finished, the Fuller Brush man walked down the Civil War–era stairs with an armload of books. He spent far more on books than R. C. had paid for the mop. R. C. said he thinks he might be the only man in America who outsold a Fuller Brush man on a house call.

R. C. also hustled the pinball machine at the local grill. If you scored a certain number of points, the pinball machine spit out tokens, which then could be retrieved for food at the grill or even turned in for cash. Most customers lost money on the pinball machine. They put in their quarter and seemed unable to reach that level for the payoff. But R. C. had figured out a way to master the game. He would cash in his tokens for more quarters, which yielded even more tokens, which then yielded money for food and coins to call a certain college dormitory at Wooster College in Ohio. Sometimes the cashier, who had gotten to know R. C., would front him the first quarter. Several games later, R. C. paid back the initial investment, had ordered food, and even left with a little change in his pocket.

Saving up that change and dollars here and there, R. C. finally had enough to buy an engagement ring. He made a trip to Wooster. They were walking through a park when R. C. pulled the box out of his pocket and handed it to Vesta. Vesta opened the box and saw the ring. R. C. does not recall that Vesta said yes. Instead he remembers her saying, "I have to get back to the dorm and show the girls."[12] The *Pittsburgh Press* reported, "At an open house Dec. 21, Mr. and Mrs. W. R. Voorhis of Pleasant Hills announced the engagement of their daughter, Vesta Ann, to Robert C. Sproul."[13] R. C. always loved Christmastime.

Early in the month of June 1960, Vesta graduated from college; then on June 11, 1960, they were married at Pleasant Hills Community

---

12 Nichols with personal interview, Sproul, April 7, 2017.
13 *Pittsburgh Press*, January 5, 1959, p. 11.

United Presbyterian Church. Dr. Paul Hudson and Dr. Thomas Gregory performed the ceremony. They went to Bermuda for their honeymoon, a gift from a Voorhis family friend. R. C. finished the summer working at a hospital. They made their first home in that apartment near the campus of Westminster. R. C. still had one more year of college. Vesta took a job on the college switchboard. 1960 was turning out to be a good year for R. C. On October 13, it got even better.

R. C. and Vesta were in the stands of Forbes Field when Bill Mazeroski hit his walk-off home run for the Pirates in the bottom of the ninth inning to win the World Series against the Yankees. It was the only time that had ever happened in a World Series. The last time the Pirates had won the World Series was in 1925. All of Pittsburgh celebrated. The newlyweds Mr. and Mrs. R. C. and Vesta Sproul did too.

That spring semester, R. C. wrote his senior thesis. He was a philosophy major, but he had also come to enjoy American literature. Much of that had to do with a professor who was a Melville scholar. R. C. had taken his course on Herman Melville and Mark Twain. R. C. combined those two interests, philosophy and literature, for his senior thesis, entitling it "The Existential Implications of Melville's *Moby Dick*." He identified himself as "Robert Sproul" on the title page. Reading this thesis, one could easily predict that a certain Robert Sproul was headed straight for a profession as a theologian, an engaging and insightful theologian.

R. C. weaves commentary on existentialist notions and ideas alongside analysis of the characters and plot twists of Melville's novel. Existentialism wrestles with the question of existence, intensified by the ever-present threat of death. Young scholar Sproul brings in Martin Heidegger: "Heidegger goes on to explain that the only way for man to have true existence, i.e., authentic being, is to have an authentic existential attitude toward death."[14] Sproul then declares, "Melville seems to have understood

---

14 Robert [R. C.] Sproul, "The Existential Implications of Melville's *Moby Dick*," unpublished senior thesis, Westminster College, New Wilmington, PA (1961), 4.

the very heart of this existential concept." In addition to authentic existence and the question of death, the existentialist wrestles, passionately, with the problem of evil.

Existentialism stresses the individual while not affirming egocentrism. The individual stands alone confronting the ultimate questions of truth, the ultimate questions of existence. In the pages of his thesis, R. C. contrasts two individuals, two main characters, Ishmael and Captain Ahab. The latter succumbs to egocentrism and, therefore, lives an inauthentic life, a "man without a 'personality.'" R. C. concludes that Ahab "failed to achieve true existential being," and ends up, in the words of Melville, a raving madman.[15]

Of course, the biblical character King Ahab informs and animates Melville's character Captain Ahab. So it is with Ishmael in Scripture. In the biblical plotline, Ishmael is an outcast, a wanderer, a loner. In the opening paragraphs of *Moby Dick*, that is the exact character we meet. And at the end of the novel, Ishmael is left alone. He's floating on an empty coffin—the threat of death is always near. The very last word of Melville's magisterial novel is *orphan*.

The main character that had R. C.'s attention, however, was the whale, the white whale. R. C. said undoubtedly *Moby Dick* is the great American novel, likely simply the greatest novel. He added that chapter 42, "The Whiteness of the Whale," might just be the greatest chapter ever written, next to Holy Scripture.

The last two paragraphs of that chapter are worth considering. They intrigued then college senior R. C. Sproul, and (I'm convinced) they lie behind what would come to be his classic text, *The Holiness of God*, from 1985. Melville's Ishmael, narrating, tells us that the whiteness of the whale "appalled him," implying that he'd rather not think or talk about it at all, but then Ishmael adds that he must explain the affect of the whiteness of the whale, lest "all these chapters might be naught." To put it another

15 Sproul, "Existential Implications," 7.

way, the "whiteness of the whale" becomes the hermeneutical key to unlock *Moby Dick*. And here's how Ishmael's narration ends in the final two paragraphs of chapter 42:

> But not yet have we solved the incantation of this whiteness, and learned why it appeals with such power to the soul; and more strange and far more portentous—why, as we have seen, it is at once the most meaning symbol of spiritual things, nay, the very veil of the Christian's Deity; and yet should be as it is, the intensifying agent in things the most appalling to mankind.
>
> Is it that by its indefiniteness it shadows forth the heartless voids and immensities of the universe, and thus stabs us from behind with the thought of annihilation, when beholding the white depths of the milky way? Or is it, that as in essence whiteness is not so much a color as the visible absence of color; and at the same time the concrete of all colors; is it for these reasons that there is such a dumb blankness, full of meaning, in a wide landscape of snows—a colorless, all-color of atheism from which we shrink? And when we consider that other theory of the natural philosophers, that all other earthly hues—every stately or lovely emblazoning—the sweet tinges of sunset skies and woods; yea, and the gilded velvets of butterflies, and the butterfly cheeks of young girls; all these are but subtile deceits, not actually inherent in substances, but only laid on from without; so that all dei-fied Nature absolutely paints like the harlot, whose allurements cover nothing but the charnel-house within; and when we proceed further, and consider that the mystical cosmetic which produces every one of her hues, the great principle of light, for ever remains white or colorless in itself, and if operating without medium upon matter, would touch all objects, even tulips and roses, with its own blank tinge—ponder-ing all this, the palsied universe lies before us a leper; and like wilful travellers in Lapland, who refuse to wear colored and coloring glasses upon their eyes, so the wretched infidel gazes himself blind at the

monumental white shroud that wraps all the prospect around him. And of all these things the Albino whale was the symbol. Wonder ye then at the fiery hunt?[16]

Ishmael found the white whale to be complex and ambiguous. He was not simply intrigued by the whale; he was terrified by it. Not so with Captain Ahab. He circumscribed the whale, and thought he, therefore, knew it and could control it—even kill it. R. C. explains. "Ahab thinks he 'knows' deity. He charts the whale; he knows its movements and its workings; yet he fails to understand its ultimate meaning. As the wicked king of old, Ahab reduces the multiplicity of deity to a concrete unit. Captain Ahab's 'Baal' becomes the great white whale." R. C. takes this one step further when he adds that Melville's use of Ahab's domesticated deity "seems to be an attack upon the shallow religious views of mankind."[17]

Against the shallow religious view stands Ishmael. Again, Ishmael sees the whale as "enigmatic, unknowable in its entirety."[18] Melville has Ishmael declare: "I know him not, and never will." Further, as a result of Ishmael coming face-to-face with the white whale, Ishmael sees himself in all of "his human frailties and finitude."[19]

This confrontation between Ishmael and Ahab mirrors, for R. C., the confrontation of God and Isaiah in the early verses of chapter 6 of the prophet. R. C.'s bachelor's thesis is a foreshadowing of R. C.'s *The Holiness of God*. In the presence of the thrice-holy God, Isaiah becomes undone.[20]

Back to the bachelor's thesis, R. C. notes how Ahab, and all of those who entirely underestimated the white whale, met their end in the confrontation: "All of these men who have reduced deity to the 'petty' cannot stand in the presence of the mighty whale."[21] Ishmael alone survived.

16 Herman Melville, *Moby Dick: Or, The Whale* (1851; repr., Norwalk, CT: Easton Press, 1977), 206–7.
17 Sproul, "Existential Implications," 20.
18 Sproul, "Existential Implications," 21.
19 Sproul, "Existential Implications," 21.
20 Sproul, *Holiness of God*, 32–38.
21 Sproul, "Existential Implications," 21.

That was what R. C. was working on during the spring semester of his senior year. Meanwhile, Vesta was experiencing a difficult pregnancy and on bed rest under doctor's orders. R. C. recalls one harrowing moment when Vesta had lost a great deal of blood. He carried her out of the apartment and down those old steps to the hospital. He thought he was going to lose her and his unborn child.

That May, R. C. graduated with his BA in philosophy. That summer he worked as an electrician's assistant in a hospital. And in that hospital in August, Sherrie Lee Sproul was born. With a new baby, R. C. and Vesta left their first apartment in New Wilmington and headed south, back to the 'Burgh, to Pittsburgh Theological Seminary.

3

STUDENT PROFESSOR
PASTOR TEACHER

Great teachers who are faithful to God's
Word are a blessing to God's church.

R. C. SPROUL

GETTING A DIVINITY DEGREE from Pittsburgh Theological Seminary
was not R. C. Sproul's first choice for his graduate education. Like his
college professor Dr. Thomas Gregory, he wanted to pursue a doctorate
in philosophy. R. C. had applied for and was accepted into the PhD
program in philosophy at Edinburgh University. Philosophy has been a
significant major at Edinburgh since it was established by royal charter
in 1582. In the 1960s it was one of the premier institutions and depart-
ments in the world. But Dr. Gregory suggested to R. C. to first take a
graduate degree in theology.

While a sophomore at Westminster College, R. C. visited Westminster
Theological Seminary in Philadelphia. He sat in on a class and then had
lunch with some faculty and students in the dining room at Machen
Hall. He was seated across from Dr. Robert Donald Knudsen, professor
of apologetics and systematic theology. Dr. Knudsen asked the prospec-
tive student, "Tell me, young man, is God transcendent or immanent?"

R. C. had just taken up a spoonful of soup, and it was all he could do not to spit it out. That is to say, he didn't understand the question, let alone the answer. R. C. had been a Christian for a short time and had never had a single theology class at that point.

Being 60 miles away, Pittsburgh Theological Seminary faculty often visited Westminster College to speak in chapel and guest lecture in classes. R. C. was struck by then president Dr. Addison Leitch. Leitch was a scholar of the first order. Having a degree from Pittsburgh-Xenia Theological Seminary, Leitch took a PhD from Cambridge University. He had taught at Pikeville College and Grove City College before joining the faculty at Pittsburgh and, for a time, serving as the seminary's president. In addition to being a good scholar and stellar communicator, Leitch also had that quality that could not always be counted on around the Pittsburgh Presbytery and on the campus of Pittsburgh Seminary. Leitch was a theological conservative.

Wipe Off the Spot

R. C. had also heard the other theological conservative from Pittsburgh Theological Seminary while at Westminster College, the inimitable Dr. John Gerstner. R. C. heard him "give a speech on predestination." R. C. then added, "which I hated." R. C. clarified that he hated the doctrine. But he wasn't all that wooed by Gerstner either. After Gerstner's lecture, R. C. approached him and asked a question. Dr. Gerstner answered the question. Then R. C. said, "That's not what I meant to ask." This exchange occurred for a while before Dr. Gerstner declared, "Young man, you need to learn to say what you mean and mean what you say." In the words of R. C., "That was not a good introduction to Gerstner."[1]

R. C. had a more positive introduction to the dean of Pittsburgh Theological Seminary (PTS). The dean had driven up to speak for chapel and then got snowed in at the campus. He left his car there and found

---

1 These quotes all come from Stephen Nichols with R. C. Sproul, personal interview, May 12, 2017.

someone to take him home. R. C. got the job of returning the dean's car to the Pittsburgh Seminary campus. R. C. remembered it was a Saab, "or some kind of foreign car that didn't work right." It wasn't the easiest drive he'd ever had. It endeared R. C. to the dean, and the dean was very friendly to him after that. R. C. came to discover that the dean was in fact one of the leading liberals at the seminary and disliked Gerstner due to Gerstner's conservative theology.[2]

R. C. offers his conclusion to the whole matter: "So it was a strange set of circumstances that got me to Pittsburgh Seminary."[3]

R. C. worked as an electrician's assistant in the hospital that summer. One evening he came home and glanced at the newspaper. The headline caught his attention, announcing that Dr. Leitch was leaving the seminary. R. C. recalled, "I didn't have one day under Leitch. That's why I went there." Leitch left PTS for Tarkio College in Missouri, and from there he went to Gordon Conwell. His first wife died, and he married the missionary widow Elisabeth Elliot in 1969. Leitch died of cancer four years later.

Recall that R. C. went to college unconverted. By his own testimony, he had two conversions while in college. A few more "conversions" awaited him in seminary. He went to seminary not a Calvinist. We have already established that he did not care much for the doctrine of predestination. He also went into seminary committed to presuppositional apologetics. And, finally, it was while he was in seminary that his "battlefield theologian" DNA began to emerge.

R. C. knew theological liberalism. He was saved out of it. He found Dr. Gregory to be an island in a sea of it at Westminster. But he wasn't ready for the politics of it. That he would come to see firsthand at PTS. Some history is in order to understand fully what R. C. got when he decided to go to PTS.

Pittsburgh, richly settled by Scotch-Irish, was full of Presbyterians. The original church building of what is now First Presbyterian Church was

2 Nichols with Sproul, personal interview, May 12, 2017.
3 Nichols with Sproul, personal interview, May 12, 2017.

a log structure built in 1773. Around that humble beginning grew up one of the largest presbyteries in the United States. Pittsburgh was also home to Western Theological Seminary. It was called "Western" because at one time Pittsburgh was the western frontier of America. Princeton and Union, in New York and in Virginia, were the seminaries to serve the Eastern Seaboard. Western would handle the frontier. It had a very significant professor in the nineteenth century, Benjamin Breckenridge Warfield, who is known as the "Lion of Princeton." But before he was at Princeton, he taught at Western Theological Seminary in Pittsburgh. The same was true of A. A. Hodge. He also first taught at Western before moving to Princeton. It was from their offices at Western Theological Seminary that Warfield and A. A. Hodge cowrote the article "Inspiration," published in the *Presbyterian Review*, April 1881. The first roar of Princeton's Lion came from Pittsburgh.

Pittsburgh Theological Seminary was the merger of two seminaries: Pittsburgh, which was formerly called Western, of the Presbyterian Church USA (PCUSA) and Pittsburgh-Xenia Theological Seminary of the United Presbyterian Church of North America (UPCNA). Pittsburgh-Xenia stretches back to 1794. Originally in Pittsburgh, it relocated to Xenia, Ohio.

The two denominations, PCUSA and UPCNA, merged in 1958. The two seminaries merged in 1959 and settled on the name Pittsburgh Theological Seminary. Drs. Gerstner and Leitch came with the merger. They were theological conservatives. Leitch got pushed out. Gerstner, bulletproof because of the fine print of the merger negotiations, hung in all the way to his retirement in 1982.

R. C. described Dr. Gerstner as a lifeline through seminary. Many could see the influence Gerstner had on R. C. Many even heard it. No doubt R. C. was the brightest shining star in the constellation of Gerstner's students over decades of teaching. You might recall, however, that R. C. began his time at PTS not all that impressed with Gerstner. That changed almost immediately.

In a fall class in his first year, Gerstner was offering a critique of the presuppositional apologetics of Cornelius Van Til of Westminster Theological Seminary in Philadelphia, when R. C. rose in defense. Earlier that spring, for a college class, R. C. had written a paper critiquing the classical arguments for the existence of God from a presuppositional viewpoint. R. C. had become a presuppositionalist under the influence of Dr. Thomas Gregory, who had been taught by Van Til himself. R. C. made his case. Then Gerstner spent the next ten minutes dismantling R. C. Or, as R. C. put it, it took Gerstner ten minutes "to wipe off the spot where I stood. And not only did he dismantle my arguments and destroy them, but the thing was I knew it. . . . I lost, and I knew I lost."[4] In that instant, R. C. had a deep-seated respect for Gerstner that continued to grow over the years.

Gerstner was the champion of orthodoxy at Pittsburgh. Jeffrey S. McDonald, Gerstner's biographer, speaks of Gerstner's isolation among the faculty: with the exception of one other moderately conservative faculty member, "nearly all of Gerstner's fellow faculty members at PTS disagreed with his doctrinal conservatism."[5] Gerstner would often simply stay quiet in faculty meetings. He knew his vote would not matter, and he also knew his colleagues "appreciated my not talking too much, because it was a waste of time."[6] But he was never quiet in class, or on the debate stage, or in the many pulpits he filled.

R. C. sensed a similar theological isolation. He recalls that there were about five other theologically conservative students at PTS at that time— one of them, David Williams, had been converted to Christ through Gerstner. R. C. also felt the tension in his classes from the theologically liberal faculty. The seminary curriculum had one course that surveyed all of the New Testament books. As they finished Acts, the professor

---

4 Nichols with Sproul, personal interview, May 12, 2017.
5 Jeffrey S. McDonald, *John Gerstner and the Renewal of Presbyterian and Reformed Evangelicalism in Modern America* (Eugene, OR: Pickwick, 2017), 101.
6 McDonald, *John Gerstner and the Renewal*, 101.

said, "Most theologians get excited about Romans, but I don't. Let's go now to 1 Corinthians."[7] These students were studying to be pastors, yet they were not taught even one minute's worth on Paul's Epistle to the Romans. It's easy to see why R. C. called Gerstner a "lifeline" during his seminary days. Gerstner, like Dr. Gregory before him, would be a model for R. C. Of Thomas Gregory, R. C. said succinctly, "He was precise, and he knew his stuff."[8] The exact same could be said of Gerstner. Precision and a high level of competency, mastery, would come to be similar hallmarks of their protégé.

Marcus Barth, son of Karl Barth, taught New Testament at Pittsburgh. If you want to see his father's desk from his office at the University of Basel and at which Karl Barth spent fifty years writing, you need to go to the Hansen Reading Room on the second floor of the library on the campus of Pittsburgh Theological Seminary. Marcus Barth arranged for it and several of his father's items to be on display at PTS in 1964, the year of his father's retirement. Pittsburgh Theological Seminary had long since shed its rich historical and confessional heritage, casting its lot with the liberal impulses of the day.

Marcus Barth was famous, or at least his father was. One of R. C.'s classmates would go on to be famous. He was Fred Rogers. Born in Latrobe, Fred Rogers's family moved to central Florida. After graduating from Rollins College, across the lake from his family home, Fred Rogers moved back to Pittsburgh. He took his degree form PTS in 1963 and became an ordained Presbyterian minister. In 1968 *Mister Rogers' Neighborhood* began its legendary thirty-three-year run on the National Education Network, which then became the Public Broadcasting Service.

The PTS neighborhood was rather charming with tree-lined streets in the East Liberty area of Pittsburgh. R. C. and Vesta, and newborn Sherrie, lived in an apartment building with other seminarians. The apartment

7 Nichols with Sproul, personal interview, May 12, 2017.
8 Stephen Nichols with R. C. Sproul, personal interview, April 7, 2017.

STUDENT PROFESSOR PASTOR TEACHER

the Sprouls moved into had belonged to Shirley Jones's mother. By 1961 Shirley Jones had a number of very successful musical movies behind her; and the television series *The Partridge Family* was ahead of her when the Sprouls moved in. Her mother had left behind a life-size painting of the actress in the apartment. The Sprouls enjoyed their young married life. Vesta described the apartment building, full of seminarians, as more like a dorm. R. C. often brought his friends to his apartment to study. The couples played "a lot of cards, a lot of bridge."[9]

'Tis Rational

In the classroom, Gerstner was putting R. C. through his paces. "I studied for his classes extra hard because he was a really hard professor," recalled R. C. A course on Jonathan Edwards (1703–1758) required R. C. to dig in.[10] There were twenty-two in the class. Twenty were auditing. Only R. C. and one other student summoned the courage to take the class for credit and to face the dreaded Gerstner examination. It was R. C.'s first time diving in to Edwards. Edwards would remain one of the major stars in the constellation of influences on R. C. In one of the many question-and-answer sessions from one of the many Ligonier conferences, R. C. would be asked, "Which figure from church history influenced you the most?" R. C. answered, "My guy is Edwards."[11]

But the colonial philosopher-theologian-pastor Jonathan Edwards was all new terrain for R. C. In that first encounter, Edwards made an immediate impression on the seminarian. R. C. noted, "Studying Edwards led me to be a convinced Calvinist."[12] R. C. went to PTS a presuppositionalist and a non-Calvinist. Through Gerstner directly, he became a classical apologist, and through Gerstner indirectly and Edwards directly, R. C. became a Calvinist. These views would come to mark the ministry

---

9 Nichols with Sproul, April 7, 2017.
10 Nichols with Sproul, April 7, 2017.
11 R. C. Sproul, "Question and Answer Session," RBC Fall Conference, September 19, 2015.
12 Nichols with Sproul, personal interview, April 7, 2017.

and teaching of R. C. Sproul and be part of his contribution to the American and even global church at the end of the twentieth and in the early twenty-first centuries. In particular, it was the weight of Edwards's arguments that convinced R. C.—not to mention Edwards's contagious passion for theology and for God Himself.

Edwards followed the typical Puritan sermon form in his preaching, which the Puritans learned from William Perkins's *The Art of Prophesying*. Prophesying meant preaching, and from the year of 1592, when Perkins's book was first published, onward his book could be found in nearly every Puritan minister's library.[13] The sermon form consisted of three elements: text, doctrine, application. The doctrine section consisted of articulating a single proposition, derived from the text. The minister would even say, "The doctrine from this text is . . ." and proceed to give the proposition, the thesis. Then the doctrine section would set about proving and demonstrating the thesis. Edwards would typically defend the text's doctrine by two lines of argument. Edwards would say "'Tis Rational," and "'Tis Biblical." With the precision of a surgeon, Edwards applied this methodology to the biblical text and to theology. This won over R. C.

R. C. would keep a card on his desk that read, "You are responsible to preach and to teach what the Bible says, not what you want it to say." R. C. had bucked the doctrine of predestination. Curiously enough, Edwards also bucked the doctrine. In his "Personal Narrative," an autobiographical recounting of his conversion experience, Edwards confesses that he hated the doctrine of predestination: "From my childhood up, my mind had been wont to be full of objections against the doctrine of God's sovereignty, in choosing whom he would to eternal life, and rejecting whom he pleased; leaving them eternally to perish, and be everlastingly tormented in hell. It used to appear like a horrible doctrine to me."[14] But

13 William Perkins, *The Art of Prophesying* (1592; repr., Edinburgh, UK: Banner of Truth, 1996).
14 Jonathan Edwards, "Personal Narrative," *Works of Jonathan Edwards*, vol. 16, *Letters and Personal Writings* (New Haven, CT: Yale University Press, 1998), 791–92.

Edwards had a conversion, which led him to have not only a conviction, "but a delightful conviction" of God's sovereignty. Edwards adds, "The doctrine of God's sovereignty has very often appeared an exceeding pleasant, bright, and sweet doctrine to me; and absolute sovereignty is what I love to ascribe to God."[15]

Through Gerstner and Edwards, R. C. saw that his own objections to the doctrine were in fact objections to Scripture. Once R. C. saw that, he submitted to the text of Scripture. "'Tis rational" and "'Tis biblical" was the powerful one-two combination that would be enough to convince R. C. Once convinced, R. C., like Edwards and Gerstner, was full-throttled in his conviction. Once R. C. knew a truth, accepted it and saw a proposition as a truth, he moved directly to defending and contending for it. And if you were in earshot of him, you would hear him proclaim it persuasively. He was known for this, and you can trace the roots of it back to his foundational years as a student.

R. C. was also learning a theological methodology on top of the theological content. To put it another way, R. C. was not only putting into place his theology; he was also forming what kind of theologian he would be. He became, as he later called it, a battlefield theologian. Augustine, in his contentions with Pelagius and a host of others, the Reformers, Edwards, the Princetonians—these were battlefield theologians all. So was Gerstner at PTS and in the Presbyterian Church in the 1960s. R. C. would remind us that Paul was a battlefield theologian in Galatians. Jude commended his original audience to contend for the faith, *earnestly*, as did Peter, John, and the author of Hebrews.

Lyndora

During his second year in seminary, R. C. worked as a youth director at the large First Presbyterian Church of Charleroi. He also was able to make connections with Dr. Robert Lamont, pastor of the historic First

15 Edwards, "Personal Narrative," 792.

Presbyterian Church in Pittsburgh. With a congregation close to two thousand, large for a northern church at the time, and a national radio program, Lamont had significant influence. Alongside Nelson Bell, Harold Ockenga, Billy Graham, and others, Lamont was part of the group that started *Christianity Today*, and he served on the original board. He served on other boards, such as the board of Gordon College, then Gordon-Conwell Theological Seminary. Lamont's homiletical style influenced R. C. Lamont was a master of the drama of the sermon and of the pulpit. Lamont also helped R. C. at moments of his early academic career. In addition to his student assistant church job, R. C. also worked in a church gym during the first two years of seminary.

In his senior year in seminary, R. C. took on a student pastorate in Lyndora, Pennsylvania, a working-class neighborhood of Butler, about thirty miles north and slightly east of Pittsburgh. R. C. described the church as a "Hungarian refugee church of a hundred members in a steel mill town." The steel mill was the Forge Steel Works, Butler, Pennsylvania. Forge Steel, part of the Standard Oil empire, was established in 1906. It was acquired by the Columbia Steel company and then absorbed by American Rolling Mill Company, ARMCO for short. Steel melts at 2,500 degrees Fahrenheit. When people speak of Pittsburgh as tough as steel, they also mean as tough as the steel worker. The factory originally manufactured large steel wheels for trains. Then it made the American Austin automobile, licensed from British carmaker Austin. Austin was acquired by Bantam. The first Jeep was made by Bantam in Butler—just in time to be deployed by the US Army for World War II.

The neighborhood around the church was Hungarian. A generation or two of Hungarians had already been in the Pittsburgh area, but the 1956 Hungarian Revolution resulted in a significant influx of new refugees. Many lived in Lyndora and worked at the steel mill and the Bantam Jeep plant. This was R. C.'s first congregation: blue collar, refugee, hardened and calloused steel workers. The neighborhood was also Catholic. There were eight or nine Roman Catholic churches and the one Presbyterian church all for this Hungarian neighborhood. R. C.'s congregation called him *Uj Papa*, the "New Pope," because most of them had been Roman Catholic. Likely many of them did not know the difference between a Catholic and a Presbyterian.

The church had a manse, so R. C., Vesta, and Sherrie left their seminary apartment and moved in next to the church. On moving day, R. C. noticed a push mower and asked the church members helping him, "Do you have a lawn mower?" They replied, "Yes. We call him 'our pastor.'" In addition to lodging at the manse, he was paid forty dollars a week as pastor.

For the academic year 1963–1964, R. C. mowed the grass for the manse and the church property, commuted an hour each way to attend his full load of courses as a senior at PTS, preached every Sunday, taught Sunday school, and accumulated a lifetime's worth of stories of frontline pastoral ministry. The faculty advisor who oversaw student ministry and student pastorates told R. C. that he had been doing so for nearly forty years, adding, "I've never heard the kinds of stories you're telling."[16] There were a lot of tangled family relations and grudges. One father made his son-in-law sleep in the chicken coop for a while. On a few occasions, R. C. posted bail for a congregant or a congregant's relative. But one story tops the list.

One woman in the church called R. C. rather late at night to come to her house because she did not like her daughter's boyfriend, and she wanted R. C. to do something about it. He walked to her home and up the few steps onto the porch and rapped his knuckles on the screen door. When she came to the door, she had a bottle of whiskey in one hand and was waving a revolver around with the other. She had relieved the bottle of much of its contents and was clearly inebriated, carrying on rather strongly about her views of the worthlessness of the boyfriend and of what she would like to do to him. All R. C. could think to say to

16   Nichols with Sproul, personal interview, April 7, 2017.

her was, "Mrs. —-, you don't want to shoot me." That worked. She gave the revolver to R. C. and calmed down.

Meanwhile in seminary, R. C. was taking an elective verse-by-verse exegesis of Romans—to make up for the earlier survey course that passed over it entirely. He also took an elective course with Gerstner on the Council of Trent. A very tattered book in R. C.'s personal library is *Canons and Decrees of the Council of Trent: Original Text with English Translation*.[17] The book is so worn that R. C. used Scotch tape to keep the covers and spine label together. It is heavily underlined with notes scattered through the margins. It was the one textbook for a whole course on the Council of Trent. Gerstner led the students through the text line by line, word for word.

The Council of Trent served as one of three responses by the Roman Catholic Church to the Protestant Reformation, the so-called Counter-Reformation. The Roman Catholic Church responded by using the Inquisition; by forming a new society or order, the Society of Jesus or the Jesuits; and by convening the Council of Trent (1545–1563). By looking at the *Canons and Decrees of Trent*, you see not only the Catholic response to the Reformation; you also see what was truly at stake in the Reformation. Reflecting on the class and reading of Trent for the first time, R. C. declared, "I've always said that the best way to understand the theology of the Reformation is to see it against the background of classical Roman Catholic theology."[18]

On the flyleaf of the book, R. C. wrote, "<u>not</u> cooperate with <u>grace</u>." R. C. explained what he meant by the note:

> In the Council of Trent's definition of justification, it says that, for the sinner to be reconciled to God and to be in a state of salvation, he must assent and cooperate with the grace of God in order to be justified. Justification, then, is not monergistic; it's synergistic—a cooperative

---

17 Henry J. Schroeder, *Canons and Decrees of the Council of Trent* (St. Louis, MO: Herder, 1941).
18 "R. C. Sproul and Schroeder's *Canons and Decrees of the Council of Trent*," *Open Book* podcast, March 15, 2018, season 1, episode 1.

venture. In my note to myself, I was opposing what was asserted by Trent. There is not a cooperative venture between nature and grace as far as salvation is concerned.[19]

Trent did not deny salvation by grace; it affirmed salvation as by grace plus merit or works. Similarly, Trent did not reject the authority of Scripture; it affirmed that authority is found in Scripture *and* tradition. Trent shines a spotlight on the significance of the word *sola* to the Reformation. The Reformers put all of the emphasis on the *sola* in the formulation of biblical authority and salvation by grace alone, through faith alone, in Christ alone, to the glory of God alone. Trent squarely rejected the *sola*. As will be seen, Reformation theology, specifically the five *solas*, became a hallmark of the teaching of R. C. Sproul. In fact, no other individual may have done more to popularize using the construct of the five *solas* to understand Reformation theology, and, hence, an orthodox understanding of the doctrines of Scripture, salvation, and Christ, than R. C. Sproul. Studying Romans line by line, while studying Trent and Roman Catholic theology line by line, was the foundation for the ministry and teaching that was to come.

R. C. also continued building on the foundation of studying philosophy. The PTS curriculum had a basic philosophy course that students could test out of. R. C. and two others scored so high that the professor asked them if they would like to do an intensive seminar on philosophy. R. C. jumped at the opportunity. R. C. called it an advanced advanced study of the history of philosophy.

As graduation approached, R. C. wanted to pastor and have a full-time job. He and Vesta had been married for four years, during which they had been living on an income of never more than two thousand dollars a year. He was ready to move on from being a student scraping to make ends meet. He made contacts with the clerks of the presbyteries around western Pennsylvania. He would have promising phone

---

19 "R. C. Sproul and Schroeder's *Canons and Decrees.*"

interviews, mention the prospects to Gerstner, and then have a flat in-person interview. He learned later that Gerstner made intervening phone calls telling the church sessions that R. C. would better serve the church by not going directly to the pastorate and, instead, pursuing doctoral work at this time. R. C., realizing what he was up against, relented his pursuit of a job. He went to see Gerstner about where to go to pursue a doctorate.

Twelve Hours

If R. C. was going to spend more years studying and pursuing a doctorate, he was going to study under the best theologian alive. When R. C. told Gerstner his plan, Gerstner directed R. C. to Amsterdam, to the Free University, to study under Gerritt Cornelis Berkouwer (1903–1996). R. C. thought to himself, but dared not verbalize, a reply: *I had in mind the best English-speaking theologian alive.* Gerstner wrote the letter of recommendation, and R. C. was accepted. He graduated from PTS; then he, Vesta, and Sherrie booked passage and set off for the Netherlands.

The Sprouls were in Amsterdam from 1964 to 1965. R. C. missed ice, meat, disposable income, and professors who spoke English, among other things. While there, they lived on peanut butter and jelly sandwiches. R. C. testified that he came home from Amsterdam weighing less than when he'd graduated from high school. One benefit in Amsterdam, not experienced in America, was the daily morning baker visit. Sherrie, at three years of age, took on the role of greeting the baker and requesting, in Dutch, the daily order: "Dag mijneer bakker, een halfje wit gesneden brood alstublieft" ("Good morning, Mr. Baker, a half a loaf of sliced white bread, please"). The bread was so fresh that steam rose from it. It had no preservatives, so it lasted only a day. R. C. said it was "the most fabulous bread I've ever eaten."[20] R. C. also likened it to the biblical manna. Any held over for the next day would be virtually inedible.

20 R. C. Sproul, *The Prayer of the Lord* (Sanford, FL: Reformation Trust, 2009), 69.

R. C. had acquired some Dutch language instructional records that he listened to as they crossed the Atlantic. That was his first exposure to Dutch. He was about to experience learning the language by full immersion. R. C. recalls his first meeting with Berkouwer to get the reading assignment for the course in the history of systematic theology. R. C. would have to read and master, to Berkouwer's satisfaction, all the books on the list, which consisted of about twenty-five in Dutch, four in Latin, four in German, and about four in French. As R. C. reviewed the list, his facial expression gave away his consternation, prompting Berkouwer to ask what was wrong. R. C. replied, "Well, I don't read French." What he didn't have the heart to tell Berkouwer was that he didn't read Dutch or German either, and that his Latin was poor. Berkouwer replied, "You can substitute four more Dutch books instead of the French books."[21]

The Sprouls lived in the small town of Bussum, about 30 kilometers to the east of the Free University in the city of Amsterdam. R. C.'s life consisted of taking classes and learning Dutch—learning Dutch as he was reading weighty Dutch philosophy and theology books. He spent most of the day sitting at a small desk in his apartment. He had a stack of index cards and a Dutch-English dictionary. He opened Berkouwer's *De Persoon Van Christus*, one of the books on the list and the first Dutch book he attempted to read. He started on page 1. In the margin of the bottom of page 1, R. C. wrote "12 hrs." That's how long it took him to read that first page. He looked up every word he did not know, which at the beginning of this process was almost every word on the page. He'd write the Dutch word on one side of an index card, and then he'd write the English dictionary definition on the back. That's how he learned Dutch, that's how he made his way through the reading list for that course, as well as his other courses, and that's how he spent most of his days and most of his hours in the Netherlands. A typical day meant R. C. would

21 "R. C. Sproul and Berkouwer's *Dogmatische Studien*," *Open Book* podcast, March 22, 2018, season 1, episode 2.

be reading or studying from 7 a.m. until 10 p.m., with short breaks for small meals.

R. C. added that Berkouwer's book on the person of Christ "was one of the most significant books that I read under his tutelage," adding that in another course he studied "in great detail" the historical Christological controversies—the controversies that led to the Nicene and Chalcedonian Creeds.[22] Another plank was being laid in the foundation of the teaching ministry of R. C. Sproul. Additionally, R. C. continued his close examination of Roman Catholic theology. Berkouwer was invited to Vatican II as an official observer. While attending one of the series of sessions, he roomed with controversial Roman Catholic theologian Hans Küng. Berkouwer wrote of the developments in his 1962 book, right as Vatican II was beginning. The book was published in English as *The Second Vatican Council and the New Catholicism* (1965). Berkouwer was and continues to be best known for his *Studies in Dogmatics* eighteen-volume series, published in Dutch from 1949 through 1976. *The Person of Christ* was published in 1952.

R. C. greatly admired the precision and the depth of analysis of Berkouwer. R. C. recognized that Berkouwer had migrated from a more conservative theological position to advocating a more "middle orthodoxy." Berkouwer, for instance, tempered his criticism of Barth as the years rolled on. R. C. also noticed that Berkouwer, though publishing prolifically on theology, lacked a systematic approach. Tellingly, Berkouwer does not have a volume on prolegomena in his *Studies in Dogmatics*. Prolegomena refers to prefatory or preliminary remarks on theological methodology and approach. Even that Berkouwer published studies, separate volumes, on theology as opposed to publishing a systematic theology reveals his unsystematic way of theologizing. Despite these shortcomings, R. C. greatly admired Berkouwer's work and was grateful for the time that he studied with him.

22 "R. C. Sproul and Berkouwer's *Dogmatische Studien*."

The study of philosophy continued as well. R. C. took a course on the history of philosophy. One of the class lectures was on Hegel. The professor, knowing R. C. to be an American, asked him after the lecture how he thought it went. R. C. said it was rather difficult. The professor replied, "Yes, Hegel is difficult in any language."[23] And there was another time when R. C. was actually singled out during a lecture. The classroom was very hot, so R. C. removed his coat and placed it on the back of his chair. As soon as he did, the professor broke from his lecture and, in English, said, "Would the American kindly put back on his coat?"

In addition to poring over his index cards and Dutch books, R. C. did work here and there in a laundry folding sheets, and he also managed to play baseball for a league team. While not having professional baseball, Holland had an amateur baseball league with teams playing on meticulously manicured fields in beautiful small ball parks. Bussum was too small for a team, but the next town over, Hilversum, had a team. R. C. was a walk-on for the Hilversum team, playing shortstop. This caught the attention of a large newspaper in Holland, landing a front-page headline in the sports section about the American minister playing baseball. In Dutch culture, the last thing you would expect to find is a minister in an athletic uniform on a ballfield. They were rarely seen in anything other than dress clothes.

They did get to Amsterdam for sightseeing on occasion, especially enjoying the Rijksmuseum, home to Rembrandt's *The Night Watch*, other works of the Dutch masters, as well as many Spanish paintings. They visited the Van Gogh Museum. They saw the charcoal sketches and paintings Van Gogh did while in Belgium. In particular, a sketch done as a study that would later be a famous painting from 1880, of a coal miner's pair of shoes, captivated R. C.'s attention: "This shoe displayed the whole pain and anguish of the life of a coal miner."[24]

---

23 "R. C. Sproul and Berkouwer's *Dogmatische Studien*."
24 Stephen Nichols with R. C. Sproul, personal interview, May 26, 2017.

As the academic year was drawing to a close, R. C. realized that he needed to return to America. Vesta, pregnant, had been told she would have to have the baby at home in Amsterdam, with a midwife. Given the difficulties encountered with the first pregnancy, that did not seem like a welcome prospect. Also, they had learned that R. C.'s mom was dying. At the same time, Westminster College asked R. C. to come for a one-year faculty appointment while a Bible faculty member, Jack Rogers, was headed for a one-year sabbatical to finish his doctorate at, ironically, the Free University of Amsterdam.

R. C. met with Berkouwer and made arrangements for supervision of his studies for that next year. They left as the spring term ended, fully intending to return to Amsterdam.

Reverend Robert C. Sproul

Shortly after the Sprouls returned, on June 30 a box was delivered to R. C.'s mother's home. Inside was a new dress that she had bought to wear for her son's ordination. She could not have been prouder. R. C. remembers her being happy and very content as she said good night and went to bed. She died the next day. That same day, July 1, 1965, R. C.'s son, R. C. Sproul Jr., was born. On July 18, 1965, R. C. was ordained into the United Presbyterian Church USA (PCUSA). The service was held at Pleasant Hills Community Presbyterian Church.

The congregation sang what was identified as "The Ordinand's Favorite Hymn," "'Tis Midnight and on Olive's Brow," a dramatic and vivid retelling of Christ's agony in the garden of Gethsemane. Dr. Gregory gave the charge to the ordinand. Then the Reverend Robert C. Sproul pronounced the benediction.

Newly ordained, R. C. was one of the founding members of Presbyterians United for Biblical Confession (PUBC), a counterweight group to the forces within the United Presbyterian Church (UPC) and PCUSA to move from the historic, confessional standards.[25] The more liberal

25 This group then changed its name to Presbyterians United for Biblical Concerns.

forces were at work in what would be the Confession of 1967. In the southern Presbyterian churches, this would lead to the formation of the Presbyterian Church in America (PCA) in 1973. Southern and northern conservative churches left the PCUSA to join the PCA. For many, these were costly moves. The PCUSA owned the property of individual and local churches. The denomination controlled ministers' pension funds. Back in 1965, this group of around thirty ministers were studying and critiquing the proposals that would eventually become the Confession of 1967. Gerstner was one of this group, as was Mariano Di Gangi, pastor of Philadelphia's Tenth Presbyterian Church. This was the first time, but it would not be the last, that R. C. became involved in the larger denominational conflict and struggle to stave off theological drift.

R. C. wrote a paper for the first meeting of the PUBC. The paper is lost, but he remembers the topic was "studied ambiguity." R. C. had just learned, from his time with Berkouwer, how studied ambiguity played a role at Vatican II. He would later see studied ambiguity at work in "Evangelicals and Catholics Together." The answer to studied ambiguity, that is, being purposefully vague so as to allow for an elastic interpretation or to allow for latitude on a particular doctrine or view, is precision. Precision and clarity, not ambiguity, serve the church best in remaining faithful to its biblical, historic, and confessional roots. R. C. was learning that in 1965 in his own denomination.

It was around this time that Vesta's parents gave R. C. a leather-bound Thompson Chain-Reference Bible. This Bible had within it a numbering system, a series of "chains," that was part of an "analytic and synthetic system of Bible study."[26] R. C. devoured it. He kept it through the years. At one point it was rebound by his Romans class, which was what those who attended his Bible study class in Cincinnati called themselves. Many pages are torn and taped. Many passages are highlighted, many words are underlined. R. C. was what you would call an active reader. It might be

---

26 Frank Charles Thompson, *The New Chain-Reference Bible*, 4th. ed. (Indianoplis, IN: B. B. Kirkbride, 1964), III–IV.

more accurate to say that reading was a bloodsport for R. C. And that was all the more true when it came to reading the pages of Holy Writ. He was not casual in his reading or studying of the Bible. Vesta testified how grateful R. C. was for the gift and how much that Bible meant to him in those formative years as he was beginning his career as a professor and a pastor. Undergirding the lectures and the sermons and the Sunday school classes that would occupy R. C.'s time from 1965 through 1971 was a solid foundation of an intense and comprehensive Bible study. As R. C. learned from Edwards, truths that ignite the passion are both rational ("'Tis Rational") and biblical ("'Tis Biblical"). R. C. was both laying a foundation for his future teaching ministry and establishing a pattern that he would follow all of his life, a pattern of Bible study, not just Bible reading.

Also in 1965, R. C., Vesta, Sherrie, and infant R. C. Jr., whom they called Craig (from Robert Craig Sproul), moved into the vacated home of Jack Rogers near the campus of Westminster College while the Rogers family lived in Amsterdam for the year. Jack Rogers would come to be known as the Rogers of the "Rogers-McKim Proposal." This proposal, put forth by Jack Rogers and Donald McKim in their book *The Authority and Interpretation of the Bible: An Historical Approach* (1979), argued that inerrancy is not a biblical or historical doctrine, but originated with the Princetonians, Hodge and Warfield, in the later nineteenth century. R. C. would come to square off directly with the Rogers-McKim proposal through his leadership of the International Council on Biblical Inerrancy. That would be later. For the academic term, 1965–1966, the Sprouls lived in the Rogers home, and R. C. worked from Jack Rogers's office.

That year, R. C. taught philosophy at his alma mater. He taught the survey course on introduction to philosophy and also upperclass electives in philosophy. Every evening he would have students in his home, a dozen or so, to talk and pray. R. C. would say sometimes they would have prayer meetings that would last late in the night. Then he would have to awake early the next day and be ready for an 8 a.m. lecture, while the students would sleep in and cut class. R. C. loved every minute of his time at Westminster. Before the year was out, the president of Westminster College wanted to hire R. C. on a permanent basis. Meanwhile, Gordon College also invited R. C. to come on the faculty, largely through Dr. Lamont, who was serving on the board. The Sprouls went to Gordon for a few days of interviews. All went very well, which served to perplex R. C. as to what decision to make.

The Mysterious Call

R. C.'s mother had a friend whose son Ed and R. C. were also friends through grade school and high school, though Ed was four years older. Ed went on to be a TWA pilot, based in Boston. During the days of interviews, they had reconnected for dinner in Boston. Weeks later, R. C. and Vesta were turning the offers over and still unsure of what to do. R. C. remembers they prayed for most of one evening regarding it and then went to bed. At 3 a.m., the phone rang. It was Ed. He was in Kansas City on a layover. He said, "Sonny" (R. C.'s old boyhood name), "I know this is none of my business and I have no reason, but I have an overwhelming burden to call you and tell you that you must go to Gordon College."[27] R. C. then told Gerstner about the mysterious call in the middle of the night. Gerstner replied, "God can intrude in a mysterious way in the most austere of Calvinistic households."[28]

The Sprouls left Westminster for Gordon College. Before they left, however, R. C. taught a summer session on a survey of theology. He used the Apostles' Creed as the structure of the course. The students seemed to really connect with the material. R. C. made a mental note to be sure to get this material onto paper. There could be a book here.

Earlier that spring, R. C. contacted Berkouwer to let him know of the developments. Berkouwer then made arrangements for R. C. to be supervised by Reformation scholar Heiko Oberman (1930–2001), who

---

27 Nichols with Sproul, personal interview, May 12, 2017.
28 Nichols with Sproul, personal interview, May 12, 2017.

was at Harvard at the time. All was settled. Then that summer Oberman left Harvard for a post at Tübingen, Germany.

R. C. and Berkouwer put together a plan for him to finish his exams and receive a Drs. In the Dutch academic system, the Drs. stands for *doctorandus*, which means "who would be called doctor." It is the degree awarded to those who finish their course of study and exams but do not write the dissertation and finish the doctoral program.

The Sproul family moved to Wenham, Massachusetts, to Gordon College, in the summer of 1966. They would live there for two years. R. C. taught the freshman Bible survey course. Old Testament in the fall, New Testament in the spring. He had 250 students. The class met in the chapel. He also taught assorted upper-level courses and electives. Gordon Seminary students heard about this new professor and sometimes would drop by to hear a few minutes of his lecture. Some of the seminarians even audited his classes. He taught another theology survey course, like the summer course at Westminster and, again, used the Apostles' Creed to structure the course lectures. He loved the students.

R. C. also enjoyed his faculty colleagues. He remembers going to an Evangelical Theological Society meeting in Boston with Dr. Roger Nicole. R. C. presented a paper on Luther, which was later published, the first published piece by R. C. The article was titled "An Analysis of Martin Luther's *The Bondage of the Will*."[29] At least five things are worth noting from R. C.'s first publication. First, in the very first paragraph, Sproul writes of Luther's thought here as having a "contemporary relevance" that "far transcends its historical significance."[30] He was not interested in pure analysis; he was interested in helping the church. Second, Sproul draws attention to Luther's claim that a theologian must make assertions. Erasmus, Luther's debate partner on the issue of the bondage of the will, made equivocations. Luther asserted. R. C. loved that. Third, R. C. raises

---

29 Robert C. Sproul, "An Analysis of Martin Luther's *The Bondage of the Will*," *Gordon Review*, vol. 10 (Fall 1967): 215–29.
30 Sproul, "An Analysis of Martin Luther's *The Bondage of the Will*," 215.

the point that this is not a sidebar or tertiary issue, as what is at stake here is fidelity to Scripture and to an essential biblical doctrine. R. C. puts it this way: "The doctrine of the bondage of the will is important then, not because it is derived from speculative philosophy but because of its integral connection with God's revealed judgment upon man's sin."[31] Fourth, R. C. sees how crucial this is to the Reformation understanding of salvation, noting the "centrality" of the issue of the bondage of the will "to *Sola Fide* and *Sola Gratia* in Luther's thought." R. C. then quotes Luther: "As long as man is persuaded that he can make even the smallest contribution to his salvation, he remains self-confident and does not utterly despair of himself."[32] Fifth and finally, Sproul ends with this sentence:

> [Luther] determined to assert and proclaim, not a neutral anthropology, but the sweetness and excellency that is found in the doxological confession: *Sola Fide! Sola Gratia! Soli Deo Gloria!*[33]

This sentence needs unpacking. The words *sweetness* and *excellency* came from Edwards. One trips over these words in the writings of Jonathan Edwards. But it also shows that R. C. was a passionate theologian. For R. C., theology not simply permeated and captivated the mind, but it also permeated the affections. When R. C. spoke of knowing God and of being transformed and renewed, he meant more than an intellectual exercise. Theology captivates and permeates the whole person—heart, soul, mind, and strength. Reading this article not only reveals what R. C. thinks; it also reveals what he feels, what he loves. You also see here the use of the *solas* as a construct to understand Reformation theology, which R. C. would say is biblical theology. Finally, you see the word *doxology*. R. C. would later say that theology is doxology; that is to say that studying God and knowing God lead to praising God and worshiping God.

---

31 Sproul, "An Analysis of Martin Luther's *The Bondage of the Will*," 222.

32 Sproul, "An Analysis of Martin Luther's *The Bondage of the Will*," 224. Citation is from Martin Luther, *The Bondage of the Will*, trans. J. I. Packer and O. R. Johnston (Westwood, NJ: Revell, 1957), 100.

33 Sproul, "An Analysis of Martin Luther's *The Bondage of the Will*," 229.

This paper, presented at ETS and published, represents R. C.'s forays into the academic community. He would come to write and teach more for laity and a broader church audience than for academe. But even here, in this first academic publication, you see the emphases and the ethos of the writing that is to come.

At Gordon, however, R. C. was generally miserable. He recalls getting ulcers. The misery stemmed from his feeling rather out of place. And he was. At the time, Gordon College reflected fundamentalist tendencies. R. C. and Vesta had never experienced fundamentalism. They played cards and smoked. All of that was against the code of conduct for students at Gordon. R. C. remembers being summoned to the dean's office. While waiting, the dean's secretary said to him, "Professor Sproul, you smell like you've been around someone who's been smoking." He replied, "Indeed, I have. It is I." She said back, "Umph, it's getting so that you can't tell who is a real Christian anymore." R. C. had a reply for that too. He said, "Well, I'm a theologian so I can tell you that a real Christian is someone who loves Jesus."

R. C. started sending out his resume. Conwell School of Theology, of Temple University in Philadelphia, needed a professor of philosophy and theology. Sixty-five scholars applied for the job. R. C. got invited for an interview. The president, Stuart Barton Babbage (1916–2012), an Australian evangelical Anglican, had read R. C.'s article on Luther and saw promise in this young professor. He interviewed R. C. and hired him on the spot. R. C. would join Philip Edgcumbe Hughes (1915–1990), another conservative Australian Anglican, teaching philosophy and theology. Before coming to America, Hughes, along with Geoffrey Bromiley and Stafford Wright, had established Tyndale Hall in Bristol as a rigorous academic and confessional school of divinity. With about ten books behind him, Hughes had just started working on what would be his massive Hebrews commentary.

The Seminary and the Sunday School

The Sprouls moved to Oreland, a bedroom community outside of Philadelphia, for R. C.'s new position at Conwell School of Theology. R. C. had a relative in Oreland, an aunt by marriage, his father's brother's wife. She had older children who helped babysit Sherrie, then in the second grade, and Craig, still in preschool. Oreland was one mile away from Westminster Theological Seminary. R. C. spent time visiting with Van Til. They would sit on Van Til's porch, talk Dutch, and eat cookies baked by Mrs. Van Til. That year, Westminster Seminary invited D. Martyn Lloyd-Jones to give a series of lectures, which he entitled "The Preacher and Preaching," which were later published under that title. It was the first and only time that R. C. met "the Doctor."

That year, 1968, was also the first year of James Montgomery Boice's (1938–2000) tenure as minister of Tenth Presbyterian Church. Boice followed Mariano Di Gangi, whom R. C. knew back in 1965 through Presbyterians United for Biblical Confession.

R. C. daily took the train into Philadelphia, then a short walk to the campus of Temple University. Temple was founded as Temple College in 1887 by Russell Conwell, pastor of Grace Baptist Church in Philadelphia and author of *Acres of Diamonds* (1890). Conwell gave a speech at the beginning of the university, which then became this best-selling book. It was a proto–prosperity gospel message. A theological seminary was established as part of the university and named in his honor, Conwell School of Theology. This is where R. C. taught the courses in the systematic theology curriculum and a course on the history of atheism.

In a history of philosophy course, while R. C. was lecturing on Kant's distinctions on the types of statements, R. C. held up a piece of chalk, furrowed his brow, and said earnestly, dramatically, "This piece of chalk is not really a piece of chalk." Then he asked his students to identify what type of statement that was. They all offered sophisticated answers. One put forth the statement that the chalk had the essence but not the substance of chalk. One student, Bishop Walters, of the African Methodist

Episcopal Church in Norristown, Pennsylvania, said, "I don't understand that kind of jive." R. C. said, "Exactly!"

At Pittsburgh Theological Seminary, R. C. had for a teacher Dietrich Ritschl, the grandson of Albrecht Ritschl. Ritschl would say to R. C. and the other students, "God is immutable in his essence, and God is mutable in his essence." All of R. C.'s classmates would be totally taken with the profundity. R. C. thought, in the words of Bishop Walters, it was nothing but jive talk. Nonsense.

Bishop Walters invited R. C. to preach at his church. It was R. C.'s first experience preaching in an African-American church. At the door, just as the service was getting underway, Bishop Walters told R. C. he had one hour and thirty minutes to preach. R. C. had never preached longer than thirty minutes up until that point. He decided he would simply string three sermons together. As he started preaching, the congregation joined in, as preaching is a team sport in this church context. They were "Amening" and saying, "Preach it, preacher man," and the like. R. C. could hardly hear himself think and was not used to this. He turned to the bishop and asked for his help to quiet down the congregation so he could preach. The next day in class the students were all curious as to how it had gone. They all asked, not R. C. but Bishop Walters, "Hey, Bishop. What happened?" Bishop Walters proceeded:

> The Prof started preaching. People were shoutin' and yelling "Amen," and calling out. And the poor Prof couldn't hear himself think, so I had to stand up and tell the congregation to quiet down and let the man preach. He got to preaching and then the Ghost came by.

R. C. said that was the highest compliment he ever received for his preaching in his entire life: "Then the Ghost came by."[34]

Conwell was a Baptist seminary, but R. C., a Presbyterian, was teaching doctrine of the church. The students were weeks away from their ordina-

---

34 Nichols with Sproul, personal interview, May 26, 2017.

tion, and they had a crisis because they were finding R. C.'s argument for a Presbyterian view of the sacrament of baptism compelling.

On July 21, 1969, Neil Armstrong walked on the moon. That week, Robert C. Sproul had an article published in *Christianity Today*, complete with a photo of the moon on the cover. His article was titled, "Existential Autonomy and Christian Freedom."[35] Vesta recalls the circumstance. As R. C. came home one day, he mentioned he'd heard that *Christianity Today* paid handsomely for articles, so he thought he would write one and send it. Vesta replied something to the effect of, "Sure, send it in. It will be sure to be published," perhaps with a little sarcasm. In the article he takes on Jean-Paul Sartre and Friedrich Nietzsche, with a little help from John Calvin and Genesis 1. Sproul ends:

> Man as covenant partner and adopted son does not lose his subjectivity or personality but is given the command (which at the same time is a privilege) to have dominion over the earth. This mandate does not annihilate man's role in the cosmos, nor does it chain him as Prometheus to the mountain. Rather it gives him a liberating task that involves the whole creation. The new man in Christ exists not as reified object but as a subject in relationship to God.[36]

R. C. recalled the moment when, after he had taken the train to Philadelphia's North Street Station and was walking the several blocks up Broadway to the Temple campus and to his office, he arrived on campus and realized, "I'm really bored. I'm bored with this."[37] He was twenty-nine, turning thirty, and he had arrived at the pinnacle of his academic career. He was a professor at a seminary. He loved teaching, but he was bored with academic life.

---

35 Robert C. Sproul, "Existential Autonomy and Christian Freedom," *Christianity Today*, July 18, 1969, 12–14.

36 Sproul, "Existential Autonomy and Christian Freedom," 14.

37 Nichols with Sproul, personal interview, May 26, 2017.

But he loved teaching Sunday school at Oreland Presbyterian Church. These were educated laity, primarily white-collar workers in Philadelphia. They were smart and capable people who loved learning and loved R. C.'s teaching. R. C. recalled, "This was my first real taste for adult education where I taught a course on the person and work of Christ to doctors and bankers and attorneys and businessmen and housewives."[38] The deeper he went, the more they listened. They wanted to learn, were eager to learn.

R. C. was shocked to discover he was bored teaching seminary. He was even more shocked at how excited he was teaching laypeople. It is not too much of a stretch to say that the vision for Ligonier Ministries was born at the moment and in that place, during 1968–1969, as R. C. Sproul taught on the person of Christ weekly in Sunday school at Oreland Presbyterian Church. He found hungry students outside the formal academic classroom. That would come to be precisely the method of operation and the ethos of Ligonier. While the vision had its first bloom in a suburb outside of Philadelphia, there would be a little bit of a detour before it would come to full flower in the Ligonier Valley in western Pennsylvania.

The announcement came that Conwell School of Theology would be merging with Gordon Divinity School. As part of the merger, Conwell would leave the campus of Temple in Philadelphia and relocate to Wenham, Massachusetts. R. C. scratched and clawed to go from there, now that the seminary he worked for was moving in toto back. R. C. decided he would not go. When word got around the Gordon faculty that R. C. had decided not to come up, William Lane, a New Testament professor, hopped on a train and headed to Philadelphia to plead with R. C. personally to stay with Gordon-Conwell Theological Seminary. When he got to Philadelphia and met with R. C., Dr. Lane likened the occasion to Farel asking Calvin to stay in Geneva. R. C. replied that Dr. Lane was not Farel, he himself was not Calvin, and Gordon was no Geneva.

38 "Sproul Memoirs," session 5, recorded 2012, Ligonier Ministries, Sanford, Florida.

Meanwhile, Jerry Kirk, senior pastor of College Hill Presbyterian Church in Cincinnati, Ohio, invited R. C. to join the pastoral staff. Jerry had been a pastor in New Wilmington, Pennsylvania, while R. C. taught at Westminster College and wanted R. C. to join him. R. C. went for the interview. For his candidacy sermon during the interview time, R. C. preached for the first time on Isaiah 6. He had heard John Guest preach on Isaiah 6 at a conference in Pittsburgh, and Guest's sermon had left an impression on R. C. He began poring over Isaiah 6 and the seraphim's thrice-holy declaration. It was the summer of 1969, and the Sprouls would move again. R. C. and Vesta, having been married for nine years, had moved eight times, with one being across the Atlantic. This time, they moved as far west as they had ever lived and ever would. The family moved to Cincinnati, to Bengals territory, a tall ask for Steelers fans.

Teacher

The position at College Hill was associate pastor of evangelism and mission. R. C. was installed on September 14, 1969, as associate pastor of evangelism, mission, and theology (R. C. had them add theology to the job description and the title). He led a weekly Bible study on Luke that drew upwards of eighty people. They ended up having so many that R. C. offered a second session. He also preached through Romans on Sunday nights. Additionally, he offered training in evangelism. For that, R. C. felt that he needed training himself. In February of 1970, he went to Florida to attend an Evangelism Explosion clinic at Coral Ridge Presbyterian Church with D. James Kennedy and Archie Parrish. Archie Parrish recalls that R. C. went back to College Hill and "in less than six months, he did what nobody else had ever done with Evangelism Explosion."[39] R. C. combined his preaching through Romans with training people in presenting the gospel. There was a network of evangelists

39 Stephen Nichols with Archie Parrish, personal interview, August 15, 2019.

through R. C.'s ministry at College Hill. His job title could have been reduced to one word: *teacher*.

Yet R. C. missed the time with college students and seemed to be yearning for something more. Since his time at Pittsburgh Seminary, R. C. had been involved in a variety of ministries in Pittsburgh. There was Young Life ministries; InterVarsity Christian Fellowship; Coalition for Christian Outreach, run by John Guest; and Sam Shoemaker's (1893–1963) The Pittsburgh Experiment.[40] Shoemaker launched the Pittsburgh Experiment in 1955 in the hopes that "Pittsburgh would be as famous for God as it is for steel." Shoemaker's prior work in Manhattan laid the foundation for what would become Alcoholics Anonymous. He was an Episcopalian priest who had a heart for business leaders and for those hard-pressed. Reid Carpenter also plied his efforts and would eventually establish the Pittsburgh Leadership Foundation in 1978.

One of the benefactors of a number of these organizations was Dora Hillman, wife of John Hartwell Hillman Jr. (1880–1959). "Hart" had turned his father's business enterprise into a small empire of manufacturing, energy and chemical companies, banking, and real estate. His main focus was Pittsburgh Coke and Chemical, now Calgon Carbon. The Hillmans, like many of the prominent families of Pittsburgh, had a home in the Ligonier Valley. R. C. once described the Ligonier Valley as the playground for all the leading families of Pittsburgh. In addition to the Hillmans, the Mellons had a home there, and nearby, at Mill Run, Frank Lloyd Wright built Fallingwater for the Kaufmann family in 1964.

Through these Pittsburgh contacts, R. C. was invited to Saranac Lake to speak to a conference of Young Life leaders in the summer of 1970. The year before, Young Life had purchased one of the old Great Camps dotting Saranac Lake. These were elaborate summer homes, with boathouses and outbuildings, for New York City's elite. This particular Great Camp

---

40 See Gary Scott Smith, *A History of Christianity in Pittsburgh* (Charleston, SC: History Press, 2019). Dr. Smith chaired the history department at Grove City College, where he went as an undergraduate. During his college days, Smith was also a student at the Ligonier Valley Study Center.

was owned by Adolph Lewisohn, an investment banker, who also, on the advice of Thomas Edison, wisely and heavily invested in copper mining. Lewisohn built his own little village nestled among the rock formations and hardwood forests on Saranac Lake in the Adirondack Mountains. The property changed hands a few times after Lewisohn's death until Young Life purchased it in 1969 and repurposed it as a retreat and conference center. The summer of 1970 was the Great Camp's maiden voyage.

R. C. decided he would teach a five-part series on the holiness of God.

4

LIGONIER

Ligonier is for learning.
TABLETALK

A CATALOG OF THE PLACES that had shaped R. C. up to this point in
his life looks something like this:

Pittsburgh
The African and Italian theaters of World War II
Forbes Field
Pleasant Hills
New Wilmington
Pittsburgh (again)
Amsterdam
An apartment in Bussum, the Netherlands
New Wilmington (again)
Wenham, Massachusetts
Philadelphia
A Sunday school classroom in Oreland Presbyterian Church
Cincinnati

The place that comes next is, however, far and away the one place that is
inextricably linked with the name and life of R. C. Sproul. The borough

of Ligonier, in western Pennsylvania, was named after Fort Ligonier, which was named after John (Jean-Louis) Ligonier, of an exiled Huguenot family. John Ligonier rose through the ranks of the British Army all the way to commander-in-chief in 1757, a title now held by the queen. Before it was Fort Ligonier, it was Fort Loyalhanna. In November of 1758, General John Forbes left Fort Loyalhanna and marched on French-held Fort Duquesne on the forks of the Ohio River. There was no battle. The French, knowing they were significantly outnumbered, blew up the fort and retreated across the Ohio River and eventually back to their northern territory. Forbes renamed Fort Duquesne "Fort Pitt," after William Pitt the Elder, prime minister at the time, and renamed Fort Loyalhanna after the aforementioned John Ligonier, his superior officer.[1]

Around the fort and the borough is a valley, the Ligonier Valley, right in the middle of the Allegheny Mountains, which are part of the vast Appalachian Mountain Range and which provide breathtaking panoramic views. As already mentioned, many of the wealthy Pittsburgh families had homes in the Ligonier Valley.

From her home perched on the summit of one of the tallest mountains in the region, Dora Hillman oversaw the estate of her late tycoon industrialist husband, J. Hartwell Hillman, and she oversaw Hilltop Farm. She had a keen interest in ministry in Pittsburgh and in western Pennsylvania and supported a long list of organizations, including Young Life.

In 1970, when R. C. was invited to speak at the Young Life conference on Saranac Lake, Dora Hillman was there. So impressed was she with this young dynamic teacher that she asked him what he would most want if he could have anything. He told her he dreamed of having a study center where he and others could teach on a broad range of subjects, all orbiting the singular subject of theology. Prior to the conference, John Guest, Dr. Robert Lamont, and Reid Carpenter had already talked to Dora about starting a study center in Pittsburgh, and

---

1   See *War for Empire in Western Pennsylvania* (Ligonier, PA: Fort Ligonier Association, 1993).

they specifically had in mind enlisting R. C. to run it. They, like R. C., envisioned that this study center would be in the heart of Pittsburgh, most likely the Oakland neighborhood, right near the campuses of the University of Pittsburgh and Carnegie-Mellon University. This was "Mars Hill" for R. C.

That was late summer 1970. The wheels were set in motion.

52 Acres

R. C. dreamed of a study center in the academic heart of Pittsburgh, but Dora had other plans for the location. She had her eye on a 52-acre property for sale only a mile or two away from her own Hilltop Farm. She bought it. It had a deteriorating structure, a stone house, up near the entrance. Beyond the house were trees, rocks, grassy patches here and there, fields, and a pond.

The closest town, two miles away, was Stahlstown, population about two hundred, with its one intersection not even necessitating a traffic light. The borough of Ligonier was a dozen miles away. Pittsburgh was 50 miles to the northwest. To say that the property Dora Hillman bought was in the middle of nowhere would be rather close to the mark.

Over the winter and spring months of 1970–1971, Dora had plans drawn up for a one-story home and began construction. She decided to knock out walls around the living room, the dining room, and the family room. Combined, this new space would accommodate groups of eighty-five or so, packed in. The bedroom walls were left standing. This structure would be called "Lecture House." It would be home to the Sprouls as well as the site of lectures for the study center and, effectively, the offices for Ligonier.[2] The structure at the entrance was appropriately called "Stone House." And that constituted the Ligonier Valley Study Center in 1971.

Meanwhile, the Sprouls were busy. They were packing up their home in Cincinnati; this would be move number nine (over eleven years).

2 Stephen Nichols with R. C. Sproul, personal interview, June 23, 2017.

R. C. met with Francis Schaeffer to learn what he could from Schaeffer's experience with L'Abri Fellowship. Schaeffer had told them the one thing to watch out for is how all-encompassing such a ministry would be for the Sprouls. They were essentially signing on to a twenty-four-hour, seven-day-a-week assignment. There would be people in their home for meals, through the evenings on into the late night, and into the weekends. R. C. recognized that whereas L'Abri was primarily evangelistic in its outreach, the study center would be aimed at a Christian audience and focus more on Christian education. Nevertheless, there were a lot of similarities between the two undertakings, and R. C. was grateful for Schaeffer's advice. R. C. and Vesta soon realized how true Schaeffer's warning was.

During that winter and spring, R. C. made many drives from Cincinnati to Pittsburgh to meet with Guest, Carpenter, Lamont, and others to lay the groundwork for the study center. He also met with officers at the Eli Lilly Foundation for a grant. While Dora provided the property, there was still the need to cover operating expenses. The study center would build up a donor base—R. C. would come to say, "Build the list, talk to the list." And there would be some revenue from the small tuition charges for the classes that would be offered. Those revenue streams, however, would take some time to cultivate. Proceeds from the grant looked promising from the initial and subsequent meetings with the Lilly Foundation. But just before the Sprouls made the move from Cincinnati, they received the call from the foundation with the unwelcome news that the study center would not be receiving the grant. This was the first, but not the last, significant financial challenge the Sprouls and the study center would face.

With the construction of the house finished, Dora mailed the keys to the Sprouls. They moved in and opened the Ligonier Valley Study Center in 1971. When they arrived, Dora had left them a housewarming gift, a pair of German Shepherds. They were brother and sister, born on Palm Sunday, from a female owned by Dora and a male from the Mellons. The dogs had a pedigree equal to their human owners. Dora had already named them: Hallelujah and Hosanna—Hallie, the female, and Hosie, the male, for short. They were, in the words of R. C., "magnificent animals." The Sprouls would own German Shepherds from 1971 until the last one, Roxie, died in 2016.

The study center was a teaching fellowship and a place for learning. R. C. was the main, but not the exclusive, teacher. One of the teachers was Jackie Shelton. She first came to the study center as a student in the summer of 1975. By the fall of 1976, she was coteaching a course entitled "Analyzing Twentieth-Century Culture." She also taught courses in Christian life and counseling, and pursued doctoral studies in psychology at the University of Pittsburgh. Stu Boehmig, a graduate of Gordon-Conwell Theological Seminary, served as a lecturer and also held the post of executive director. Bill White taught psychology and counseling. Tim Couch taught various courses and oversaw vocational counseling for the students. Art Lindsley taught theology, ethics, and apologetics. Art joined R. C. and John Gerstner for the writing of *Classical Apologetics*, published in 1984. R. C. and these five other teachers constituted the residential faculty. Additionally, the study center regularly hosted visiting faculty and lecturers from a variety of colleges and seminaries. Bible and theology were the hub of the teaching, alongside courses on counseling, vocation and career counseling, relationships, ethics, philosophy, and physical education. The study center offered weekly Bible studies, tailored study programs for anywhere from two weeks to two years, and, eventually, courses for college credit. Church groups came on the weekends, and everybody's favorite was the Monday night "GabFest," where no question was off-limits. The study center students ranged from teens to retirees.

One such teen was just walking around the parking lot of the Monroeville Mall, one of the earliest shopping malls built in Pennsylvania. A car drove up full of fellow teens; some he knew, and some he didn't. They said to him, "We're going to a Bible study in the mountains. Want to come along?" He piled in, and they got on the Pennsylvania Turnpike. A few miles after the Donegal exit, they pulled into the study center. Then he was sitting cross-legged on the floor of R. C. Sproul's living room hearing teaching like he'd never heard before. That teen came back many times. He went on to study engineering, and eventually he moved to Denver. A layman, he would occasionally teach Sunday school, and he raised his family. When R. C. came on the radio a few decades later, he listened in daily. He is a lifelong laystudent of theology. That story could be told literally thousands of times over.

Right Now Counts Forever

The Ligonier Valley was the place. It was hard to get to, much more so in the winters when the snow piled up. But its seclusion allowed for students to focus, without distractions, on the topic and on the people at the study center. It was important to R. C. that theological education take place in a life-on-life context. He enjoyed teaching, he enjoyed the prayer times, he enjoyed the meals, and he enjoyed the legendary softball games. It was close enough to Pittsburgh for R. C. and the study center to have a larger impact on the city.

The 1970s was the time. This was the time of hippies, Woodstock, and the sexual revolution. This was the "tune in, turn on, drop out" culture. The 1970s seemed to be a time when people were fixated on the present and wanted little to do with the past. It was a time when people lived for the moment, with little regard for future consequences, or even a future. It was also the culture of the underground church and of the Jesus Movement. Many young people, caught up initially in the cultural revolution, got saved at concerts or on the street or at any one of the storefront churches in America's cities. Then they ended up at the study center to be taught and discipled.

R. C. was interested in a countercultural movement that was at root theological and ecclesiological. In his column in the second issue of *Tabletalk*, from July 1, 1977, R. C. took on the sexual revolution. He asked the question, after cataloging the upheaval caused by the sexual revolution, "How does the Christian deal with all this?" He then offered:

In the final analysis we are left with the deterrent we started with—the Holiness of God and His authority to command obedience from us. We need a new and clear vision of who God is. We need encouragement from the Christian community as a model. We need to see "the more excellent way." . . . How we as Christians deal with the revolution now, will count forever.[3]

The Sprouls were not alone in the work at the study center. Jim and Kathy Thompson moved with them from Cincinnati. Jim was an executive at Procter & Gamble and compiled a lending library of cassette tapes of R. C.'s teaching. He assisted with operations and also recorded R. C. on reel-to-reel tape and then oversaw the production and distribution of R. C.'s teaching on cassette tapes. After a few years of accumulating tapes, Ligonier Ministries purchased the back catalog from the Thompsons and took over the tape ministry. The catalog added the other study center teachers' tapes. Cassette tapes were going out all over the country from the tiny rural Stahlstown post office.

Steve and Janice Gooder also joined the staff at Ligonier. Janice was the first editor of a newsletter that went out from the study center. The first volume, published June 1, 1977, consisted of six 11x17-inch pages folded in half and center-stapled for a total of twelve pages. It was mailed out to about one hundred people, with another hundred or so distributed at the study center. It has been published monthly by Ligonier Ministries ever since under the original title, *Tabletalk*. That first edition had a column by R. C. He entitled his column "Right Now Counts Forever." The first installment of the column was "The Pepsi Generation." The prevailing worldview of secularism held that right now counts for right now. R. C. disagreed and instead asserted that right now counts forever.

The formula for those first years of *Tabletalk* was a headline story on the front page; R. C.'s column on the second page; a profile of a student

---

3   R. C. Sproul, "Right Now Counts Forever: The Sex Revolution and the Christian," *Tabletalk*, vol. 1, July 1, 1977, 2.

or two; an article by one of the teaching staff, usually on a biblical topic; a meet-the-staff page profiling one of the study center's staff; then a two-page spread, in the center, that announced the upcoming lecture series and seminars to be offered at the study center; followed by a page of Ligonier tape ministry offerings; followed by R. C.'s answer to a question in a section titled "Ask R. C." Next came some news items of the study center in a column entitled "The Field Mouse." Here you would learn, for instance, that "Sherrie Sproul is a junior in high school and has her learner's permit for driving. Clear the way folks!"[4] In another you would learn that R. C. has a new jogging suit and may be seen jogging around the hilly roads of the Ligonier Valley or doing jumping jacks on his porch. Quaint to be sure, "The Field Mouse" gave people a sense of being there, and that's what people enjoyed so much about the study center. It was the teaching, but it was the ethos, the context, and the place that were so special to all of the students who visited. No one else was doing anything quite like it.

In one sense, R. C. saw the study center as bridging a gap—the gap between the Sunday school and the seminary. R. C. was not interested in starting a seminary. In fact, Stuart Babbage had tried in vain to get R. C. to be a seminary president in Philadelphia when Conwell pulled up and moved to Massachusetts and merged with Gordon. There was a venture to start a seminary in a downtown Philadelphia venue that would serve primarily the pastors already ministering there. R. C. had no desire to do that. He'd left the academy. R. C. was also concerned about the overwhelming liberalism that marked some of the once confessional and convictional seminaries, like Pittsburgh Theological Seminary or Princeton. At the same time, R. C. also realized that great numbers of young and old laypeople desired deep biblical, theological, and philosophical teaching. Some might be interested in pursuing some form of full-time ministry, but many were not. They were preparing for careers in other areas but wanted to be thoughtful and informed Christians. Vesta put the

4 "The Field Mouse," *Tabletalk*, vol. 1, October 1, 1977.

whole purpose of Ligonier rather succinctly when she said they wanted it to be a place where people could get answers—trusted, reliable, biblically and confessionally faithful answers.

Another Cincinnati couple that loved R. C.'s teaching was Jack and Linda Rowley. Jack had retired from the Air Force, then worked for General Electric, overseeing its television education program for engine mechanics. Using the brand-new technology of the videocassette recorder, Jack filmed and produced teaching tapes for mechanics and engineers. General Electric sold jet engines to the Israeli Air Force, for instance. Jack led a team that would produce step-by-step instructional videos. During the summer, the Rowley family took their vacations at the study center. Once in 1974, Jack brought along his recording equipment and asked R. C. if he minded if he taped the teaching sessions to take back with him for his Bible study class in Cincinnati. The lecture series that Jack taped was on the holiness of God.

A couple from Wichita, Kansas, visited. When they heard about the possibility of the videotaping, they purchased equipment to outfit an entire studio. At that point, Jack announced his retirement from General Electric, and the Rowleys moved to Ligonier permanently. Jack took up the position of media director. More often than not, he could be found behind a video camera. Soon VHS packages were being shipped all over the country with the Stahlstown postmark.

There was very little material available for adult Bible and theological study at this time. No one was producing video material. Ligonier found that they had to give churches VCRs so that churches could order VHS tape series. Ligonier even produced a short booklet entitled "Is Your Church Ready for Video Tapes?" It was an avant-garde piece for avant garde technology.

The Sprouls were feeling the constant pressure of the ministry, with nowhere to escape in their own house. If they wanted privacy, the only place they could go was their bedroom. R. C. recalled, "There would be an occasional weekend when we didn't have a seminar and we would have a Sunday off. And here would come 'the tourists.' They wanted to see the study center. They wanted to see our house."[5] After residing three years in the lecture house, they moved out. They kept the big rooms for lectures and converted the other rooms into offices. R. C. and Vesta built another house on the property 500 yards up on the hill. They lived there for three years, but it still did not provide them much sanctuary. The Rowleys moved in, and the Sprouls built a third house about a half-mile away, tucked back in the woods on seven acres. One remodel consisted of adding a room that popped out of the back, which provided a floor for R. C. and Vesta to practice their hobby of ballroom dancing. They had weekly staff meetings in the house, which always ended with praying over requests that were sent in to the study center.

Making Connections

One of the audiocassette tapes was ordered by Michael Cromartie (1950–2017). Cromartie first met and heard R. C. when R. C. visited Covenant College and Lookout Mountain Presbyterian Church on Lookout Mountain, straddling the Tennessee and Georgia line overlooking Chattanooga. R. C. was invited there by an assistant pastor at the church. He had been on staff with Young Life before he went to Lookout Mountain Presbyterian Church. He was one of the conference attendees at Saranac Lake back in the summer of 1970. He invited R. C. to preach at the church and conduct a conference series. On that trip, additionally, R. C. gave a lecture to businessmen in Chattanooga, and he spoke in chapel at Covenant College. It was the beginning of many trips to Chattanooga. The Sprouls loved that city and met people who became lasting friends. Over time, they met members of the Maclellan family. The Maclellan Foundation would later support Ligonier Ministries.

Michael Cromartie was president of the student body at Covenant College and served as R. C.'s host on that first visit. After chapel, R. C. went

5 "Sproul Memoirs," session 8, recorded 2014, Ligonier Ministries, Sanford, Florida.

to the home of Gordon Haddon Clark (1902–1985) for a dinner. This was a great honor for R. C. He had used one of Clark's books, *From Thales to Dewey*, as a textbook and thought it an excellent analysis of the history of ideas. He was on the side of the presuppositionalists when it came to apologetics and opposed both Gerstner's and R. C.'s classical approach. During dinner, Clark attempted to criticize R. C.'s approach, hanging him out on the same line as Aquinas and Warfield, but R. C. took it as the highest compliment.[6]

Cromartie graduated and took a position as Chuck Colson's (1931–2012) personal assistant. Cromartie drove Chuck to speaking engagements and meetings. On one long drive, he asked Chuck, who sat in the back and worked while they drove, if he minded if he played a teaching tape he had just received in the mail. It was R. C.'s series on the holiness of God. Chuck's attention was given to the papers he had brought along, so he was barely listening. Then he was half-listening, then he put down his papers altogether. Chuck told Cromartie that he'd like to speak with this man, R. C. Sproul.

Chuck made a visit to the study center. That was the start of a deep friendship. Prison Fellowship used R. C.'s audio- and videocassettes to train their staff and to take into prisons. Through the friendships Chuck had in DC, he had arranged work release for federal prisoners two weeks each year. One week he had them in DC, and he'd take them to the study center for the second week. The study center was not a secure facility— no fence, no gate, no cameras—and they never had a single issue with the prisoners on site.

R. C. and Chuck also served on each other's boards. After the runaway success of his book *Born Again* (1976),[7] Chuck kept writing books. He gave his manuscripts to Carl F. H. Henry and R. C. to check the theology. They were friends and had a deep respect for each other. One year, Chuck invited R. C. and Vesta to join him for some vacation time in Chuck's

---

6 Nichols with Sproul, personal interview, June 23, 2017.
7 Charles Colson, *Born Again* (Old Tappan, NJ: Chosen, 1976).

home in Naples. If you were to have asked R. C., he would have told you that his favorite city in the world was Prague, but his favorite place to vacation was Naples. He once said that while he had been a priest in this life, he hoped that in the life to come he would be a king in Naples. The Sprouls enjoyed the time with the Colsons immensely. At one point the conversation turned to work, and they began to entertain the idea of a merger between the two ministries, Prison Fellowship and Ligonier, and the two boards. The merger would be an equal share of everything.

R. C. took the plan back to his board, and they were in support as it had been outlined. When they came to the meeting of the two boards, however, the details were such that the merger was not equal share. The Ligonier board, not including Chuck, would not go along with the plan. It was a grim meeting, but afterward the two ministries kept working together, and R. C. and Chuck remained friends.[8]

Value of the Person

Another Ligonier board member was a former basketball coach of R. C.'s, Wayne Alderson. R. C. wrote Alderson's biography, *Stronger than Steel: The Wayne Alderson Story*, which was published in 1980.[9] Alderson was from Pleasant Hills, R. C. and Vesta's old neighborhood. He was an assistant coach of a basketball team in a church league across metropolitan Pittsburgh that R. C. had played on during high school. Later, Alderson was vice president of operations at Pittron Foundry, a steel mill within inches of closing its doors. Alderson came to the study center with a church group for the seminar. R. C. truly enjoyed a time of reunion with his former coach. Alderson explained to R. C. the situation he was in and the dire condition of the mill. Alderson wanted to put his faith to work and apply his biblical worldview and ethic to the mill. He thought about how he could go about doing that quite intensely. He started with the basic tenets of human dignity and respect. He began to approach all aspects of his

8   Nichols with Sproul, personal interview, June 23, 2017.
9   R. C. Sproul, *Stronger than Steel: The Wayne Alderson Story* (New York: Harper & Row, 1980).

work from this perspective, and Pittron started to turn around and then became very successful. Industry analysts were tempted to use the biblical language of miracle to describe what Alderson pulled off. Alderson came to call his approach the "Value of the Person," which stressed dignity and respect. R. C.'s biography chronicles how absenteeism declined to almost zero among workers and an unprecedented level of productivity. Executives visited workers or their relatives if they were in a hospital. Alderson started a Bible study among the mill workers and organized labor-management prayer breakfasts. At Pittron, Alderson brought a culture of dignity and respect. He then wanted to replicate that at other steel mills and across other industries in Pittsburgh. R. C. joined him.

They were also joined by Francis John "Lefty" Scumaci, a union representative for the International Steel Workers. Before that, Scumaci was a ballplayer in the farm system for the Boston Red Sox. He had a mean streak. He was fired multiple times and was involved in several wildcat strikes. He was sent to Pittron essentially to spy on Alderson. Lefty attended one of the Bible studies to see what was really going on. He found himself coming back, and then he was converted. He and Alderson became quick friends. Alderson introduced him to R. C. Scumaci would eventually serve on Ligonier's board.

Alderson, Lefty, and R. C. were a formidable team. They visited Fortune 500 companies across Pittsburgh and western Pennsylvania and lectured and led seminars among executives. Then they would visit union halls in "Steel Valley." White-collar in the morning, blue-collar in the afternoon. R. C. would start off the day with a coat and tie. On the way to the union hall he'd shed the coat and tie and roll up his shirtsleeves. When they walked through the door of the union hall he was ready.

Sometimes management teams came to R. C. Ahead of Volkswagen's opening of their plant in New Stanton, Pennsylvania, where they would make the Rabbit, they sent a team of fifty-six supervisors to the study center for four days of seminars. R. C. explained, "One of society's greatest areas of pain is in labor-management relations, and that's where people hurt the most, because problems on the job affect a person's whole life. We'd like to reduce the hostilities and the suffering in the work world." One of the supervisors testified, "I came to these seminars a total skeptic. Now I want to be the best supervisor I can possibly be and I want to learn all I can about Jesus and God."[10]

The study center had a fascinating list of students. Richard Lints helped on the ground crew and studied there. He went on to become a professor of theology. Howard Griffith taught at Reformed Theological Seminary until his death in 2019. Bill Hybels took classes at the study center. Tim Keller and his wife, before they married, both studied there. In fact, R. C. Sproul married Tim and Kathy Keller. Rebecca Manley, later to become Rebecca Manley Pippert, studied there. Mike Ford, President Gerald Ford's son, studied there for several months, as did Russ Pulliam, award-winning journalist of the *Indianapolis Star*.

Russ had graduated and had already worked for a few years as an Associated Press reporter in New York City. After he left that post, he "was looking for opportunities to develop a better knowledge of the Bible and its application to journalism, politics, culture, race, and inner city issues." He found it at the study center. He took one seminar, then he returned for a two-month study of supervised reading, adding, "I also enjoy the chance to go barefoot around here and split an infinite number of logs."[11]

Lee Baker was looking for a place that would help her connect biblical studies to art, having taken her bachelor of fine arts. She went to the study center seven times, saying that she'd be back. She noted about the study center, "My appetite for reading has been awakened, and I gained valuable insight into how culture arrived at the state it's in and our responsibility to understand what our culture is thinking."[12]

College students who came to the study center wanted more, and soon colleges approached R. C., asking him to offer January-term courses for

10 "It's Rabbit at Ligonier," *Tabletalk*, vol. 2, April 1978, 1.
11 "Student Life," *Tabletalk*, vol. 1, September 1, 1977, 4.
12 "Student Life," *Tabletalk*.

credit. About a dozen colleges across western Pennsylvania and into Ohio would grant college credit for courses taken from R. C. Students from Geneva College, Grove City College, Westminster College, and other places took courses on philosophy or Bible and took those credits back with them. R. C. remembers how the students enjoyed the time. They had only the one class, so they could concentrate in it, and, with all of the snow around, they could get in a little skiing. R. C. enjoyed teaching them as well. He found college students to be very teachable. Seminarians sometimes had the distraction of work or family, and, as R. C. observed, they already had their positions and views solidified for the most part. But college students were like sponges, and R. C. loved the challenge of impacting them.

Of all the students who came to the study center, Harvey stood out in R. C.'s memory. He had cerebral palsy, and he came to the study center over a few summers and a few January terms. Back at his college, a group of charismatic students had tried to heal Harvey. When their efforts didn't work, they told Harvey that he wasn't healed because he lacked faith and that, likely, he wasn't even a Christian. The next time he came to the study center, he told R. C. what had happened. R. C. assured him that he did not lack faith and that he was a Christian. And they prayed together. Somewhere in the middle, R. C. prayed this line: "Lord, please help this man understand that he is fully justified in your sight and is clothed with the righteousness of Christ." When they finished, R. C. noticed tears streaming down Harvey's face. R. C. asked what was wrong, and Harvey replied, "That was the first time in my life that anybody ever called me a man." "We love Harvey," R. C. said, and they continued to stay in touch decades later.[13]

Ligonier also provided for three of R. C.'s hobbies: hunting, golf, and the Steelers. The Steelers held training camp at nearby Saint Vincent College in Latrobe, and this was the time of the Steelers' dominance, winning the Super Bowl in 1975, 1976, 1979, and 1980.

13 "Sproul Memoirs," session 8.

Western Pennsylvania was known for hunting. School districts considered the first day of deer season a holiday. The property around Ligonier provided plenty of opportunities, and the dogs always went along. The dogs' puppies would come too. Sometimes this would get in the way of the objective of actually capturing game. So to keep the dogs contented at home, R. C. would have to put one of his teaching tapes in the cassette player and turn it on so the dogs would think he was in the room behind the closed door. Then he would slip out his study window, and the dogs were unaware that he had left. On occasion, Vesta would go hunting with him. She could do a good impression of an owl. When turkeys hear a certain owl hoot, they take it as a signal to get up and get about the day.[14]

In seminary, R. C. started playing golf. Near their apartment there was a little course that let ministers play for free. When R. C. went in to sign up for the ministerial plan, the person behind the counter said, "You don't look like a minister."[15] He didn't fit the image. He would go out early in the morning and find golf balls that had been hit off the course. Since they had very little money, it was the only way he could play. He loved golf. Not far from the study center was the Ligonier Country Club where he later played, and also Arnold Palmer's Latrobe Country Club. That's where R. C. first met the legendary golfer. R. C. kept a picture of Arnold Palmer in his office, along with a picture of Luther, of course.[16]

Those were his hobbies. His vocation was running Ligonier, teaching, and writing.

The Symbol

You may recall that before R. C. left Westminster College to go teach at Gordon College, he taught a doctrinal survey course over the summer using the Apostles' Creed as the structure of the course. He taught through similar material again at Gordon. He had hoped to write the material in

---

14 Stephen Nichols with Vesta Sproul, personal interview, May 1, 2018.
15 R. C. Sproul, *The Prayer of the Lord* (Sanford, FL: Reformation Trust, 2009), 8.
16 Nichols with Vesta Sproul, personal interview, May 1, 2018.

book form. He was able to do that while in Cincinnati. He edited the text and sent it to Presbyterian & Reformed Publishing Company, the same company he'd worked for as a book salesman while a student in college. He called the book *The Symbol: An Exposition of the Apostles' Creed*.[17] Presbyterian & Reformed published it. A graphic designer friend of R. C.'s drafted a potential cover, which R. C. sent along to the publisher merely as an idea, fully intending to have his friend finish the draft if the publisher liked it. Presbyterian & Reformed published it with the draft cover that was sent, and then later R. C. found out that *Christianity Today* designated it among the significant books published that year. The words come back from his writing teacher: "Don't let anyone tell you you can't write." R. C. dedicated the book to Vesta, the inscription bearing these words:

TO VESTA
To the Romans, a pagan goddess;
To me, a Godly wife.

It was his first book, and his first book dedicated to Vesta. It would certainly not be his last book, nor would it be the last book dedicated to Vesta. It was the only book dedication of R. C.'s, however, that used the words "pagan goddess."

In the preface, R. C. takes a few sentences to explain his style and approach, noting that he uses a semipopular literary style, and that he "sought in many cases to deal with highly complex theological matters in a manner that will simplify them for the reader."[18] These would be the telltale signs of R. C. Sproul's teaching. While he sought to simplify for his beloved readers, he never patronized them. Additionally, he liked to make his readers smile. Still in the preface, he writes that he avoided "academic technicalia," to which he adds a footnote. The footnote reads: *Semper*

---

17   The first printing has a different subtitle on the front cover than on the title page inside the book. The front cover reads, "A Contemporary Exposition of the Apostle's Creed," whereas the title page reads, "An exposition of the Apostles' Creed," leaving out "Contemporary" and putting the apostrophe in the proper place.

18   R. C. Sproul, *The Symbol* (Phillipsburg, NJ: Presbyterian & Reformed, 1973), vii.

ubi, sub ubi, which translated means, "Always where, under where." In English it sounds like, "Always wear underwear."

On page 1, he notes that the Apostles' Creed begins with the words "I believe." He then observes, "The present is an hour of non-faith for much of American culture. To say, 'I believe,' smacks today of a fundamental flight into a make-believe world where reality is softened by faith." R. C. goes on to argue that faith is not a leap. As Christians we are not each "a 'Tiny Alice' who closes her eyes and holds her breath, hoping to believe her wishes into fulfillment."[19] No, "the New Testament does not call man to crucify his intellect." He further exclaims, "Faith is reasonable."[20] He goes on to say that faith involves "more than being persuaded of the truth; it involves loving the truth. . . . Faith wills the exaltation of Christ."[21] Faith also results in living: "The faith that justifies is the kind of faith that results in holy living."[22] Faith involves thinking and knowing, loving and delighting, and obeying and living. So R. C. concludes the first chapter, "If the church is to be the church, she must continue to be a confessing body."

By page 10 R. C. writes of ice cream cones, actually of "God and Ice Cream Cones." He then is on to Thomas Aquinas and analogical language. Understanding who God is leads R. C. to discuss who we are and our need for a savior. All of the themes that R. C. would continue to unfurl over the next five decades may be found in his first book.

Near the end of the book R. C. observes that the "future of the visible church appears to be a grim one." But then he holds out hope for renovation and renewal, adding:

Perhaps the greatest hope for the future lies in the present revolution of the laity. A new dimension of lay involvement, lay education, and lay mobilization is informing the major churches of America. Maybe

19 Sproul, *The Symbol*, 2.
20 Sproul, *The Symbol*, 3.
21 Sproul, *The Symbol*, 6.
22 Sproul, *The Symbol*, 7.

a new Moses stands among them, a new Luther, a new Augustine, or Calvin who will lead us out of the impasse as we stand between Migdol and the Sea.[23]

R. C. first heard that challenge—to stand between Migdol and the Sea—in seminary. In seminary, he also heard Gerstner say, many times, that for the church "it is an age of _illiteracy_," as R. C. double-underlined that word in one of his lecture outlines penned in one of his private notebooks from the early study center days. R. C. continues, observing that the "clergy [are the] most 'incompetent' of all 'professionals' [and] have little knowledge of God." R. C. experienced that firsthand when the New Testament survey class he'd taken as a student skipped Romans.

A dearth of well-trained clergy in the pulpit meant poorly fed congregants in the pew and an anemic church. R. C. saw Ligonier as the place where he could stand between Migdol and the Sea and lead laypeople, mostly, into theological and biblical literacy.

What R. C. was attempting to do at the Ligonier Valley Study Center was ignite a theological revolution. In the face of the turbulent 1970s as institutions crumbled, R. C. looked to the solid and sure plank of the authority of God's Word. In a time when the past was disdained and the present moment was celebrated, R. C. looked to the ancient Apostles' Creed, Aquinas, the Reformers, and Jonathan Edwards to overflow with contemporary relevance. And in a moment when the power of the now and present satisfaction eclipsed the eternal, R. C. declared "right now counts forever." Everything that happened at the study center arced back to one thing: the diligent study of God's Word. R. C. did not want the study center to be a place of mere opinion, but a place of knowledge, the acquiring and teaching of knowledge that led to transformation. It was a place to go to learn who God is.

The study center was a particular place and it started at a particular time.

---

23 Sproul, _The Symbol_, 140.

The time was the 1970s, a peculiar moment in American history, culturally revolutionary. The place, the Ligonier Valley Study Center, was also a peculiar place in church history, theologically revolutionary. There was nothing quite like it. It was not like Schaeffer's L'Abri. The closest kin would be Luther's Black Cloister, the monastery Frederick the Wise gifted him and Katie as a wedding present. Known as the "Lutherhalle" or the "Lutherhaus," it was here that Luther studied, taught, and lived with his family in the company of students. That was the study center.

When the Sprouls moved onto the property in 1971, there was the old Stone House and the brand-new Lecture House—where R. C. studied, taught, and lived with his family in the company of students. You entered the gravel driveway off Old Distillery Road. Like all of Pennsylvania's rural roads, this one had no berm and never had any painted lines, but it did have ups and downs, twists and turns, and potholes. You entered the property facing the sunrise, Stone House to the left, Lecture House to the right. Cedar Lodge, which would provide housing, was added later, and it would boast wide cedar planks, harvested from Dora Hillman's land. A lake and fields lie behind it, running north until they give way to the tree line and the undulating hills. There was Pine Lodge, which housed the studio, production facility, and offices. It boasted pine boards, harvested, again, from Dora Hillman's property. Staff houses lined up in a row flanking Pine Lodge. Above them a tree-capped dome provided the stage for sunrises. Looking south, just past Lecture House, there stands an old log chapel. Dora found it and had it moved onto the property. Carved into the hill, Ligonier was a place for learning and living theology. Ligonier was a place for learning and living theology. While a cultural revolution was taking place out there, a quiet reformation was beginning here.

5

INERRANCY

The full trustworthiness of sacred Scripture must be
defended in every generation, against every criticism.

R. C. SPROUL

THE LAURELVILLE MENNONITE RETREAT CENTER sits not far from the
study center at the bottom of Three Mile Hill, which is literally a three-
mile descent on PA Route 31, from the top of which you can see the city
of Pittsburgh 50 miles away. This particular center, like any number of
places, offers camp and retreat facilities for mostly church groups in and
around western Pennsylvania. It is not an overstatement to claim that
for a few days in October of 1973, it played a historic role in American
church history, serving as the setting for a conference on biblical inerrancy. Big rocks, boulders really, and sturdy pines dot the hilly grounds
and surround wood-sided buildings, meeting rooms, and cabins. Cool
mountain streams run through it, with a more formidable creek at one
point offering a small but still impressive waterfall. If you were looking
for the perfect place for a weekend retreat in the woods, you'd have found
it. The study center could host large groups for lectures, but it could not
feed and house three hundred people. And that was the group that came
to what was the first large-scale conference put on by Ligonier.

It was called the "Conference on the Inspiration and Authority of Scripture," and it brought together a group of scholars as speakers to address an audience of mostly pastors. The essays were published in 1974 as *God's Inerrant Word: An International Symposium on the Trustworthiness of Scripture*, edited by John Warwick Montgomery (1931–). The book was dedicated to Dora Hillman. J. I. Packer (1926–2020), conference speaker and contributor, was from the UK. Peter Jones was also from the UK and had just started as a professor at the Reformed seminary in Aix-en-Provence, France. Rounding out this international symposium were the American speakers John Warwick Montgomery, John Gerstner, Clark Pinnock, John Frame, and the conference convener, R. C. Sproul, at age thirty-four.

Montgomery collected degrees, eleven in all, in such fields as philosophy, library studies, theology, and law. He holds a PhD from the University of Chicago, a doctorate in theology from Strasbourg, and his JD degree is from Cardiff. In 1973 he published a collection of essays under the title *Christianity for the Tough-Minded*. Packer's classic text, *Knowing God*, was published that same year as well, but that was not the book that got him invited to the conference. Packer's first book, *Fundamentalism and the Word of God* (1958), was the reason he was invited. Of course, R. C. would invite his mentor, Dr. Gerstner. Clark Pinnock had published *A Defense of Biblical Infallibility* (1967), a book on apologetics, and another book on the doctrine of Scripture. John Frame taught at Westminster Theological Seminary in Philadelphia, the tough-minded seminary that stood tall for biblical fidelity and confessional conviction. Peter Jones had recently completed his doctorate at Princeton and was beginning his career as an apologist and theologian. If you wanted to draw a line in the sand, this was a good group to do it.

The book's preface declares that the conference, and the essays in this book, served "as an adrenal injection for the faint-of-heart who question the place of inerrancy in historic Christian theology or doubt the modern research is compatible for an errorless Bible." The preface continues observing that the essayists "hold in common the historic Christian confidence in an entirely trustworthy Bible." They hoped that through these essays they would impart that confidence to the readers and to the church, to pastors in the pulpit and to people in the pews.

It was certainly R. C.'s goal to impart that confidence to the audience at Laurelville. For R. C., the subject of inerrancy was not an abstract doctrine, and this conference was not a quaint gathering of theologians and pastors to discuss ivory-tower matters. The storms of war had gathered and were continuing to gather in denominations that were historically and confessionally committed to an inerrant and authoritative Bible. The Princetonians, Charles and A. A. Hodge, B. B. Warfield, and J. Gresham Machen, battled for the Bible as modernism ricocheted through culture and spawned liberalism in the churches. In the 1950s, the teachings of Rudolf Bultmann and Karl Barth had impacted an entire generation of academics, who then impacted pastors and denominational leaders. Eventually the trickle down reached the pew. R. C. had experienced it firsthand at Pleasant Hills Community Presbyterian Church, although he didn't even realize it at the time.

The Bible and History

In 1967 R. C.'s denomination, the United Presbyterian Church USA (UPCUSA), published the Book of Confessions. The plural is important. The Westminster Standards had been the confessional statement for the various Presbyterian denominations. From the 1640s, the Westminster Standards consist of the Westminster Confession of Faith, the Shorter Catechism, the Larger Catechism, and the Directory for Public Worship. The Book of Confessions added to these documents various historical confessions, as well as the Confession of 1967.

R. C.'s issue with this new confession was not so much what it said, but what it didn't say. For instance, the confession affirms the resurrection of Jesus Christ but does not use the word *bodily*. This allows for those who, following Rudolph Bultmann, would claim the nonsensical position that Christ rose again merely in the realm of faith; they deny the bodily, in space and time, resurrection of Christ. Bultmann argued that the New Testament Gospels are a mixture of the historical and the mythological, and for the Bible to have any relevance for modern man, a biblical interpreter—and a pastor—must get past the historical in order to preach the mythological. In an article in *Tabletalk*, R. C. explains it this way:

> The historical character of Judeo-Christianity is what markedly distinguishes it from all forms of mythology. A myth finds its value in its moral or spiritual application, while its historical reality remains insignificant. Fairy tales can help our mood swings, but they do little to give us confidence in ultimate reality. The twentieth century witnessed a crisis in the historical dimension of biblical Christianity. German theologians made a crucial distinction between ordinary history and what they called "salvation history," or sometimes "redemptive history." This distinction was based in the first instance on the obvious character of sacred Scripture, namely, that it is not only a record of the ordinary events of men and nations. It is not a mere chronicle of human activity but includes within it the revelation of God's activity in the midst of history. Because the Bible differs from ordinary history and was called "salvation history," it was a short step from there to ripping the biblical revelation out of its historical context altogether. No one was more important in the snatching of the Gospels out of history than the German theologian Rudolf Bultmann. Bultmann devised a new theology that he called "a theology of timelessness." This theology of timelessness is not interested in the past or in the future as categories of reality. What counts according to Bultmann is the *hic et nunc*, the "here and now," or the present moment. Salvation doesn't take place on the horizontal plane of history, but it takes place vertically in the present moment or what others called "the existential moment."[1]

1   R. C. Sproul, "An Historic Faith," *Tabletalk*, vol. 30, February 2006, https://www.ligonier.org/learn/articles/historic-faith/.

Then Dr. Sproul counters succinctly, "The Bible is the record of God's historic works of redemption within the context of space and time. Take the Gospel and its message out of the context of history, and Christianity is destroyed altogether."[2]

Here we see the doctrine of Scripture and the doctrine of salvation intertwined. A belief in the historical veracity, the complete and entire veracity, of Scripture has everything to do with the person and work of Christ and a completely and entirely true account of His virgin birth, life of perfect obedience, crucifixion, resurrection, and ascension.

R. C. wanted the church to make no mistake about what was at stake here: accept Bultmann's approach to Scripture, adjust doctrine and confessional statements accordingly, and you lose the gospel. You lose the church's raison d'être, the reason for its very existence.

In addition to Bultmann, the church in the 1960s and 1970s was confronted with the influence of Karl Barth. Barth stressed that human beings err, so if God were to override the human authors of Scripture, the result would be biblical Docetism. Docetism was the heretical view that the Christ was not truly human. The Greek word *dokeo*, means "to appear." This heresy taught that Christ appeared to be human but was not truly human. Christ's divine nature, as it were, swallows up any human nature. When Barth charged that the view of inerrancy was biblical Docetism, he was saying that the inerrantist view requires the divine authorship of Scripture to gobble up the human authorship. Instead, he held the dialectical position that Scripture is God's word that does not err and also man's word that does err. R. C. explains Barth's next move:

> Barth said the Bible is the "Word" (*verbum*) of God, but not the "words" (*verba*) of God. With this act of theological gymnastics, he hoped to solve the unsolvable dilemma of calling the Bible the Word of God, which errs. If the Bible is errant, then it is a book of human reflection

2   Sproul, "An Historic Faith."

on divine revelation—just another human volume of theology. It may have deep theological insight, but it is not the Word of God.[3]

Barth's view had a significant impact. What emerged was so-called neoorthodoxy, and it could be felt in nearly every European and Anglo denomination and had adherents on the faculty across major seminaries.

So in 1973 R. C. convened a conference to respond to the frontal attacks of Bultmann and Barth on inerrancy.[4] But for R. C. this was no mere academic endeavor. The doctrine of Scripture, as mentioned, directly impacts the doctrine of salvation. The doctrine of Scripture also directly impacts living the Christian life, the Christian's obedience to God, and the Christian's ethic. In short, inerrancy, and the authority of Scripture, has everything to do with salvation and with life.

Bread, Not Stones

Herman Bavinck, who preceded R. C.'s professor G. C. Berkouwer at the Free University, recalled his time at Leiden as a student. The faculty there had all come under the spell of higher criticism. Bavinck reminisced sadly that he went to Leiden to receive bread and was given stones instead.[5] R. C., too, had been given stones. He knew what was preached in the pulpits, because it was preached to him. He knew what was taught in some of the denominational colleges and seminaries, because it was taught to him. He knew there was a steady diet of stones being offered, and there appeared to be even more to come. Also disconcerting was the subtlety of the newer arguments against inerrancy, which meant that challenges to inerrancy were impacting fellow evangelicals, evangelicals who should have known better.

---

3 R. C. Sproul, "Foreword," *The Inerrant Word: Biblical, Historical, Theological, and Pastoral Perspectives*, ed. John MacArthur (Wheaton, IL: Crossway, 2016), 10.

4 In his essay "The Case for Inerrancy: A Methodological Analysis," R. C. devotes four pages to refuting Barth's "docetic" argument against inerrancy.

5 Herman Bavinck, "Modernism and Orthodoxy," cited in John Bolt, "Grand Rapids between Kampen and Amsterdam: Herman Bavinck's Reception and Influence in North America," *Calvin Theological Journal*, vol. 38 (2003): 267.

At the conference, R. C. unveiled the Ligonier Statement, written by him and signed by all of the presenters. In one paragraph, the statement declares:

> We believe the Holy Scriptures of the Old and New Testaments to be the inspired and inerrant Word of God: We hold the Bible, as originally given through agents of revelation, to be infallible and see this as a crucial article of faith with implications for the entire life and practice of all Christian people. With the great fathers of Christian history we declare our confidence in the total trustworthiness of the Scriptures, urging that any view which imputes to them a lesser degree of inerrancy than total, is in conflict with the Bible's self-testimony in general and with the teaching of Jesus Christ in particular. Out of obedience to the Lord of the Church we submit ourselves unreservedly to his authoritative view of Holy Writ.

The statement begins with a reference back to the basic argument of the Princetonians and Warfield. Warfield argued that if inspiration is true, then inerrancy is the proper conclusion. To put the matter more succinctly, if inspiration, then inerrancy. If the Bible is God's word, breathed out by Him (inspiration), then the Bible is true (inerrancy), as God cannot err. The Ligonier Statement affirms that inerrancy is consistent with historical orthodoxy and with the Bible's own self-understanding, specifically with Christ's view of Scripture. The statement ends with a declaration to submit "unreservedly" to Scripture.

This was the 1970s, the era of Joseph Fletcher's "situational ethics." He had published *Situation Ethics: The New Morality* in 1966. Fletcher declared flatly, "The morality of an action depends on the situation." Relativism run amok. Additionally, there was an erosion of the institutions people relied upon as America was embroiled in the Watergate scandal from 1972 through 1974. This caused another fault line to emerge regarding authority. How does one know what is the right? And further, how does one do the right? These crucial questions need to be answered from a solid foundation.

The early 1970s was a time of ethical crisis. At the study center, R. C. and the other teachers confronted these ethical issues, challenges, and questions directly. R. C. cared deeply about how people live, how they live *right now*, because of the eternal consequences. R. C. realized the disobedient life is not worth living. The obedient life is. The only way we know if a comprehensive world- and lifeview and ethic is sound and cogent is for the basis of that worldview and ethic to be sound and cogent. Thinking about how to live in this world is what drove R. C.'s doctrine of Scripture. He wanted the church to know that there is a sure and solid foundation for doctrine and life, theology and ethics, studying and knowing God, and also obeying God and worshiping him in all of life. An authoritative Scripture is the key. From that basis, you can offer from the pulpit and the lectern bread, not stones.

The Ligonier Valley Study Center addressed a number of subjects, but none was more important than the study of the Bible. R. C. stressed that reading the Bible is one thing, studying the Bible is another thing, and obeying the Bible is another thing altogether. The argument followed a logical chain:

(1) We submit to every word of the Bible (obedience), which requires

(2) every word of the Bible to be studied, preached, and taught (the whole counsel of God), because

(3) every word of the Bible is true (inerrancy), because

(4) every word of the Bible is from God (inspiration), because

(5) God is truth (doctrine of God).

Accordingly, R. C. convened the conference on inerrancy.

Meanwhile, the PCA

R. C. had other matters to contend with while planning and hosting the inerrancy conference. His denomination allowed for the ordination of women. R. C. opposed this. His denomination allowed him, and others who were like-minded, such as Gerstner, to hold his view. The denomination would not bind his conscience by requiring him to attend the ordination service of a woman, which would require him to join the other elders in the laying upon of hands and signifying approval. That practice changed with the "Kenyon decision." The Kenyon decision required ministers of the UPCUSA to follow the polity and decisions of the denomination. The denomination decided that women could be ordained to the position of teaching elder, as pastor. Prior to the Kenyon decision, the denomination allowed for ministers to follow their conscience. Ministers could choose not to participate in the ordination service of women. The Kenyon decision ended that practice, letting ministers know that they should leave the denomination if they cannot support the rulings and polity of the denomination.

Walter Wynn Kenyon was a student at Pittsburgh Theological Seminary, a student at the study center, and was mentored by both Gerstner and R. C. Holding the same view as R. C. and Gerstner on women's ordination, as well as many others, Kenyon's ordination nevertheless kicked off a landmark judicial case. While awaiting the decision by the general assembly, R. C. and Gerstner hosted a meeting in Pittsburgh's William Penn Hotel for like-minded pastors and seminarians. R. C. presented his position, which was to leave the denomination and transfer the credentials elsewhere to denominations like the much more conservative Presbyterian Church in America (PCA). Gerstner advocated the position to stay and wait and see if the denomination would bring them up on charges, potentially leading to a church trial that would end in defrocking them of their credentials.

To disagree with Gerstner was difficult for R. C. He did not relish being on the other end of an issue from his mentor. "You can't imagine," R. C. recalled, "what an experience it was for me to be standing in opposition to my mentor."[6] The disagreement with Gerstner, however, "was not in any way a hostile difference." After they had presented their two sides,

6 "Sproul Memoirs," session 7, recorded 2013, Ligonier Ministries, Sanford, Florida.

"Dr. Gerstner sat down next to me, put his arm around me, and said, 'Can you live with that, Roberto?' He always called me Roberto. I looked at him and smiled and I said, 'No, I can't.'"

That the relationship came through this difference of opinion intact can be seen in R. C.'s serving as editor of the book that honored the life and work of Gerstner in 1976. Scholars call this kind of a book a *festschrift*, which means festival writing. They are published to mark retirements or special occasions. R. C. and the group of scholars assembled to write essays honoring Gerstner's twenty-five years of teaching.[7] The bond between Gerstner and Sproul ran deep. Their differences discussed that day in the William Penn Hotel would not break it.

Returning to the issue in 1974, R. C. took the position he did because of seminarians coming up and some of the younger pastors. He did not think the denomination would come after him or Gerstner, but he wasn't as sure for the others. The Kenyon case likely, as R. C. interpreted things, only portended more to come. In the end, Gerstner decided to stay in (until 1990), whereas R. C. wrote a letter to the Presbytery of Redstone stating that he felt it was his duty to withdraw peaceably from the ministry. The Presbytery, glad to see him go, replied that he was a minister in error. R. C. recalled how that made him feel a little bit of what the Reformers felt. It is a painful irony to be one who has to leave because the church is not faithful to her calling. R. C. transferred his credentials to the PCA, remaining a minister in good standing in that denomination until his death in 2017.

The conference on inerrancy and the tangle with the denomination were preparing R. C. for a larger leadership role to come, as was the work at the study center. The budget for the first year of the Ligonier Valley Study Center was $85,000. From day one in August of 1971, R. C. had help on the operations side and various directors, executive directors, and presidents. At times, however, R. C. stepped into those roles. But even when he did not have the title, the brunt of the leadership, decision

---

7   R. C. Sproul, ed., *Soli Deo Gloria: Essays in Reformed Theology, Festschrift for John Gerstner* (Phillipsburg, NJ: Presbyterian & Reformed, 1976).

making, budgeting, and the actual meeting and balancing of the budget fell upon him.

Not to mention the fact that R. C. was raising a family in the midst of the study center. The staff at the study center all lived on the property or nearby. The kids grew up together. It was enjoyable and intense all at the same time. It also meant that R. C., except when he was traveling, was with his family all day long. Everyone knew that it was not only R. C.; it was always R. C. and Vesta. They modeled marriage, much like Martin and Katie Luther.

Given that priests were, in theory, celibate, Martin and Katie effectually modeled the first parsonage and the first married life for clergy. As mentioned previously, when they married, Frederick the Wise gave them the Black Cloister, the former monastery, as their home. Rather large, it was also a lecture hall and classroom, a refectory, and a hotel for traveling dignitaries. The Luthers raised their children among students and colleagues of the University of Wittenberg, and amidst a constant stream of visitors. Luther studied, wrote, and taught in the same dwelling in which he ate, slept, and lived.

Ligonier called its newsletter-turned-magazine, *Tabletalk*, after a publication of Luther by that same name. *Tischreden* in the German, Luther's dinner always had theological conversation going, "table talk" in the context of life, with spouses and children and students and colleagues all chiming in. Even the Luther family dog was a subject of the *Tischreden* on a few occasions. They would ask questions, and Luther would answer them. Students started transcribing Luther's answers and comments, providing us with one of the most fascinating texts in church history.

That was all true of the study center. Theology was taught in the context of life. Rather, theology was lived. Even the family dogs, and the occasional cat that R. C. would let Sherrie keep, were also part of it.

Historians have pointed out that one of the unique elements of the portraiture of Martin Luther is that you often see his portrait alongside Katie's portrait. That typically didn't happen in those days. Most historic portraiture is singular, the great man alone. Rarely do we have portraits of wives unless they were queens. The combined portraits of Martin and Katie, which were common to see from the sixteenth century on, signify the centrality of the relationship to Luther's life and legacy. That is true of the centrality of the relationship of R. C. and Vesta to R. C.'s life and legacy. Not only did they model marriage, but R. C. and the other study center teachers also taught marriage courses and led marriage seminars often. R. C. collected his material and published it in his third book, *Discovering the Intimate Marriage* (1975).

R. C.'s first book was released in 1973. In 1974 *The Psychology of Atheism*, which grew out of a course he taught at Conwell School of Theology and lectures at the study center, was released. That same year his essay was published in the inerrancy book of essays from Ligonier's conference. Then the marriage book. From then onward to his death, and posthumously, there were only a handful of years when he did not publish a book. Most years, he published several.

R. C. was teaching many hours every week. He wrote out lecture notes in spiral-bound notebooks, then stepped before an audience to teach, usually without the notebook. And R. C. was traveling to speak. In those days, he felt "like I was traveling here, there, and everywhere."[8] He frequently made road trips around western Pennsylvania and into Pittsburgh to speak, and also traveled by air to speak all over the country. He was gaining a reputation as a clear and cogent communicator. He kept his ear close to the ground and had a keen sense of the issues facing both the church and the culture. He pulled on his knowledge of the Bible and theology, as well as philosophy and the history of ideas, to speak to those issues in a compelling manner—and with conviction. People listened. "I can't think of another place in America where I could get teaching like I got here tonight," testified one student after spending the evening at the study center listening to R. C. lecture.[9]

8   "Sproul Memoirs," session 8, recorded 2014, Ligonier Ministries, Sanford, Florida.
9   "Ligonier Packs Them In on Monday Nights," *Tabletalk*, vol. 2, September 1978, 9.

In 1975 he drove the Pennsylvania Turnpike east to Philadelphia. He had been invited to speak at the Philadelphia Conference on Reformed Theology at the historic Tenth Presbyterian Church right off Rittenhouse Square. This was the second year of that conference. James Boice had started the conference in 1974. R. C. first met Boice in 1968, when R. C. taught at Conwell in Philadelphia. Boice was one year older than R. C. He, too, was from Pittsburgh, and he, too, played all sports in his elementary through high school years. Because R. C. was bused to Clairton High School, he and Jim would have been in rival school districts, but Boice's father sent him to Stony Brook, a boarding school in New York. Then Boice went to Harvard University, Princeton Theological Seminary, and then to the University of Basel in Switzerland for his doctorate. He was senior minister at Tenth from 1968 until his death from cancer in 2000. R. C. and Boice were brothers-in-arms. They were true friends, and over the years the Sprouls and the Boices spent much time together. From 1975 through the early 1990s, R. C. spoke at most of the Philadelphia Conference on Reformed Theology gatherings. They were always held in the spring. The opening session on Friday evening always began with a packed congregation singing "A Mighty Fortress," with the organ in full tilt, and the windows open, as Luther's lyrics lifted over Philadelphia. R. C. sometimes took his daughter, Sherrie, with him on those trips. Philadelphia had far better shopping for a young girl than the borough of Ligonier.

For R. C.'s many accomplishments, Geneva College, in Beaver Falls, Pennsylvania, awarded R. C. an honorary doctorate in 1976. Geneva was north and west of the study center. It was not quite as far north as his college alma mater, Westminster. As Geneva's president Dr. Jack White awarded the degree, he noted in the citation that R. C. "is a capable teacher," and then he listed the books R. C. had written up to that point in time and the various places where he served and taught. The local paper, the *Ligonier Echo*, ran a picture of R. C. in his robe and hood, holding his degree and smiling. After the ceremony, R. C., Vesta,

Sherrie, and Craig drove back to the study center. The staff threw a big party of celebration for him. That summer the whole nation celebrated the nation's Bicentennial. Everything turned red, white, and blue. Fort Ligonier garnered quite the attention.

In 1977 R. C. published *Knowing Scripture* with InterVarsity Press. Inter-Varsity Press, the British imprint, had published Packer's *Knowing God* with a great deal of (unexpected) success. The American publishing division specifically titled Sproul's book to catch the wave. They invited Packer to write the foreword. He penned a clever first line: "If I were the devil (please, no comment), one of my first aims would be to stop folk from digging into the Bible."[10] That is exactly what R. C. wanted folk to do: to dig deeply in the Bible. The book grew out of lectures he had given over the preceding decade, but especially over the previous three or so years at the study center. It's full of practical tips on how to interpret the Bible, as well as nuggets of theological reflection. He speaks of Bible study as a duty:

> We live as human beings under an obligation by divine mandate to study diligently God's Word. He is our sovereign, it is His Word, and he commands that we study it. A duty is not an option.

On the exact same page, he also tells us that "the secret to happiness is found in obedience to God. . . . Thus the top and the tail of it is that happiness cannot be fully discovered as long as we remain ignorant of God's Word."[11]

The doctrine of Scripture remained front and center for R. C. for the next few years, not only because he cared so deeply about Bible study, but also because of the theological and ecclesiastical climate of the time. You could say that a storm was brewing at the time, and R. C. would be in the center of it all.

---

10 J. I. Packer, "Foreword," in R. C. Sproul, *Knowing Scripture* (Downers Grove, IL: InterVarsity Press, 1977), 9.

11 Packer, "Foreword," 14.

Chicago

The controversy over inerrancy intensified after the conference in 1973. In addition to R. C.'s denominational context of the PCUSA, other hot spots included the Evangelical Lutheran Church in America, the Southern Baptist Convention, and such seminaries as Fuller Theological Seminary and Gordon-Conwell Theological Seminary—where R. C. taught as an adjunct professor of apologetics. In 1976 Harold Lindsell (1913–1988), who had taught at Fuller and at Wheaton and was then editor of *Christianity Today* magazine, published his bombshell, *The Battle for the Bible*. Lindsell named names and called for the church to respond to this crisis. Fervid reviews of his book appeared in journals and magazines. Some of those whom Lindsell called out threatened to sue. This was a crisis moment in the church.

In the midst of lecture notes in one of his spiral-bound notebooks, with a $2.38 price tag from G. C. Murphy, R. C. sketched an outline for discussing inerrancy. It starts off with "Present Crisis—Lindsell—rupture." Next follows "Historical Bkgrd [Background]," which notes "Evangel. Heritage, Sola Fide—Sola Scriptura." At the end of this outline he writes:

Need Evangelical summit.

Then he adds:

May fail but must try it.[12]

R. C. reached out to Lindsell and suggested that Lindsell, from his post at *Christianity Today*, convene such a summit, reaching across denominational lines, on inerrancy. Lindsell wrote back that while he thought such a summit was vital, he was not in a position to lead it.

R. C. and fellow 1973 Ligonier conference speakers Packer and Gerstner joined Norman Geisler and Greg Bahnsen for a conference on the authority of Scripture at Mount Hermon, California, in February of 1977. That

---

12 R. C. Sproul, lecture notebook (no title/date). This outline sketch is most likely from 1975 or 1976.

group of five met with Jay Grimstead, Audrey Wetherell Johnson of Bible Study Fellowship, and Karen Hoyt. They prayed and deliberated. Out of the meeting of the original "advisory board" came the decision to launch what would come to be called the International Council on Biblical Inerrancy.

The ICBI launched in 1977. The idea was to impact the church and produce materials on inerrancy for a period of ten years, then dissolve. Joining that original group that met in California were Roger Nicole, Earl Radmacher, Harold Hoehner, Paige Patterson, Robert Preus, Donald Hoke, Gleason Archer, Edmund Clowney, and James Montgomery Boice.

The group invited Billy Graham to join the council. In a letter to Jay Grimstead, stamped "Private and Confidential," Graham said he would take the invitation under advisement but added that his "work as an international evangelist is considerably different than the others you have on your list. I must work with all kinds of Christians that hold varying positions, and certainly would not break fellowship with a fellow believer on the basis of inerrancy." He then added, "I think probably I can best help by continuing to proclaim the Bible both in my writings and preaching to be the infallible Word of God, rather than becoming drawn into this issue at this time." He also mentioned that the Billy Graham Evangelistic Association will be sending a check in the amount of $10,000, and he requested that it be itemized "as an anonymous gift."[13] In the end Graham declined the invitation and never signed the Chicago Statement. The ICBI council did reference the gift in correspondence and in a newsletter, mentioning an anonymous gift from a well-known evangelist. Most could figure that one out rather easily.

The council soldiered on. Boice was elected chairman, and R. C. was elected president. Karen Hoyt ran the ICBI office in Oakland, California. They held a meeting to plan the first big summit. They each were given a card to fill out their lunch order from a selection of sand-

13 Billy Graham to Jay Grimstead, June 21, 1977, ICBI Archives, Dallas Theological Seminary Archives.

wiches. Ham and cheese, turkey, Reuben. R. C. handwrote his order for a "Hamburger—well done, K[etchup]., French Fries." According to the minutes, R. C. at one point said succinctly, "Luther: 'When the Bible speaks, God speaks," They planned to convene a summit. The first location discussed was Atlanta. (It could have been named the Atlanta Statement.) Instead, they agreed upon the more centrally located Chicago, specifically locking in the Hyatt Regency at Chicago's O'Hare Airport. The summit would take place October 26–28, 1978.

This was the summit that R. C. knew the church needed. It might fail, but they must try.

The council intended to present a draft of an extended statement on inerrancy at the summit itself, allowing for response, interaction, and discussion with the participants. When the summit attendees arrived, they found a welcome letter from Jim Boice in their registration packet: "In spite of our diversity we have one great thing in common. We all hold to the absolute authority, integrity, and full inerrancy of God's Word, and we want to present the case for this conviction and win others to it by the grace of God. Indeed, we are convinced that the health of the church depends on it."[14]

The council had appointed a drafting committee and divvied up writing responsibilities so that a draft document could be presented at the summit. When the council members met the night before the council convened, the person assigned the articles of affirmation and denial revealed to the group that he did not have them. The group looked to R. C. They continued their meeting, finishing just before midnight. R. C. went to his room in the Hyatt Regency and from midnight until about 4:00 a.m. wrote a draft of the nineteen articles of affirmation and denial. They were presented, rather hot off the press, later that day at the plenary session of the summit. In addition to the sessions presenting and discussing the Chicago Statement, the summit schedule included six sermons and fourteen major papers.

14 James M. Boice to summit participants, October 26, 1978 (on ICBI letterhead).

R. C. preached a sermon, "Hath God Said," and presented a paper, "The Internal Testimony of the Holy Spirit." He had a busy few days in Chicago.

Twelve countries were represented among the summit participants, over thirty colleges and over thirty seminaries, and over a dozen denominations. The participants included a father and son team, Drs. John MacArthur Sr. and Jr. The summit included a moment for participants to be original signers. In the twentieth century it was hard to get evangelicals to agree on anything. To have such a hearty agreement about such a detailed, complex, and comprehensive statement might tempt one to call it a miracle. The official newsletter, "The ICBI Update," reported, "A remarkable spirit of unity and anticipation marked the Summit which culminated in signing the finished statement on Saturday." R. C. preached the final sermon, "Hath God Said" from Genesis 3 and Matthew 4. They sang "A Mighty Fortress," followed by the formal signing of the document.[15] Those present "were deeply moved and went from that place rejoicing in what God had done."[16]

R. C. had the summit he had hoped for, and it had not failed.

The Chicago Statement consists of four parts: a preface of five paragraphs, the statement proper consisting of five points, an exposition comprised of elaborations on six issues, and nineteen articles of affirmations and denials.

The statement proper in its five points reads:

1. God, who is Himself Truth and speaks truth only, has inspired Holy Scripture in order thereby to reveal Himself to lost mankind through Jesus Christ as Creator and Lord, Redeemer and Judge. Holy Scripture is God's witness to Himself.

2. Holy Scripture, being God's own Word, written by men prepared and superintended by His Spirit, is of infallible divine authority in all matters upon which it touches: it is to be believed, as God's instruction,

---

15 "Summit Agenda,—Page 3" in Billy Graham Archives 192, Wheaton College, Wheaton, IL, box 7, folder 13.

16 "Summit Report," ICBI Update, December 1978, No. 2, 1.

in all that it affirms: obeyed, as God's command, in all that it requires; embraced, as God's pledge, in all that it promises.

3. The Holy Spirit, Scripture's divine Author, both authenticates it to us by His inward witness and opens our minds to understand its meaning.

4. Being wholly and verbally God-given, Scripture is without error or fault in all its teaching, no less in what it states about God's acts in creation, about the events of world history, and about its own literary origins under God, than in its witness to God's saving grace in individual lives.

5. The authority of Scripture is inescapably impaired if this total divine inerrancy is in any way limited or disregarded, or made relative to a view of truth contrary to the Bible's own; and such lapses bring serious loss to both the individual and the Church.

The Articles of Affirmation and Denial, written by R. C. with some editing during the summit, read:

Article I. WE AFFIRM that the Holy Scriptures are to be received as the authoritative Word of God.
WE DENY that the Scriptures receive their authority from the Church, tradition, or any other human source.
Article II. WE AFFIRM that the Scriptures are the supreme written norm by which God binds the conscience, and that the authority of the Church is subordinate to that of Scripture.
WE DENY that Church creeds, councils, or declarations have authority greater than or equal to the authority of the Bible.
Article III. WE AFFIRM that the written Word in its entirety is revelation given by God.
WE DENY that the Bible is merely a witness to revelation, or only becomes revelation in encounter, or depends on the responses of men for its validity.

Article IV. WE AFFIRM that God who made mankind in His image has used language as a means of revelation.

WE DENY that human language is so limited by our creatureliness that it is rendered inadequate as a vehicle for divine revelation. We further deny that the corruption of human culture and language through sin has thwarted God's work of inspiration.

Article V. WE AFFIRM that God's revelation within the Holy Scriptures was progressive.

WE DENY that later revelation, which may fulfill earlier revelation, ever corrects or contradicts it. We further deny that any normative revelation has been given since the completion of the New Testament writings.

Article VI. WE AFFIRM that the whole of Scripture and all its parts, down to the very words of the original, were given by divine inspiration.

WE DENY that the inspiration of Scripture can rightly be affirmed of the whole without the parts, or of some parts but not the whole.

Article VII. WE AFFIRM that inspiration was the work in which God by His Spirit, through human writers, gave us His Word. The origin of Scripture is divine. The mode of divine inspiration remains largely a mystery to us.

WE DENY that inspiration can be reduced to human insight, or to heightened states of consciousness of any kind.

Article VIII. WE AFFIRM that God in His work of inspiration utilized the distinctive personalities and literary styles of the writers whom He had chosen and prepared.

WE DENY that God, in causing these writers to use the very words that He chose, overrode their personalities.

Article IX. WE AFFIRM that inspiration, though not conferring omniscience, guaranteed true and trustworthy utterance on all matters of which the Biblical authors were moved to speak and write.

WE DENY that the finitude or fallenness of these writers, by necessity or otherwise, introduced distortion or falsehood into God's Word.

Article X. WE AFFIRM that inspiration, strictly speaking, applies only to the autographic text of Scripture, which in the providence of God can be ascertained from available manuscripts with great accuracy. We further affirm that copies and translations of Scripture are the Word of God to the extent that they faithfully represent the original.

WE DENY that any essential element of the Christian faith is affected by the absence of the autographs. We further deny that this absence renders the assertion of Biblical inerrancy invalid or irrelevant.

Article XI. WE AFFIRM that Scripture, having been given by divine inspiration, is infallible, so that, far from misleading us, it is true and reliable in all the matters it addresses.

WE DENY that it is possible for the Bible to be at the same time infallible and errant in its assertions. Infallibility and inerrancy may be distinguished, but not separated.

Article XII. WE AFFIRM that Scripture in its entirety is inerrant, being free from all falsehood, fraud, or deceit.

WE DENY that Biblical infallibility and inerrancy are limited to spiritual, religious, or redemptive themes, exclusive of assertions in the fields of history and science. We further deny that scientific hypotheses about earth history may properly be used to overturn the teaching of Scripture on creation and the flood.

Article XIII. WE AFFIRM the propriety of using inerrancy as a theological term with reference to the complete truthfulness of Scripture.

WE DENY that it is proper to evaluate Scripture according to standards of truth and error that are alien to its usage or purpose. We further deny that inerrancy is negated by Biblical phenomena such as a lack of modern technical precision, irregularities of grammar or spelling, observational descriptions of nature, the reporting of falsehoods, the use of hyperbole and round numbers, the topical arrangement of material, variant selections of material in parallel accounts, or the use of free citations.

Article XIV. WE AFFIRM the unity and internal consistency of Scripture.

WE DENY that alleged errors and discrepancies that have not yet been resolved vitiate the truth claims of the Bible.

Article XV. WE AFFIRM that the doctrine of inerrancy is grounded in the teaching of the Bible about inspiration.

WE DENY that Jesus' teaching about Scripture may be dismissed by appeals to accommodation or to any natural limitation of His humanity.

Article XVI. WE AFFIRM that the doctrine of inerrancy has been integral to the Church's faith throughout its history.

WE DENY that inerrancy is a doctrine invented by scholastic Protestantism, or is a reactionary position postulated in response to negative higher criticism.

Article XVII. WE AFFIRM that the Holy Spirit bears witness to the Scriptures, assuring believers of the truthfulness of God's written Word.

WE DENY that this witness of the Holy Spirit operates in isolation from or against Scripture.

Article XVIII. WE AFFIRM that the text of Scripture is to be interpreted by grammatico-historical exegesis, taking account of its literary forms and devices, and that Scripture is to interpret Scripture.

WE DENY the legitimacy of any treatment of the text or quest for sources lying behind it that leads to relativizing, dehistoricizing, or discounting its teaching, or rejecting its claims to authorship.

Article XIX. WE AFFIRM that a confession of the full authority, infallibility, and inerrancy of Scripture is vital to a sound understanding of the whole of the Christian faith. We further affirm that such confession should lead to increasing conformity to the image of Christ.

WE DENY that such confession is necessary for salvation. However, we further deny that inerrancy can be rejected without grave consequences, both to the individual and to the Church.

R. C. said the crucial element is the denial. You may recall that R. C. had acute antenna for "studied ambiguity." Statements can be taken to mean, or to allow for, different things by different readers. The denial portion puts boundaries on the interpretation. The denials preclude a certain latitude of interpretation. The council made it clear that the Chicago Statement should be looked at as an entire document, taken in toto.

The Chicago Statement on Biblical Inerrancy proved to be a line in the sand. Historically, creeds, confessions, and statements do that. The Chicago Statement still does that. In 2016 Roger Olson wrote:

> When I look at the Chicago Statement on Inerrancy and its signatories I believe it is more a political (in the broad sense) statement than a clear, precise, statement of perfect agreement among the signatories. In other words, what was really going on there, in my humble opinion, was driven by a shared concern to establish and patrol "evangelical boundaries."[17]

The Chicago Statement on Biblical Inerrancy made and makes some wince. For others, it serves to fortify. In fact, the Chicago Statement galvanized an entire generation, instilling confidence that an inerrantist position is not an embarrassment but rather buoyed by cogent rational arguments and by historical precedent. One immediate impact was the retaking of the Southern Baptist Convention in the 1980s. Ousting Barthians from the leadership was one thing. They were fairly well entrenched as tenured professors in the seminaries. This was especially true of the Southern Baptist Convention's flagship seminary The Southern Baptist Theological Seminary in Louisville, Kentucky. R. Albert Mohler, who first listened to R. C. on cassette tapes as a teenager, mounted his battle

---

17 Roger Olson, "Is Real Communication as Perfect 'Meeting of Minds' Possible? Some Radical Thoughts on Words Like 'Inerrancy,'" February 17, 2016, https://www.patheos.com/blogs/rogereolson/2016 /02/is-real-communication-as-perfect-meeting-of-minds-possible-some-radical-thoughts-about-words -like-inerrancy/.

for the Bible in Louisville when he took office as president of SBTS in 1993. He carried the flag of the Chicago Statement.

One paragraph from the preface should not be overlooked.

> We offer this Statement in a spirit, not of contention, but of humility and love, which we purpose by God's grace to maintain in any future dialogue arising out of what we have said. We gladly acknowledge that many who deny the inerrancy of Scripture do not display the consequences of this denial in the rest of their belief and behavior, and we are conscious that we who confess this doctrine often deny it in life by failing to bring our thoughts and deeds, our traditions and habits, into true subjection to the divine Word.

Two things stand out. First, though this is a boundary-making statement and polemical in nature, the drafters and signers intend an irenic spirit. It was written for people who confess belief in God and a trust in the Bible. ICBI was convinced that such a belief and trust could lead only to one possible conclusion: inerrancy. It was intended to foster true dialogue—by drawing attention to what the Bible says about itself. Second, the concern for the drafters to connect the dots from biblical authority to obedience is also evident. Ultimately, confessing the full trustworthiness, authority, and inerrancy of the Bible is lived out when one obeys it.

ICBI held another summit in 1982, again at the Hyatt Regency O'Hare, on biblical hermeneutics. R. C., again, wrote the articles of affirmation and denial. He wrote a dozen and sent them along to the drafting committee with this note:

> These working articles have been hastily conceived and produced from a sick bed while antibiotics are rushing through my blood system on a search and destroy mission to liberate my body from its present state of infection. My mind is also muddled at the moment (though some discern a more permanent affliction) but my heart is without fog about the importance of your task. I pray that the Holy Spirit will be pleased

to grant the same or even greater level of assistance in refining these points as He did in Chicago.[18]

ICBI hosted a third and final summit in 1986 on biblical application. ICBI also produced books, including both scholarly collections of essays and popular books. R. C. wrote one of the pamphlets, "Implications of the Abandonment of Inerrancy." The original text, per his style, was written out longhand on lined, yellow legal paper (he later switched to lined, yellow 8.5x11 paper). The council produced pamphlets and booklets, held conferences, and served as a "speakers bureau" of sorts for council members to address inerrancy at churches and for other groups.

R. C. spoke at the Cincinnati seminar on the topic "What Difference Does an Inerrant Bible Make?" Toward the end he made a point with rather dramatic hyperbole:

> But there's one objection to this [insistence on inerrancy] that when I hear it, it starts at the base of my spine and goes right up my neck, right out my ears, and it takes all the self-control I can muster not to slam somebody over the head with a book or a chair and that's when they say to me, "Why should we worry about this doctrine, let's get on with the ministry of the church. I'm not going to get bothered with the doctrine of Scripture." I want to say, "How naïve can you be?"[19]

ICBI also held a large conference, with forty-three speakers, which was dubbed a "Congress on the Bible," in San Diego in 1982. (San Diego in February has sunshine, not snow, like at the study center.)

As they planned, ICBI dissolved having completed its ten-year run in 1987. They marked the occasion by hosting a Congress on the Bible II, this time in Washington DC, the final ICBI event.

Back on April 17, 1979, R. C. reluctantly resigned as president, citing two factors that prompted his difficult decision. One was that executive

18 R. C. Sproul, "Personal Note to Working Committee," n.d.
19 R. C. Sproul, "What Difference Does an Inerrant Bible Make?," Cincinnati Seminar, manuscript, n.d., 15, ICBI Archives, Dallas Theological Seminary.

director at Ligonier, Stu Boehmig, had resigned to take a pastorate, which then led the Ligonier board to task R. C. "to assume full responsibility for the administration of LVSC. Second, the rapid growth of the Labor-Management Ministry [Value of the Person] has placed a heavy time burden on me." He was quick to add, "By no means does my resignation, to be effective immediately, indicate any loss of zeal or earnest concern for the goals and objectives of ICBI."[20]

His zeal can be seen in an article R. C. wrote for *Moody Monthly*, "What Inerrancy Is All About: The Truth of Scripture Demolishes Speculation," in the January 1980 issue. His first sentence declares, "I love my Bible—both Old Testament and New. I must have it—and I must have it without error." The Word "comes to us from a transcendent personal God," so it "dwarfs all human conjecture and renders finite speculation impotent."[21] That's vintage R. C. Every doctrine arcs back to the doctrine of God, to who God is. It's also battlefield theologian language.

Of course, R. C. spoke at various ICBI events and conferences and also continued writing for them into the 1980s. But as he wrote, the work back at Stahlstown swarmed. In 1977, eighteen thousand students, and eight hundred resident students, passed through the grounds of the study center, numbers that steadily increased.[22]

R. C. started the Ligonier Valley Study Center in August of 1971 with a lot of land, one large single-family house, and a deteriorating structure. R. C. spent much of that summer not only preparing lectures but also clearing fields of scrub brush and rocks, and sowing grass seed. Then, during those early years, he mowed it, and in the winter he cleared the sidewalk and some parking areas with a snowblower and a shovel. One picture has R. C. with trowel in hand, helping to put up a cinder block

20 R. C. Sproul to [ICBI] Committee Members, April 17, 1979.
21 R. C. Sproul, "What Inerrancy Is All About: The Truth of Scripture Demolishes Speculation," *Moody Monthly* (January 1980), 13.
22 "Ligonier Celebrates Sixth Year," *Tabletalk*, vol. 4, September 1, 1977, 1.

wall—Vesta suspected that he did not do that particular task often, but there did happen to be a camera present the one day that he did.

During many of these early years, the budget was not met. Occasionally staff had to go without paychecks. LVSC had its full share of the difficulties that any start-up organization has. There was no model for what R. C. was trying to do, no playbook. But there was also no model for R. C. He was as much at home in a union hall as in high-church liturgy. There was likely not a single biblical trivia that escaped him. There was no topic in theology that he could not teach on extemporaneously—without any notes. There was likely no topic in philosophy that he could not teach on either. He was conversant with modern film, with modern novels, and with current politics. From the time of his conversion in September of 1957, a foundation was being laid, the infrastructure carefully put in place. In the 1970s, you could start to see the structure emerge.

As the 1970s drew to a close, R. C. had seven books to his credit and a place on the national platform in the American church. He had a reputation that extended beyond his beloved Pittsburgh, a growing reputation as a trusted teacher and compelling communicator. But more awaited on the horizon.

6

APOLOGETICS

Christianity is rational.

R. C. SPROUL

IN R. C.'S PERSONAL COPY of *Aquinas on Nature and Grace*, he underlines this sentence:

Now when an effect is more apparent to us than its cause, we reach a knowledge of the cause through its effect.

On the next page he not only underlines this sentence, but emphasizes it in the margin with a squiggled line:

The existence of God, and similar things which can be known by natural reason as Rom. Ch. I affirms, are not articles of faith, but preambles to the articles.

These two sentences from Thomas Aquinas (1225–1274) are a matter of debate among Christians, resulting in different apologetics camps. The underlining means that R. C. agrees with it, and the squiggled line in the margin means that R. C. *really* agrees with it. It also means that he is squarely in the classical apologetics camp.

R. C. relied heavily on classical theism for his thought and teaching. In fact, in the fall of 2017, merely months before his passing, R. C. observed, "What I've said since we started Ligonier forty-six years ago is that the biggest crisis that the church faces today is our understanding of the nature of God." R. C. went on to explain that he was talking about the simplicity, the eternality, and the aseity of God. At the mere mention of the aseity of God, R. C. said, "Now that's one of my favorite words. I get chill bumps. God is self-existent. He's eternally self-existent. And He's Pure Being."[1] When asked directly, "What is your legacy? Is classical theism at the center?" he responded, "Absolutely."[2]

R. C. learned classical theism from the living and the dead, from the ancient philosophers, the scholastic and Reformed theologians, and from his teachers. R. C. stood in the line of Plato and Aristotle, Augustine, Aquinas, the Reformers, Turretin, Edwards, and Hodge and Warfield. He was introduced to these titans by Thomas Gregory, John Gerstner, and G. C. Berkouwer. R. C. then sought to teach others through in-person lectures, tapes, and books.

R. C. published three works that have come to be classic texts in three successive years: *Classical Apologetics* in 1984 (with John Gerstner and Art Lindsley), *The Holiness of God* in 1985, and *Chosen by God* in 1986. *Chosen by God* explores the sovereignty of God. *The Holiness of God* explores the thrice-holy God, as well as God's justice, love, wrath, mercy, truth, and beauty, alongside other dimensions to God's character. *Classical Apologetics* deals with a fundamental question regarding God, namely, that He *is*. This book from 1984 deals with the question of His existence: that God is known, what kind of God is known, and how God is known.

For R. C. every thread you pull on traces back to God. That's theology. It's also apologetics.

---

1   "R. C. Sproul and Dolezal's *All That Is in God*," *Open Book* podcast, April 12, 2018, season 1, episode 5. The episode was recorded on October 13, 2017, in R. C.'s home.

2   Stephen Nichols with R. C. Sproul, personal interview, October 20, 2017.

R. C. the Apologist

The first page of the February 1979 issue of *Tabletalk* speaks of the thirty-nine college students, from nine different colleges, as well as a group of adults, who took R. C.'s classical apologetics class in the January term. It then points out, "Apologetics (knowing what you believe and why you believe it) is Dr. Sproul's major area of interest."[3] The study center decided to repeat the same course in January 1980.

Later that year, *Eternity* magazine ran an article entitled, "Where'd You Get Those Ideas? A Round-Up of Fifty Evangelical Thinkers Who Influence You."[4] Caricatures of eighteen of the fifty provided accompanying artwork for the article. R. C. made the cut, wearing a football uniform sans helmet and holding a tulip, representing his reputation as an athlete and a Calvinist. In the article, he was counted among the apologists. The article mentions that "R. C. Sproul, a Pittsburgh-area, free-lance theologian, has influenced a small circle, including Charles Colson."[5] The reference to "a small circle," misses the point of his efforts. The article was concerned with identifying the influencer behind the influencers, the platform figures on the American evangelical scene. Colson was the one the editors identified. But in truth, R. C. was influencing a very large circle, not of platform figures but of the rank-and-file laity. He was teaching business executives, managers, and workers how to defend the faith in the workplace. He was teaching college students how to respond to their biology professors and liberal Bible and religion professors. He was helping neighbors learn how to answer the questions of their neighbors. His circle of influence was in the tens of thousands and climbing. The influence came through the classes he taught and through his books. There was also a "staged" debate with his mentor and colleague John Gerstner.

3 "New Year Starts Big," *Tabletalk*, vol. 3, February 1979.
4 "Where'd You Get Those Ideas? A Round-Up of Fifty Evangelical Thinkers Who Influence You," *Eternity* magazine, November 1980, 29–31.
5 "Where'd You Get Those Ideas?," 31.

R. C. invited Gerstner to join the teaching staff as professor-at-large at the study center in 1980, as Gerstner retired from his post at Pittsburgh Theological Seminary. Gerstner had been a frequent lecturer at the study center prior to this appointment; the study center would see more of him, and he and R. C. could do more together as well. R. C. remembers how he and Gerstner were sometimes called "the Pittsburgh Mafia" in the Reformed world. In 1982 they put on a debate for the John Ankerberg Show, filmed in Chattanooga. R. C. played the part of *advocatus diabolic*. The *Chattanooga Times* ran a lengthy article covering the event, with pictures, including R. C. with "arms flaying." Despite all the drama R. C. could muster, he was no match for Gerstner. R. C., playing the role of the skeptic/atheist, lost. After the "debate," R. C. and Gerstner took questions from the packed house gathered in Brainerd Baptist Church. The article reports that in one of his answers, R. C. "said the 'concept of blind faith was utterly repugnant.'"[6]

The idea of blind faith or of "a leap of faith," smacked of fideism to R. C. Of course, R. C. loved the notion of *sola fide*, of faith alone. *Fideism* is not a reference to justification by faith alone. Fideism is the idea that you cannot offer any reason for faith, that you should avoid any kind of rational argument. R. C. called fideism "irrationalism." He believed Christianity is rational and that Christians have reason for the faith they profess. He believed that you could prove God's existence and the basic reliability of Scripture through reason. He also believed that what was said of the nation of Israel through the prophet Hosea could be said of the modern church: "My people perish for lack of knowledge" (Hos. 4:6). R. C. lamented this in his "Right Now Counts Forever" column in the August 1979 *Tabletalk*, which he entitled "My People Perish . . ." He discussed the need for theologians to speak directly to the laity, enlisting the example of the Reformers in the process, and also the need to discuss the knowledge of God.

6 "Theologians Tape Debate Here," *Chattanooga Times*, May 22, 1982.

R. C. did just that, "get the message to the people," in his books.[7] In 1974 he had written *The Psychology of Atheism*.[8] In 1978 he published *Objections Answered*.[9] This book grew out of a request from his friend Archie Parrish. Through his work at Evangelism Explosion (EE), Parrish had kept careful records of reports back from the field. He had long lists of objections that the door-to-door evangelists of EE were getting. It was soon obvious that the objections could be grouped into about ten categories. Archie turned the list of ten over to R. C. to see if R. C. might be interested in answering these objections. The next year the book was published. The ten chapters are:

> "The Bible Contradicts Itself. It's Just a Fairy Tale."
>
> "All Religions Are Good. It Doesn't Matter What You Believe."
>
> "What about the Poor Native Who Never Heard of Christ?"
>
> "Christianity Is a Crutch for Weak People."
>
> "The Church Is Full of Hypocrites."
>
> "I Don't Need Religion."
>
> "There Is No God!"
>
> "If There Is a God, Why Is There So Much Evil in the World?"
>
> "Why Does God Allow Suffering?"
>
> "When You're Dead You're Dead! There Is No More."

R. C. had heard these questions and objections before. He had asked and made some of them himself. R. C. waxes autobiographical in the book's introduction, offering an account of his "Personal Pilgrimage." He notes, "As a youth I had two consuming passions. One was sports and the other the 'why' questions."[10] He mentions how he was a "wartime

7   R. C. Sproul, "My People Perish . . ." *Tabletalk*, vol. 3, August 1979.

8   Originally published by Bethany, this book was republished as *If There's a God, Why Are There Atheists?: Why Atheists Believe in Unbelief* (Wheaton, IL: Tyndale, 1988).

9   Originally published by Gospel Light-Regal, this book was republished as *Reason to Believe: A Response to Common Objections to Christianity* (Grand Rapids, MI: Zondervan, 1982). References that follow are from this edition.

10 Sproul, *Reason to Believe*, 11–12.

child." So his first big "why question" was "Why are there wars?" A big question for a four- to five-year-old to be asking. Then came his dad's suffering and death and the difficult years of high school. He became an angry and bitter young man. He did not see Christianity as the answer. To a teenage R. C., Christianity was weak: "Christian was a synonym for 'sissy.'" Then came his conversion in his freshman year of college. His objections "dissolved into repentance."[11] Next, he recalls how he was thrown into liberalism in college and seminary. Is all that he believed objectively true?

All that personal experience stacks up to R. C.'s having existential sympathy for the questions and objections of the unbeliever and the believer alike. Coming to faith and theology the hard way gave him both a tough-mindedness and a gracious demeanor.

In 1983 R. C. published *In Search of Dignity*.[12] Here R. C. discusses human dignity. Calvinists like to discuss human depravity. But thumbing through Calvin's *Institutes*, one realizes that before Calvin himself discusses human depravity, even he first makes the case for human dignity based on the first chapter of Genesis and the image of God in man. R. C. follows suit. He declares, "Man's dignity rests in God who assigns an inestimable worth to every person."[13] R. C. sees this as an essential plank in the Christian worldview. Every person he met with deserved his respect because they were endowed with dignity, because they were in the image of the Creator.

That same year, 1983, he published two other short books with Tyndale House: *Ethics and the Christian* and *Who Is Jesus?* R. C. was continuing to provide answers. Then came 1984, a year that had R. C. publishing two short books and two big books. The short books were on prayer and on God's will, both for Tyndale. The first big book was his novel, *Johnny*

---

11 Sproul, *Reason to Believe*, 15.

12 Originally published by Gospel Light-Regal, this book was reprinted as *The Hunger for Significance* (Phillipsburg, NJ: P&R, 2001), and in a revised edition by P&R in 2020.

13 Sproul, *Hunger for Significance*, 109.

Come Home. The second big book, which came out near the end of the year, was *Classical Apologetics.* And while these four books were moving through the pipeline of writing and editing and on to publication, R. C. and Ligonier moved.

A Novel, a Move, and a Textbook

R. C. had written the biography of Wayne Alderson, which also told the turnaround story of Pittman Steel, published by Harper & Row. During a conversation with his "very competent" editor at Harper, R. C. mentioned how much he enjoyed writing narrative. The editor suggested that R. C. consider writing a novel, further advising him, "You want to write from your own experience."[14] R. C. wanted to write a novel on the doctrine of election. Of course he would.

Johnny is the central character.[15] R. C. has him marrying Leah La-banson, then marrying his second wife, Rochelle. R. C. then exclaimed, "And you'd think somebody would get the point: Leah and Rachel and Laban—and nobody got the point."[16] As if to warn the reader, R. C. has a note on the very first page declaring, "This is a work of fiction . . . a fiction that is more than a gossamer veil of real history." Gossamer, indeed. The next page is a dedication to Johnny, the real-life Johnny Coles, R. C.'s childhood friend and freshman college roommate. The next page cites Genesis 27:11 with a reference to Jacob and Esau. What does the prophet Malachi say? Jacob have I loved, Esau have I hated. The former, scheming, plotting, wrestling—yet chosen. Then there's Esau. From the one brother comes Israel, from the other brother comes Edom. How did readers miss the point?

Johnny is the central character, but the book's main character is "Scooter." R. C. did confess that the main character, "Scooter," who goes

---

14 Stephen Nichols with R. C. Sproul, personal interview, September 8, 2017.

15 R. C. Sproul, *Johnny Come Home* (Ventura, CA: Regal, 1984); republished as *Thy Brother's Keeper* (Brentwood, TN: Wolgemuth & Hyatt, 1988).

16 Nichols with Sproul, personal interview, September 8, 2017.

on to become the Reverend Doctor Richard Evans, a preacher of national acclaim, is a "composite of John Guest, Jim Boice, [chuckle and then big smile] and me."[17] Early Scooter seems to be all R. C. We start off with him finishing high school. It's all about sports, his car, and his friend Johnny. They go off to college, Witherspoon, "a Presbyterian church–related college in Northwestern Pennsylvania."[18] Westminster College can be seen through the gossamer veil. Scooter and Johnny are each converted, having been stopped by a star of the football team as they were trying to sneak off to a bar. They each write letters to their girlfriends. But soon, Johnny drifts away, barely even remembering the moment. Not Scooter. Scooter goes on to have a second conversion in the college chapel after a midnight trek. He changes his major to philosophy—all very familiar sounding. But he, that is the Reverend Doctor Richard Evans, ends up in Phoenix and on a weekly television program.

There is a love interest, "Pamela," and even another, "Patricia." Neither is Vesta. Vesta is not in the novel. It ends with Richard Evans returning home to give a grand sermon in the grandest church in his hometown. The church is packed. Christians are there to hear a sermon, many non-Christians are there to see the hometown boy who made it big. He preached on the holiness of God, Isaiah 6. Johnny is there.

R. C. loved writing the novel: "Oh, it was great fun," he recalled. He had so much fun that he started on a second novel. He was going to call it "Sin Stones." The novel begins with a WWII pilot in a P51 Mustang on a mission over Germany. R. C. had an older cousin who flew the P51 Mustang, and R. C. learned from him what great planes they were, with the one vulnerability being the radiator. So the opening scene has the pilot's P51 Mustang shot in the radiator and the pilot parachuting out. He lands safely on the ground, but then is pursued by German soldiers. A priest comes to his rescue, but in the process he is fatally shot, his last act being to hand over a precious document to the pilot—a document

17 Nichols with Sproul, personal interview, September 8, 2017.
18 Sproul, *Thy Brother's Keeper*, 42.

revealing the hidden location of the two tablets handed down to Moses, the Sin Stones. R. C. wrote out the first few pages. And that was it. Other work and duties and book contracts set in. He threw out the first few pages he had written, and he moved on. The one novel that he did write earned an Angel Award. Elisabeth Elliot called it "a page turner." It really is. It could be turned into a movie.

R. C. wrote the novel while teaching seminary classes at Jackson, Mississippi. While still maintaining his Ligonier responsibilities, R. C. and Vesta relocated to Jackson for three to four months at the beginning of the year. He taught a full year's worth of a full-time professor's course load in those three to four months. In addition, in those three to four months, he wrote a book or two and started to sketch out a few more. He also golfed, and they kept up with their ballroom dancing.

In addition, there was a move in 1984. From the beginning, the study center at Stahlstown had challenges. Additional buildings were required to accommodate overnight guests, meals for groups, groups meeting on campus, staff housing, a recording studio, and office space. It soon became quite a drain on the operations budget to have so many buildings and such a large property to maintain. Additionally, while the seclusion of the study center made for great experiences for the students who did get there, the isolated location proved difficult.

Additionally, R. C.'s tape ministry—both cassette and video—was really taking off. He could impact far more by focusing his energy on producing teaching series, which could then be watched again and again, than by teaching small classes at the study center. They started scouting strategic locations to which they could move the ministry. The board met three times, apart from R. C. and without his knowledge of the meetings. They narrowed their list to three cities: Dallas, Atlanta, and Orlando. R. C. and Vesta would have liked to see Philadelphia or Memphis on the list. R. C. loved Philadelphia. As for Memphis, they thought it was a strategic and central location to the entire US (a point on which FedEx agreed). What's more, they would so have enjoyed having John Sartelle as their pastor and Independent Presbyterian Church as their church. But neither Memphis nor Philadelphia made the cut.

When presented with the three choices of Atlanta, Dallas, or Orlando, R. C. responded, "Any one of those three is fine with me, as long as it's not Dallas or Atlanta." The September 1984 issue of *Tabletalk* was the last issue mailed from Stahlstown. The November issue was sent out from Altamonte Springs, ten miles directly north of Orlando in central Florida. Ligonier Ministries moved into office space on North Lake Boulevard and used a nearby television station for taping.

Everyone thought Ligonier moved to Florida so R. C. could golf. The truth was that he golfed plenty in the winter already, especially since he resided January through March in Jackson, Mississippi. The move to Florida was, instead, because the board, after doing an intensive feasibility study, found central Florida to be family friendly, easy to get to, and a premier travel destination not only for the US but for the world. Disney opened its theme park in 1971, the same year the Ligonier Valley Study Center began. Tourists, visitors, and convention goers streamed in. After Ligonier Ministries moved to Orlando, several other national ministries also moved, including Campus Crusade and Wycliffe. Orlando proved to be a wise choice. R. C. said, "We fell in love with Florida the first fifteen minutes we were here."[19] He only regretted they did not relocate sooner.

R. C. and Vesta moved into a home in Sabal Point in nearby Wekiwa Springs for two years. Then they settled into a home in Longwood. Up to moving into their home in Longwood, they had been married for twenty-nine years and lived in thirteen different dwellings over that time. They would live in their fourteenth home for the next twenty-eight years. It was a large home, and it needed to be. Sherrie and her husband and three kids lived with them, as also did Vesta's mom for a time. It put R. C. near Ligonier and near some exceptional golf courses.

19 Nichols with Sproul, personal interview, September 8, 2017.

Also in 1984, R. C., along with fellow study center teachers John Gerstner and Art Lindsley, published a textbook on apologetics. It was published by Zondervan's Academic imprint, and it had a rather academic subtitle: *Classical Apologetics: A Rational Defense of the Christian Faith and a Critique of Presuppositional Apologetics.*

Three Views

There are three major views of apologetics: evidentialism, presuppositionalism, and classical apologetics. Evidentialism, as its name indicates, uses evidences, both rational and empirical evidence, to prove the existence of God and the truth claims of Christianity. Josh McDowell popularized evidentialism through his books *Evidence That Demands a Verdict* (1972); *More Evidence That Demands a Verdict* (1981); and *More Than a Carpenter* (1977). R. C. has noted that evidentialism tends to be held by those evangelicals who tilt more toward Arminianism. Those who are more Reformed tend toward the classical approach or the presuppositional approach. In fact, and R. C. lamented this, presuppositionalism has "swept the allegiance of Reformed people throughout America."[20] R. C. adds that it "is the prevailing view in most Reformed circles today, and it is a circle around which I have not been willing to dance."[21]

Presuppositionalism also, as its names indicates, centers around the notion of presupposition. This view is associated with its founder, Cornelius Van Til, with whom on his porch R. C. used to have conversations and eat cookies. Van Til said, "We argue by 'presupposition,'" adding "The only 'proof' of the Christian position is that unless its truth is presupposed there is no possibility of 'proving' anything at all."[22] Van Til further contended that any other view necessarily admits human autonomy and compromises God Himself.[23]

20 R. C. Sproul, *1–2 Peter: St. Andrew's Expositional Commentary* (Wheaton, IL: Crossway, 2011), 119.
21 Sproul, *1–2 Peter*, 120.
22 Cornelius Van Til, "My Credo," in *Jerusalem and Athens: Critical Discussions on the Theology and Apologetics of Cornelius Van Til* (Phillipsburg, NJ: Presbyterian & Reformed, 1980), 21.
23 Van Til, "My Credo," 9, 11, 18.

That leaves the classical view. While R. C. laments that it is the minority report on the contemporary scene, it has been the majority view through church history. As a classical apologist, R. C. declares, "I believe that the case for the existence of God is not just highly probable but it is absolutely logically compelling."[24] R. C. will say plainly in the first sentence of the preface to *Classical Apologetics*, "Christianity is rational."[25] He would be sure that we noticed a difference between being rational and rationalism. He rejects the presuppositionalist claim that to assert a proof or argue a proof for Christianity bows to human autonomy unless that proof is presupposed. The presuppositionalist's claim confuses being rational or making a rational argument as rationalism. They are quite different. R. C. then defines apologetics as "the reasoned defense of the Christian religion."[26] That's what classical apologists do—they offer reasons and arguments.

The book *Classical Apologetics* had a twofold purpose. One was to offer a full discussion of the classical view, to lay out the case for God and for Christianity. The other purpose was to critique presuppositionalism. The book was written by R. C. and Arthur Lindsley, and John Gerstner. R. C. wrote the first part, "Classical Natural Theology: An Overview of Problem and Method." Arthur Lindsley wrote most of the second part, "Classical Apologetics: The Theistic Proofs, the Deity of Christ, and the Infallibility of Scripture." Gerstner wrote part 3, "The Classical Critique of Presuppositional Apologetics."

The book is dedicated to Cornelius Van Til, with this inscription: ". . . who has taught a generation that Christ is the Alpha and Omega of thought and life." When Van Til received his copy, he sent R. C. a letter thanking him and expressing what an honor it was to have the book dedicated to him. R. C. did respect Van Til. He enjoyed those times they were together back in 1968 and 1969. It provided opportunities for R. C.

24 R. C. Sproul, *1–2 Peter*, 119.
25 John Gerstner, Arthur Lindsley, and R. C. Sproul, *Classical Apologetics* (Grand Rapids, MI: Zondervan, 1984), ix.
26 Sproul et al., *Classical Apologetics*, 13.

to keep up with his Dutch. It does reflect on both R. C. and Van Til that they could be diametrically opposed and yet remain friendly, respectful, and constructive. They were gentlemen scholars.

R. C. recalled how *Classical Apologetics* came about. He had hoped to write a book called "Rational Christianity." R. C. started in on it but interrupted the writing to take on the book *Stronger Than Steel: The Wayne Alverson Story*. R. C. then discussed with Gerstner the idea of the rational Christianity book. It eventually morphed into the longer, joint-authored *Classical Apologetics*. Since all three taught different apologetics courses at the study center, it made sense for the three to cowrite it.

R. C. remembers that when the first edition came out, the editors at Zondervan used a computerized spell-checker that changed all occurrences of "noetic effects" of sin to "poetic effects." R. C. has a far more painful memory regarding Gerstner's footnotes. Gerstner lost all of his footnotes to all of the citations of Van Til for that third part of the book. R. C., who was the lead in putting the book together and getting it to the publisher, had to go back and find them. The third part has 228 footnotes in total. Well over half are citations of Van Til. R. C. had to go back through every one of Van Til's books and find the citation and rewrite the footnotes. All of them. At the time, many of Van Til's books had no index, so R. C. didn't even have that much to help him. R. C. said, "I can't tell you how many hours and hours and hours I had to research everything that Van Til ever wrote."

Classical apologetics, according to R. C., contends that the fundamental question is, Why is there something rather than nothing? And the moment you start pulling on the thread to account for the "something" for existence, you will be led to the only rational conclusion: there was a beginning and a Beginner. Any other view is irrational. The classical apologetics view looks to the classical arguments to defend and prove the existence of God.

These arguments are the cosmological, the teleological, and the ontological. These arguments may be seen in the ancient philosophers, Plato and Aristotle, and are also developed by the medieval thinkers Anselm (the ontological argument specifically) and Thomas Aquinas. They sometimes constitute what is called "natural theology," which "asserts that people can and do gain valid knowledge of God by means of natural reason reflecting upon natural revelation."[27]

This takes us back to the underlined passages from Thomas Aquinas. Those passages come from Aquinas's magnum opus, the *Summa Theologica*. Aquinas said, "When an effect is more apparent to us than its cause, we reach a knowledge of the cause through its effect."[28] To illustrate that, when a meal is brought to your table at a restaurant, the meal is the effect, and it is apparent to you. What is not apparent is the cause of the meal. But you have the effect, so you know there's a cause. You begin to reason from the cause to the effect that lies behind it. You eventually realize there are chefs in the kitchen, and there is food in the kitchen, brought to the kitchen by a web of a food distribution system, and that eventually traces back to a farmer or a cattle rancher, or a fisherman. Aquinas is clear: "A cause must exist if its effect exists."[29] Then Aquinas says, "We can demonstrate God's existence in this way, from his effects which are known to us, even though we do not know his essence."[30] Aquinas will proceed to offer "Five Ways" that God's existence can be demonstrated. These five ways lay out the cosmological and teleological argument for God's existence. R. C. loved every one of them, but the third way, the argument from necessity, was to him the key.

R. C. explains this argument from Aquinas in his later book *The Consequences of Ideas*: "If there was a time when nothing existed, then nothing could ever start to exist and nothing would exist now. But if something *does* exist now, there must have always been something in

27 Sproul et al., *Classical Apologetics*, 27.
28 Aquinas, *Nature and Grace*, ed. and trans. A. M. Fairweather (Philadelphia: Westminster Press, 1954), 52.
29 Aquinas, *Nature and Grace*, 53.
30 Aquinas, *Nature and Grace*, 53.

existence; something must exist that possesses *necessary* existence—its existence is not merely possible but necessary."[31] This being must *be*, and must be independent of any other being, and must be eternal. Aristotle called the being "Pure Act." Edwards called this being "the Being with the Most Being." Aquinas will come to call this being the *ens perfectissimus*, the most perfect being. The necessary being is God, and God must exist. Why? Because there is something and not nothing. R. C. points out that while the five ways, taken together, form the cosmological and teleological argument, the third way, the argument form necessary being, actually reflects the ontological argument.

A Fourfold Foundation

Key to understanding R. C.'s apologetics is what he calls the four basic epistemological principles. These are all in part 1 of *Classical Apologetics*. In that book, he speaks of three nonnegotiables but spends a great deal of time discussing a fourth.[32] In his later book *Defending Your Faith* (2003), he makes explicit that fourth nonnegotiable.[33] The four principles are:

1. The law of noncontradiction
2. The law of causality
3. The basic (although not perfect) reliability of sense perception
4. The analogical use of language

It is crucial to note that these are not the four foundational principles for apologetics. R. C. sees these as foundational to epistemology, to all knowledge and all knowledge claims. It is these principles that allow for the adjudication of conflicting truth claims. It is these principles that allow for the distinction between what is mere opinion and what counts as truth. But when applied to apologetics, it is these four principles that

31 R. C. Sproul, *The Consequences of Ideas: Understanding the Concepts That Shape Our World* (Wheaton, IL: Crossway, 2000), 73.
32 Sproul, *Classical Apologetics*, 72–90.
33 R. C. Sproul, *Defending Your Faith: An Introduction to Apologetics* (Wheaton, IL: Crossway, 2003), 30–33.

allow R. C. to make the claim that Christianity is rational. These four principles can keep at bay the recourse to "a leap of faith."

The law of noncontradiction is a way of simply saying "logic." It states that "A cannot be non-A at the same time and in the same relationship."[34] This is "crucial for theology as it is for all intellectual disciplines," and "is the necessary precondition for any and all science."[35] R. C. then explains that the law of noncontradiction and logic "monitor the formal relationships of propositions."[36] When a disagreement arises, when a hypothesis gets tested, when a proposition is claimed to be true and factual and not mere opinion, logic steps in and monitors the discussion. Logic allows us to have meaningful discourse. Logic keeps us from devolving into absurdity.

In one of his notebooks, R. C. sketches out longhand a short note called "The Tension of Disagreement: Disagreement and the Law of Noncontradiction." He sets up a scenario of disagreement over the answer to the question of God's existence. Without the law of noncontradiction, the fallback to evaluate propositions and conflicting truth claims is personal meaningfulness. He explains, "Thus the question of the existence of God is reduced to the question of practical meaningfulness in the life of individuals. If truth is defined by that which is meaningful to the believing subject, then, of course, anything that is meaningful to the believing subject may be regarded as true." He then observes that the debate, at this point, descends into "emotional hostility." The answer to the most profound question of all time—Does God exist?—is reduced to "You say to-*may*-toe, I say to-*maa*-toe."

The formal rules of verification and falsification only serve in the Christian's interest. Without the law of noncontradiction, any debate over any truth claim will devolve to a power play or a shouting match.

The law of causality is at the root of the cosmological argument for the existence of God. The law of causality states that every effect has an

---

34 Sproul et al., *Classical Apologetics*, 72.
35 Sproul et al., *Classical Apologetics*, 72.
36 Sproul et al., *Classical Apologetics*, 73.

equal or greater cause. The world, the cosmos, is the effect. It begs the question of origins: where did the world come from? Or, again, why is there something rather than nothing? As the law of noncontradiction takes us back to Aristotle, so does the law of causality. Aristotle first started with motion, then moved on to causality. Motion is apparent. In order for there to be motion, there needed to be first motion, what Aristotle called an "Unmoved Mover." So every cause has an effect, which you trace back to the "Uncaused Cause," or "First Cause." Aquinas simply uses those two arguments as the first two of the five ways. God can be proven by the argument from motion (first way), from cause (second way), and from the necessary being (third way).

Next follows the third nonnegotiable, the basic reliability of sense perception. We acquire knowledge through sense perception. R. C. is careful not to say *infallible* reliability of sense perception.[37] But we are "physical, sensory-equipped creatures," and through our senses knowledge of the external world is possible.[38]

Last is analogical language. This view stands in between the polar opposites of univocal language and equivocal language. And here we are ultimately talking about our language of God. Univocal means identical (one voice), and equivocal means different. These are understood best by considering how they apply to ontology, the nature of being. The univocal view sees a oneness between God and everything else. This is pantheism. The equivocal view sees God as wholly or totally other, *totaliter aliter* in Latin. God is incomprehensible. R. C. explains, "Many theologians and philosophers have argued that God is so entirely different from us that any attempt to speak about him is futile."[39] Neither of these views is desirable. In between these two opposite views is a middle way.

Aquinas pointed to the image of God to help us understand what he called the *analogia entis*, the analogy of being. There is a point of

37 Sproul et al., *Classical Apologetics*, 87.
38 Sproul et al., *Classical Apologetics*, 87.
39 Sproul, *Defending Your Faith*, 32.

connection between God and man, the image of God. And because there is an analogy of being, we can have meaningful talk of and about God. Analogy of being leads to analogical language. R. C. informs us, "It is by virtue of God's creating us in his image and likeness that there is an analogy between the Creator and the creature, thus enabling us to speak of God in a meaningful way even within the limits of our finitude."[40] R. C. then adds, "Without this bond, we could have no understanding of the created world and its testimony to the greatness of the Creator's hand. What is more, we could have no understanding of God's special revelation through the Word—both written and made flesh in Jesus Christ his Son."[41]

R. C. builds his classical apologetics on these four nonnegotiables, with a little help from his friends Aristotle and Aquinas.

Not only did R. C. believe that you can make a rational argument for the existence of God, but in the full scope of his apologetics, he also believed that you can make a rational argument for the infallibility of Scripture. If so, then you are making a rational case for Scripture's truth claims regarding Christ and the gospel. R. C. sketched an argument of five premises and a conclusion for such an argument in his book *Objections Answered* (1978):

Premise A—The Bible is a basically reliable and trustworthy document.

Premise B—On the basis of this reliable document we have sufficient evidence to believe confidently that Jesus Christ is the Son of God.

Premise C—Jesus Christ being the Son of God is an infallible authority.

Premise D—Jesus Christ teaches that the Bible is more than generally trustworthy; it is the very Word of God.

Premise E—The Word, in that it comes from God, is utterly trustworthy because God is utterly trustworthy.

Conclusion—On the basis of the infallible authority of Jesus Christ, the church believes the Bible to be utterly trustworthy, i.e., infallible.[42]

40 Sproul, *Defending Your Faith*, 33.
41 Sproul, *Defending Your Faith*, 69.
42 R. C. Sproul, *Objections Answered* (Ventura, CA: Gospel Light-Regal, 1978), 31.

Contra Secularisma

While the book *Classical Apologetics* was concerned with showing the merits of classical apologetics over presuppositionalism, the book, and R. C., were mainly concerned with equipping the saints to contend for the faith in light of Christianity's biggest and fiercest opponent of the day, secularism. From his very first column in *Tabletalk*, R. C. took on secularism. He plunged into the topic back in the 1960s, when he prepared extensive notes on *The Secular City*, a book by Harvey Cox that had made quite a splash. He prepared the notes, thirty-two handwritten pages in all, for his ethics *tentamen* at the Free University. The *tentamens* were his examinations in several areas. R. C. was given reading lists for each of the areas. Published in 1965, Cox's book sold over a million copies in its first few years on the market. The book offered an in-depth sociological-philosophical-theological analysis of the impact of secularism on culture. R. C. summed up the conclusion of the matter in the first chapter of *Classical Apologetics*: "Secularism is a *post*-Christian phenomenon carrying in its baggage a *conscious* rejection of the Christian worldview."[43] In his 1986 book *Lifeviews*, R. C. writes, "The dominant *ism* of American culture, the *ism* reflected in the news media, the film industry, the novel, and the art world is *secularism*."[44] It is important to note that there is a vast difference between the words *secular* and *secularism*. The Christian is called to be secular, to be in the world. And, lest we forget, it's God's world. Secularism is the poisonous worldview.

In one of his personal notebooks with lecture notes for study center lectures, he outlines a lecture on the topic "Does God Exist?" He notes this is an "age of skepticism" and a "Post-Christian Era," where "churches are mausoleums." He acknowledges, "People still affirm 'something greater,'" but he notes, "<u>practical atheism</u> is [the] order of

43 Sproul et al., *Classical Apologetics*, 4.
44 R. C. Sproul, *Making a Difference: Impacting Culture and Society as a Christian* (1986; repr. Grand Rapids, MI: Baker, 2019), 26. Originally published as *Lifeviews*.

the day."[45] He explains, "People live as if there were no God." R. C. would want us to notice the "were" and not "was." *Were* is used for a condition contrary to fact. Because there is a God. The very next outline point is "Hard Evidence." R. C. believed in apologetics, because R. C. believed there is a God, and people believe and live as if there *were* not.

In that same notebook R. C. observes that "the only way to disprove Christianity is to disprove God," adding "but such attempts boomerang." He gives the argument for evil as an example. To call something "evil," or to speak of justice and injustice, is to appeal to some transcendent standard, to some absolute standard. That immediately begs the question of the origin of an absolute standard, the origin of our sensibility of evil and justice and injustice—in an ultimate sense.

Abandoning God, secularism is not able to deal with either origins or with destiny; both the past and the future are eclipsed, disdained. What matters is the present, the here and now. Right now, says secularism, counts for right now. Consequently, "There is no eternity, there is no eternal perspective. There are no absolutes."[46] R. C. says, "This is precisely where Christianity and secularism collide."[47] He countered with "Right now counts forever." He added:

> If there is one message that I can give to my generation it is this: Right now counts forever. What you and I do now has eternal significance. The now is important because it counts for a long, long time. The secular is important because it is linked forever to the sacred.

Luther gets credited for saying, "If you're not defending the gospel at precisely the point it is being attacked, then you're not defending the gospel at all." What R. C. was doing in *Classical Apologetics*, and in other books and in his teaching and preaching, is defending the gospel at the point at

---

45 Here and throughout, the underlines are R. C.'s.
46 Sproul, *Making a Difference*, 29.
47 Sproul, *Making a Difference*, 29.

which it was being attacked. In his first column in *Tabletalk*, R. C. observed that if there is only the now, then "even the now is meaningless."[48] Raising his prophetic, and apologetic, voice against secularism was the one message he gave to his generation. Like John the Baptist, with outstretched arm he pointed to God, he pointed to eternity, and he pointed to the Lamb of God who had come.

In the 1200s Thomas Aquinas saw the threat to the church of his day as Islam. He wrote yet another magnum opus entitled *Summa Contra Gentiles*, encompassing four books written between 1259 and 1265. Aquinas wrote it for those on the front lines, the missionaries who would be encountering Islam, and also Judaism. He identified the dissenting points—where the gospel was being attacked. Then he offered reasons for the faith, a defense of the faith in light of the opposition and attack. On page 1 of chapter 1 of *Classical Apologetics*, R. C. heralded that the Christian task in the modern epoch was "to produce a *Summa Contra Secularisma*."[49]

What You Believe, Why You Believe It

Apologetics is not only for Christians to use in engaging non-Christians in an increasingly pluralistic and secularistic world. Apologetics is for Christians too. In R. C.'s discussion of the task of apologetics in *Classical Apologetics*, he observes, "The pervasive contemporary skepticism is not without its deleterious effect on Christian faith. Apologetics can be used by God as a liberating force in the life of the Christian plagued by the darts of doubt."[50]

He mentions that Christian laity sometimes sees apologetics as "an unnecessary and undesirable complication of the simple Christian life."[51] R. C. goes on to mention recalling hearing a radio debate of

---

48 R. C. Sproul, "Right Now Counts Forever: Roots in the Pepsi Generation," *Tabletalk*, vol. 1, May 6, 1977, 1.

49 Sproul et al., *Classical Apologetics*, 3.

50 Sproul et al., *Classical Apologetics*, 22.

51 Sproul et al., *Classical Apologetics*, 22.

scholars over the existence of God. When the phone lines opened, one woman called in exclaiming, "Ain't you guys got your eyes open? Look out the window. Where do yins think this all came from?"[52]

The "ain't" and "yins" is classic western Pennsylvania dialect. R. C. points out that her argument is classic, as in the cosmological argument. There is a rational answer to the question, Where did everything outside your window come from? Every other answer, or avoiding the question altogether, is irrational.

An advertisement for his January-term course on classical apologetics at the study center raises the question, "What Will It Do for Me?" The answer is:

> This course is for you. If you are looking for a solid foundation for your faith, if you are looking for ways to defend your faith in the classroom, or if you are looking for ways to defend your faith with your friends then this course can unlock for you the tools of apologetics to help you defend your faith and give you reason to know why you believe what you believe.[53]

In a notebook, on the cover of which R. C. wrote "History of Apologetics," he has a three-page outline for a lecture called "Reason and Faith." He notes that "apologetics rises out of historical crises." This can be seen in the first century, even while the New Testament was being written and the church was under the specter of Rome. The crisis was "Caesar *Kurios*," Caesar as Lord versus Jesus as Lord. R. C. mentions the early apologists Justin Martyr and Polycarp.

Then R. C. lists a long line of "apologists" who confronted culture: "Paul, Augustine, Aquinas, Luther." That brings R. C. up to the current age. He calls our time the "Age of Impressionism." It is a culture that is consumed with being "Entertained," in which there is "crisis of Content."

---

52 Sproul et al., *Classical Apologetics*, 23.
53 January Term Advertisement, *Tabletalk*, vol. 3, September 1979, 4.

Then he turns to the response. He declares, "Christians <u>think</u>!" He then says not rationalism, but also not irrationalism, adding that we are "not called to crucify intellect," and we do not have to settle for "barren speculation." Instead, R. C. advocates for a position that sees that "<u>Truth provokes passion</u>." He cites the example of Søren Kierkegaard. R. C. could not agree with Kierkegaard on faith and could not follow down the path Kierkegaard took, but he always admired Kierkagaard's passion for truth. More, he admired Paul, so he jotted a note: "Paul— I am <u>persuaded</u>—See II Cor. 11." Then he offers his concluding point: "We're Playing for Keeps." R. C. was an apologist committed to knowing what he believed and why he believed it. He had been asking, according to his own personal account, the *why* questions all his life. He labored to help others know what they believe and why they believe it, because, as he would often say, it's not a matter of life and death; it's a matter of eternal life and eternal death.

The Arc of His Teaching

For each year from 1975 through 1979, R. C. spoke at the Philadelphia Conference on Reformed Theology (PCRT). In 1975 the conference theme was "Knowing God." R. C. spoke twice, titling his sessions "Why Don't We Know?" and "Why Must We Know?" In 1976 the theme was "Our Sovereign God." R. C. spoke three times, along with Jim Boice, John Stott, and C. Everett Koop. R. C. spoke again in 1977 on topics orbiting the doctrine of man, the topic for that year. In 1978 the conference discussed "The Cross, Our Glory." R. C. spoke twice; one lecture was titled "Sacrifice and Satisfaction." The 1979 PCRT concerned "The Names of Christ." Again, R. C. spoke twice. It is curious that this conference progression mirrors R. C.'s major theological contributions over the decades of his ministry and also reflects his classic texts and much of his books.

The topics here are the doctrines of God, man, salvation, and Christ. R. C. aimed all of his efforts at a single vocation orbiting a single topic: teaching people who God is. Thinking about who God is immediately raises the question, Who am I? R. C. would give a straightforward answer to both: God is holy. We are not. Once that's realized, the next question is, Who is my substitute? Who is the sacrifice on my behalf? Who will make satisfaction?

All of these are crucial questions, and all of them fall under the category of apologetics. The Greek word *apologia* means "to give an answer." R. C. and Vesta always envisioned the study center as a place where people could get answers, and where Christians could be equipped to answer the questions they are asked. Apologetics was a crucial feature of the study center from its inception and of R. C.'s teaching and preaching prior to his tenure at Stahlstown. It was a particular brand of apologetics at that.

R. C.'s name is synonymous with classical apologetics. For years, decades, he felt that he was the lone voice in the wilderness as he taught and wrote on the subject. Others seem to be catching on in recent days, and history may very well come to show that R. C. was on the right side of the question.[54]

It is also worth noting that his PCRT talks not only arc back to apologetics; they also arc back to the doctrine of God. R. C. would often say there is no difference whatsoever between the confessional understanding of Roman Catholics, Lutheran, or Reformed when it comes to the doctrine of God. Then he would say that there is every difference in the world between these views on the doctrine of God. He disdained double talk. So how could he say both statements? He would go on to explain that these different views all say the same thing about God on page 1 of a systematic theology but they don't carry the full doctrine of God over to

---

54 This may be seen in the following: the lengthy essay by Keith Mathison "Christianity and Van Tillianism, *Tabletalk*, August 21, 2019, http://tabletalkmagazine.com; James Dolezal, *God without Parts: Divine Simplicity and the Metaphysics of God's Absoluteness* (Eugene, OR: Pickwick, 2011); Dolezal, *All That Is in God: Evangelical Theology and the Challenge of Classical Christian Theism* (Grand Rapids, MI: Reformation Heritage, 2017); J. V. Fesko, *Reforming Apologetics: Retrieving the Classic Reformed Approach to Defending the Faith* (Grand Rapids, MI: Baker, 2019). These books have spawned a host of reviews and blog posts.

page 2, when you talk about the doctrine of man, or to later discussions of the doctrine of Christ and of salvation. The Reformed classical tradition carries the doctrine of God all the way through the rest of systematic theology, and all the rest of the topics of systematic theology bend back to the doctrine of God.

Not only did R. C. feel like a lone voice in the wilderness calling out classical apologetics; he also felt like a lone voice proclaiming the holiness of God. That was the next book to come.

7

HOLINESS

Shadows in a cave are given to change. They dance and flicker with ever-changing shape and brightness. To contemplate the truly holy and to go beyond the surface of creaturely things, we need to get out of our self-made cave and walk in the glorious light of God's holiness.

R. C. SPROUL

THE WEEKENDER SECTION OF *The Tribune-Democrat* for Saturday, September 20, 1980, has a large picture of R. C. on the front cover. Taken at the study center, R. C.'s wearing a coat and tie and leaning back on a fence post under the headline: "Dr. R. C. Sproul: Teaching People Who God Is." Four years later, the June–July issue of the sardonic *The Wittenburg Door* ran an interview. The first question and answer were these:

Door: What does the Church need today?
Sproul: I am passionately convinced that the biggest need of the church is to develop a deeper understanding of the character of God. People need to know, cognitively and intellectually, who God is.[1]

An advertisement in a 1979 issue of *Tabletalk* for R. C.'s six-part teaching series on the holiness of God contains, in large Gothic script, "Holy. Holy. Holy." followed by this:

---

1 R. C. Sproul, "Interview," *The Wittenburg Door*, vol. 79, June–July 1984, n.p.

It's a shame. What God repeated most we understand least.[2]

The advertisement proceeds: "In the entire Bible there is only one word that God repeated three times to describe himself. Holy. Holy. Holy. That word describes God's most elusive and frightening characteristic: His Holiness. It's a subject so awesome that few have dared to approach it."[3]

R. C. did not approach it. It approached him.

Recalling that pivotal moment in college, R. C. was "compelled" to leave the comfort and warmth of his bed in his dorm room at Westminster College. Feet crunching through snow as the clock struck midnight, R. C. entered the chapel, having passed through the oaken door under a Gothic arch. From that moment on, the holiness of God gripped R. C. It found him, and it did not let him go.

When R. C. went on the air for the first time for his national radio show, *Renewing Your Mind*, on October 3, 1994, the very first broadcast was the first lecture of the "Holiness of God" teaching series. R. C. ended the first broadcast by recalling that turning-point moment; then he delivered these last lines:

> That private and personal experience that I had in that chapel was a life-changing experience for me, and it was the beginning of a lifelong pursuit of the holiness of God. . . . It is not only vital to my life, but is central to the biblical revelation of the character of God, and it's absolutely crucial for every Christian's personal growth to investigate, to reflect upon, to seek an understanding of what the Scriptures mean when they declare that God is holy.[4]

In a Mission Statement (and a Note on the Hair)

The October 1981 edition of *Tabletalk* ran a unique "Ask R. C." column. Those who have known R. C. over the years, or have seen video

---

2   *Tabletalk*, vol. 3, March 1979, 5.

3   *Tabletalk*, vol. 3, March 1979, 5.

4   R. C. Sproul, "The Otherness of God," *Holiness of God* radio format, lecture 1. Originally aired on *Renewing Your Mind*, October 3, 1994.

clips, have likely observed his clothing styles change and, what's more, his hairstyle change. The hair took on a life of its own. It has become part of the story. This particular column from R. C. deals with the hair directly. It was coarse, full, and flat. Then came a trip to a barber shop in Arizona. The barber, a woman, asked R. C., "Why don't you let me do something with your hair?" He thought to himself, *You already are. You're cutting it.* But what he said was, "Like what?" And the rest is history. Everyone asked: "What in the world did you do to your hair?" That was the pressing question in the "Ask R. C." column. It was the pressing question R. C. got in 1981. The response to the coiffed mane was mixed. R. C. kept track. Tongue-in-cheek, he offered:

> J. I. Packer uttered a soft and dignified word of encouragement; Jim Kennedy raised his eyebrows in consternation; Francis Schaeffer looked at it quizzically and moved his lips to form a response until he caught me staring at his knickers; Charles Colson wrote the Second Book of Lamentations as he cried all the way to L. L. Bean; Ron Sider thought it looked nice but wondered if it didn't cost a little too much; and John Gerstner hasn't noticed it yet.[5]

But the opinion expressed in a following and final sentence had the last word on the matter: "But . . . Vesta said, 'I love it' . . . so it stays." To the list of influencers who truly impacted R. C.—his dad, Mrs. Gregg, his coaches, Dr. Gregory, and Dr. Gerstner—we need to add an unknown female barber in Arizona. That's the origin of the hair. That same October 1981 issue of *Tabletalk* also sheds light on the origin of the mission statement of Ligonier.

The mission statement for Ligonier evolved over the years. Beginning with that October 1981 issue, the *Tabletalk* masthead included "The Mission of Ligonier," which was:

---

5   R. C. Sproul, "Ask R. C.: The Crisis of Image Change, Or, A Funny Thing Happened on the Way to a Barber Shop," *Tabletalk*, vol. 5, October 1981, 5.

To contribute to the cause of spiritual renewal and reformation through a teaching ministry designed to inform masses of people with Biblical content and to train key church and paraministry leaders in Biblical truth including doctrine, practice, and cultural interpretation (theology, ethics, practical theology, and apologetics).[6]

The February 1983 issue had a new and much shorter version of the mission statement:

To teach the Christian faith to as many people as possible.

The February 1985 issue ran another new mission statement, which trended back longer:

To teach biblical truth to adult Christians and to encourage them to achieve a world and life view that will yield mature, obedient Godliness, thereby contributing to a renewal of the church and culture.

The mission statement in the late 1980s became:

To help awaken as many people as possible to the holiness of God in all its fullness.

The mission statement currently reads:

To proclaim the holiness of God in all its fullness to as many people as possible.

The August 1996 issue of *Tabletalk* celebrates the twenty-fifth anniversary of Ligonier. R. C. devoted that month's "Right Now Counts Forever" column to the event and took the occasion to reflect on the purpose of Ligonier. He titled that column, "Why Ligonier?" He noted that since the early days, they'd forged purpose statements, adding, "The expressions changed but the underlying purpose never did."[7] That underlying

---

6 Actually, that first occurrence in October had a typo, "partical theology." That was fixed in the next issue.

7 R. C. Sproul, "Why Ligonier?," *Tabletalk*, vol. 20, August 1996, 6–7.

purpose has to do with reckoning with who God is, in His holiness, and then teaching and living that. That underlying purpose goes back to a time early in Ligonier's history when they brought in a consultant.

The final version of the evolved mission statement was the result of a collaboration with that consultant and R. C. The consultant sat with R. C. and asked him to describe himself. R. C. replied that he is a theologian. Then the consultant asked, "What do you do?" R. C. said that he teaches. Then the consultant asked him what he teaches, and R. C. replied that he teaches people who God is. Then the consultant asked him, "Who do you teach?" R. C. said he mainly teaches people in the church but also reaches and teaches people in culture. The consultant had just two more questions. First, he asked, "What do people in the church most need to know about God?" R. C. said, "He is holy." Then the consultant asked the last question: "What do people in the culture need to know about God?" R. C. said, "He is holy." That has always been the foundation of the underlying purpose and is reflected in the final form of the refined mission statement.

The night before the memorial service for R. C., a group of theologians and pastors who had shared many conference platforms with R. C. gathered for a reception. As different memories were brought up, John Piper, with a laser focus, thought of R. C. and the holiness of God. He exclaimed, "What other ministry has the phrase the holiness of God in its mission statement?"

The holiness of God was central to R. C. The doctrine that gripped him began with a personal experience, but it was nurtured and fostered by a lifetime of study and pursuit. One book that caught R. C.'s attention was by the German Lutheran theologian Rudolf Otto.

The Idea of the Holy

Rudolf Otto published his book *Das Heilige* in 1917. The first English translation appeared in 1923 with the title *The Idea of the Holy: An Inquiry into the Non-Rational Factor in the Idea of the Divine and Its Relation to the Rational*. Otto notes that we tend to use the term *holy* in relation to moral perfection, "the consummation of moral goodness."[8] Then Otto observes, "But this common usage of the term is inaccurate."[9] R. C.'s copy, which he picked up sometime in the 1960s, has this sentence underlined, with double-underlining of the word "inaccurate." To be sure, God's holiness means purity and moral perfection. Holiness entails that, but it is more; something above and beyond that speaks to the essence of who God is. Otto suggests the word *numinous*, from the Latin *numen*, meaning divine power.[10] As *omen* becomes *ominous*, so *numen*, Otto surmised, can become *numinous*. Otto further suggests that it takes our "creature-consciousness" to fully appreciate the notion of the numinous, of the holy. That "Creature-Consciousness" enables us to feel "submerged and overwhelmed by its own nothingness in contrast to that which is supreme above all creatures."[11] R. C. underlined that sentence too. The creature feels powerless, like "nothingness before an overpowering absolute might of some kind."[12] One more sentence gets underlined as Otto finishes chapter 3: "The numinous is thus felt as objective and outside the self."[13] Hearing these sentences, one thinks of Abraham before the burning bush and Isaiah before God's throne.

R. C.'s active reading notches up a bit at chapter 4, "Mysterium Tremendum." You do not have to know Latin to know that *mysterium* means mystery. Before you think of "tremendous" *for tremendum*, however, you should think first of the word *tremor* or *tremble*. It is tremendous, but in a way that shakes you to your very core. This expression means the "tremendous, tremor-inducing and awe-inspiring, mystery." For this chapter in Otto's book, R. C. underlined, circled, and drew his squiggly line. At one point he folded over the pages for the entire chapter—a sure

---

8 Rudolf Otto, *The Idea of the Holy: An Inquiry into the Non-Rational Factor in the Idea of the Divine and Its Relation to the Rational*, trans. John Harvey (New York: Oxford University Press, 1958), 5.

9 Otto, *The Idea of the Holy*, 5.

10 Otto, *The Idea of the Holy*, 6–7.

11 Otto, *The Idea of the Holy*, 10.

12 Otto, *The Idea of the Holy*, 10.

13 Otto, *The Idea of the Holy*, 11.

sign that he wanted to come back to the chapter again, maybe even use it in a book someday. These are some of the sentences from that fourth chapter that captivated him and his pen:

> The feeling of [*mysterium tremendum*] may come sweeping like a gentle tide, pervading the mind with a tranquil mood of deepest worship. . . . It may become the hushed, trembling, and speechless humility of the creature in the presence of—whom or what? In the presence of that which is a mystery incomprehensible and above all creatures. . . . *Tremor* is in itself merely the perfectly familiar and "natural" emotion of *fear*. The Hebrew *hiqdish* (hallow) is an example. To "keep a thing holy in the heart" means to mark it off by a feeling of peculiar dread. . . . Specifically noticeable is the *enah* of Yahweh ("fear of God"), which Yahweh can put forth.[14]

Otto is sometimes accused of teaching that God is "wholly other," a total mystery, entirely unknowable. That is not a fair assessment. His translator says, "God for him is not, so to speak, wholly 'wholly other.'"[15] Otto himself says, in a foreword for the English edition, that while he is pursuing the irrational, better to say "supra-rational," he is actually venturing to study "that rational aspect of that supreme Reality we call 'God.'"[16]

In one of his lectures for his holiness series, R. C. testified:

> One of the most fascinating studies that I've ever read and I would commend to you for your careful attention is a book that appeared early in the Twentieth Century by a German theologian who was also an anthropologist. His name was Rudolf Otto, and he wrote a very little book, but a book that many theologians consider one of the most important books of the Twentieth Century.[17]

14 Otto, *The Idea of the Holy*, 13.
15 John Harvey, "Translator's Preface," in Otto, *The Idea of the Holy*, xviii. (Yes, R. C. underlined that sentence.)
16 "Foreword by the Author to the First English Edition," in Otto, *The Idea of the Holy*, xxi.
17 R. C. Sproul, "The Meaning of Holiness," *Holiness of God* radio format, lecture 5.

R. C. appreciated Otto's concept of the numinous. He appreciated the concept of the *mysterium tremendum* even more. The holy invokes dread, fear. R. C. found a parallel in the Negro spiritual "Were You There?" The refrain stops us in our tracks: "Sometimes it causes me to tremble, tremble, tremble." God is "Awe-ful" and we tremble before Him.[18]

Well-Meaning Uzzah

In addition to reading the German theologian, R. C. also found himself enraptured by two biblical texts:

> I remember reading a Sunday school curriculum in one of the denominations I used to work with. It came from our headquarters, and . . . it said: "Now we understand that these kinds of stories that we read in the Old Testament, like Uzzah and Nadab, like God's destroying the whole world with a flood—men, women, and children—of God's ordering the *herem*, telling the Jewish people to go into the land of Canaan and to slaughter all of the inhabitants of Canaan—men, women and children—can't possibly be a manifestation of the real character of God. We have to understand these stories in the Old Testament simply as ancient, primitive, pre-scientific, semi-nomadic Jewish people who interpreted the events they saw in light of their own peculiar theology. Probably what happened was that Uzzah had a heart attack, and he died, and the Jewish writer attributed the cause of his death to an unmerciful expression of this vicious wrath of God.[19]

No, that's not at all what happened. God struck "well-meaning" Uzzah instantly dead. R. C. put it this way: "Uzzah touched the ark, and *wham!* God exploded in fury."[20] R. C. first preached on Uzzah from 1 Chronicles 13 at a chapel at Gordon College while he was a professor there.

---

18 R. C. Sproul, *The Holiness of God* (1985; repr., Carol Stream, IL: Tyndale, 1998), 50–54.
19 R. C. Sproul, "Holiness and Justice," *Holiness of God* radio format, lecture 3.
20 Sproul, *Holiness of God*, 127.

He preached on it many times. The story strikes the reader as incredibly unjust. When David heard of the incident, he was angry at God. Uzzah was protecting the ark, which held the Ten Commandments, which was covered with the mercy seat. The ark's home was in the temple, God's holy temple. And at that, it was in the Most Holy Place, secluded from all except for that one day out of the year when one man, the high priest, would dare enter and stand before it. Rings were affixed to it so poles could be inserted for carrying. The ark was never, ever to be touched. But an oxen stumbled, and Uzzah reached out his hand to stop the ark from falling to the ground. It was the last thing Uzzah ever did on earth. R. C. notes that Uzzah committed the "sin of presumption. Uzzah assumed that his hand was less polluted than the earth."[21]

The other text that captivated R. C. was Isaiah 6. R. C. heard John Guest preach a sermon on this text, sometime around 1969. R. C. kept mulling the text over. When he was invited to give the lectures at Saranac Lake, he decided he would use Isaiah 6 as the hub for his five lectures on the holiness of God. That was the first time he preached on Isaiah 6, but it would not be by far the last. His novel ends with the fictional Reverend Doctor Richard Evans delivering a sermon on Isaiah 6. Isaiah and his chapter 6 form the warp and woof of chapter 2 of R. C.'s *The Holiness of God*.

Before R. C. read any Christian book, he read the Bible through. He devoured the Old Testament as a brand-new Christian. He realized that "this God of the Bible is a God who plays for keeps." He added, "In that very first couple of weeks I had an awakening to the biblical concept of God that informed my whole life after that."[22]

In addition to Otto, Uzzah, and Isaiah 6—and many other biblical texts such as any number of passages from the Psalms—the other strand of influence here on R. C. is the Reformed classical tradition, again. The footnotes in *The Holiness of God* contain the usual suspects: Luther, Calvin,

21 Sproul, *Holiness of God*, 130.
22 Stephen Nichols with R. C. Sproul, personal interview, October 20, 2017.

and Edwards. Near the very end of the book, R. C. also references the "Medieval theologians" who "used the phrase *ens perfectissimus* to refer to God."[23] That's Aquinas. It would be poor English grammar to say the "perfectest" or the "mostest." Perfect and most are already superlatives. You cannot add the superlative suffix *-est* to a superlative.

Latin is not troubled by such a grammar rule. *Perfect* is a superlative. The suffix *-issimus* is a superlative. This Latin expression would be literally (though poorly) translated into English as the *perfectest*. We would just say "most perfect." The Latin word *ens* means "being." God is the most perfect being. R. C. picks it up from here:

> To say that something or someone is the most perfect being involves a redundancy. Real perfection does not admit to degrees. Something that is truly perfect in every respect cannot become more perfect or most perfect. We speak like this because we have become accustomed to dealing with things that are imperfect. Imperfect things can be improved, but the perfect cannot.[24]

So all of this questioning of superlatives and degrees raises a question: "Why then did the theologians use the superlative degree to speak of God's perfection?"[25] R. C. replies:

> The answer must be found in their desire to underscore the reality of God's perfection so clearly that they would eliminate any possibility of suggesting the slightest lack of perfection in God's character. It was a legitimate use of hyperbole to speak of most perfect.[26]

In the *Summa Theologiae* Aquinas writes, "Now God is the first principle, not material, but in the order of efficient cause, which must be most perfect . . . because we call that perfect which lacks nothing of the

23 Sproul, *Holiness of God*, 241.
24 Sproul, *Holiness of God*, 241.
25 Sproul, *Holiness of God*, 241.
26 Sproul, *Holiness of God*, 241–42.

mode of its perfection."[27] Aquinas adds, "All created perfections are in God. Hence He is spoken of as universally perfect, because he lacks not any excellence. . . . He is all, as the cause of all."[28]

Aquinas here is expressing the fundamental identity of God, the essence of God. This is the core, the heart, of the Reformed classical tradition. R. C. said, "Augustine, Thomas Aquinas, Luther, Calvin, Edwards—All of these were intoxicated by the transcendent majesty of God." He added, "I was so gripped by that. That was one of the reasons why I wrote *The Holiness of God*, and why my concern throughout my ministry has been recovering the doctrine of God."[29]

This is important to grasp. When R. C. focused on the holiness of God, he focused not on a singular attribute of God but on the being of God, the essence of God.

When Moses approached the burning bush, he was told that he was standing on holy ground, standing in the very presence of God. The Most Holy Place is where God "dwelt" with His people; where God met them—"There I will meet you," at the mercy seat, on the ark in the *sanctum sanctorum*. The seraphim sing in God's presence the thrice-holy anthem, because God *is* holy.

The holiness of God is one way to get at the *ens perfectissimus*. It was the path R. C. took. We sometimes hear the God of wrath of the Old Testament pitted against the God of love of the New Testament. God is a God of holy wrath. God is a God of holy love. To zero in on the holiness of God as R. C. did was exactly what the church needed.

God, Man, Christ

R. C.'s theology—his distinct theological method and contribution to the Christian tradition—is to move from the doctrine of God to the doctrine

---

27 Thomas Aquinas, *Summa Theologiae, Prima Pars 1–49*, trans. Fr. Laurence Shaupcote, O. P. (Lander, WY: Aquinas Institute for the Study of Sacred Doctrine, 2012), 37–38.

28 Aquinas, *Summa Theologiae*, 39.

29 Nichols with Sproul, personal interview, October 20, 2017.

of man to the doctrines of Christ and salvation. He does this precisely and poetically in *The Holiness of God*. He starts with where the Bible starts:

> The Bible says, "In the beginning God." The God we worship is the God who has always been. He alone can create beings, because he alone has the *power of being*. He is not nothing. He is not chance. He is pure Being, the one who has the power to be *all by Himself*. He alone is eternal. He alone has power over death. He alone can call worlds into being by fiat, by the power of His command. Such power is staggering, awesome. It is deserving of respect, of humble adoration.[30]

That is the *ens perfectissimus*, the most perfect being. R. C. continues, "The idea of holiness is so central to the biblical teaching that it is said of God, 'Holy is his name' (Luke 1:49). His name is holy because He is holy."[31]

That is the doctrine of God, the eternal, immutable, omnipotent, majestic, holy God. Next comes the doctrine of man. Consider the example of Isaiah. What happens to Isaiah after he encounters the thrice-holy God? He says, "I am undone" (Isaiah 6:5 NKJV). R. C. elaborates:

> To be undone means to come apart at the seams, to be unraveled. What Isaiah was expressing is what modern psychologists describe as the experience of personal disintegration. To disintegrate means exactly what the word suggests, *dis integrate*. . . . [Isaiah] caught one sudden glimpse of a holy God. In that single moment, all of his self-esteem was shattered. In a brief second he was exposed, made naked beneath the gaze of the absolute standard of holiness. As long as Isaiah could compare himself to other mortals, he was able to sustain a lofty opinion of his own character. The instant he measured himself by the ultimate standard, he was destroyed—morally and spiritually annihilated. He was undone. He came apart.[32]

---

30 Sproul, *Holiness of God*, 13.
31 Sproul, *Holiness of God*, 15.
32 Sproul, *Holiness of God*, 35–36.

God's holiness revealed Isaiah's sinfulness. On cue, a seraphim took a coal from the altar and purged Isaiah's lips. Atonement. This was a foreshadowing, a type, of the God-man to come who would make full atonement for sin, who ends our "holy war" and brings peace. So R. C. moves from God's holiness and our sinfulness to Christ's work and the gift of salvation:

> When our holy war with God ceases, when we, like Luther, walk through the gates of paradise, when we are justified by faith, the war ends forever. With the cleansing from sin and the declaration of divine forgiveness we enter into an eternal peace treaty with God. The firstfruit of our justification is peace with God. This is a holy peace, a peace unblemished and transcendent. It is a peace that cannot be destroyed. . . . It is the kind of peace that only Christ can bestow.[33]

Christ's holiness swallows up our unholiness. Christ's purity swallows up our uncleanness. Christ's righteousness swallows up all our transgressions. "He took our filthy rags and gave us His righteous robe."[34] R. C. says, "This is the legacy of Christ: *peace*."[35] It all starts with the proper view of God's holiness. A shallow view of God will distort the views held on all other doctrines.

Shallow Views

In his 1994 book, *God in the Wasteland*, David Wells observed, "The fundamental problem in the evangelical world today is that God rests too inconsequentially upon the church. His truth is too distant, his grace is too ordinary, his judgment is too benign, his gospel is too easy, and his Christ is too common."[36] Wells's comment sounds like an echo of R. C.'s 1961 bachelor's thesis on Melville's *Moby Dick*. Melville, R. C. astutely

---

33 Sproul, *Holiness of God*, 183–84.

34 "The Word Made Flesh: Ligonier Statement on Christology," 2016.

35 R. C. Sproul, *Holiness of God*, 185.

36 David F. Wells, *God in the Wasteland: The Reality of Truth in a World of Fading Dreams* (Grand Rapids, MI: Eerdmans, 1994), 28.

observed, offers what "seems to be an attack upon the shallow religious views of mankind."[37]

Whiteness of the whale:

All Christian priests derive the name of one part of their sacred vesture, the alb or tunic, worn beneath the cassock; and though among the holy pomps of the Romish faith, white is specially employed in the celebration of the Passion of our Lord; though in the Vision of St. John, white robes are given to the redeemed, and the four-and-twenty elders stand clothed in white before the great-white throne, and the Holy One that sitteth there white like wool; yet for all these accumulated associations, with whatever is sweet, and honorable, and sublime, there yet lurks an elusive something in the innermost idea of this hue, which strikes more of panic to the soul than that redness which affrights in blood.

This elusive quality it is, which causes the thought of whiteness, when divorced from more kindly associations, and coupled with any object terrible in itself, to heighten that terror to the furthest bounds. Witness the white bear of the poles, and the white shark of the tropics; what but their smooth, flaky whiteness makes them the transcendent horrors they are? That ghastly whiteness it is which imparts such an abhorrent mildness, even more loathsome than terrific, to the dumb gloating of their aspect. So that not the fierce-fanged tiger in his heraldic coat can so stagger courage as the white-shrouded bear or shark.[38]

Whiteness stands for purity, the unblemished, like the crispness of a pure white garment, David cries out in repentance, pleads to be washed, so that he would be "whiter than snow" (Ps. 51:7). Yet Melville's "*ghastly whiteness*" is akin to Otto's numinous. It entails purity, moral perfection, but also encompasses more. Both Otto's numinous of the divine

---

37 Robert C. Sproul, "The Existential Implications of Melville's *Moby Dick*," bachelor's thesis, 1961, Westminster College, New Wilmington, PA.

38 Herman Melville, *Moby Dick, or The Whale* (Norwalk, CT: Easton Press, 1977), 200.

being and Melville's whiteness of the whale ignite fear and excitement. It is too much; it causes one to tremble, tremble, tremble. The whiteness is, for Melville, transcendence, not the common or the ordinary or the domesticated or the conquerable. Ahab misjudged the white whale.

R. C. saw confronting this casual view of God as the need of the day, the need of every day. In the few years before R. C. died, he referenced how little he enjoyed traveling a certain stretch of Interstate 4, just north of Orlando. While it did have something to do with the notoriously bad traffic on the I-4, it had more to do with a billboard put up by a central Florida megachurch. The billboard declared in bold white letters on a stark black background "God Is Not Angry at You." R. C., a meticulous driver, testified how every time he saw that message glaring at him, it nearly caused him to drive off the road. R. C. lamented the depths to which the view of God "as a consuming fire" had sunk in the church and in the culture. Otto spoke of the *numinous*, a word he invented. Melville spoke of whiteness, intrigued and terrified by its manifestation in nature. R. C. used a word straight from the Bible—*holiness*.

If the keystone of the doctrine of God is in place—and honored— then all other doctrines will fall into place, will be sound. If the doctrine of God is off-kilter, forgotten, or diminished, then all other doctrines will go awry. Holiness reminds us who God is and who we are. We are Uzzah, profanely misguided in thinking we know better than God. We are Isaiah, unclean and undone.

This is what R. C. was trying to teach the church, and the culture, all those decades through the sermons, teaching series, and books. When *The Holiness of God* was published in 1985, there was really nothing like it on the popular Christian book market. In the book, R. C. notes that Jonathan Edwards's "consuming need was to preach about God's holiness, to preach it vividly, emphatically, convincingly, and powerfully."[39] That was R. C.'s consuming need as well.

39 Sproul, *Holiness of God*, 212.

The Holiness of God kicked off a virtual series of books by R. C. on the doctrine of God in quick succession. Consider this book release list:

1985 *The Holiness of God*
1986 *Chosen by God*
1987 *One Holy Passion: The Consuming Thirst to Know God*
1988 *Pleasing God*

These books don't simply rehash the same topic. Each one explores a different facet of the multifaceted diamond that is the doctrine of God.

R. C. found it odd that readers who liked *The Holiness of God* did not like *Chosen by God*. He would want to tell them, if that's the case, you need to go back and reread *The Holiness of God*.

A Perplexing and Perilous Doctrine

In *Chosen by God*, R. C. explores God's sovereignty over all things, including our salvation. As *Holiness* is one long, compelling, and persuasive argument for the transcendence of God, so *Chosen* is one long, compelling, and persuasive argument for predestination. R. C. first published on predestination in the essay he wrote for the book he edited to honor the work of his mentor, Dr. Gerstner. In fact, R. C. tackled one of the truly thorny theological issues by writing "Double Predestination," the title of his essay.[40]

Since that first essay in 1978 and, in fact, throughout all his years of teaching, inevitably the question of predestination would arise and, just as inevitably, people would express their difficulty with it and would be perplexed by it. R. C. wrote *Chosen by God* to help: "I wrote the book for people who are committed to struggling with this difficult, complicated doctrine."[41] John Calvin himself pointed out, "The subject of predestination, which in itself is attended with

---

40 R. C. Sproul, "Double Predestination," in *Soli Deo Gloria: Essays in Reformed Theology, Festschrift for John H. Gerstner* (Phillipsburg, NJ: Presbyterian & Reformed, 1976), 63–72.
41 R. C. Sproul, "Interview with R. C. about *Chosen by God*," *Tabletalk*, vol. 10, December 1986, 4.

considerable difficulty, is rendered very perplexing, and hence perilous by human curiosity."[42]

Like Calvin, R. C. was sympathetic to those tackling the doctrine of predestination because of its complexity. R. C. was also sympathetic for an existential reason. You might recall that R. C. struggled with this doctrine in the first several years of his own Christian life. To help people understand the sovereignty of God and the doctrine of predestination, he started *Chosen by God* by pointing out that it is indeed a biblical doctrine and by recounting his personal narrative and retracing how he came first to a tolerable understanding and then to a joyous embrace of the doctrine.

R. C. marshals Ephesians 1 and Romans 8 as the biblical proof for the doctrine. He concludes, "If the Bible is the Word of God, not mere human speculation, and if God himself declares that there is such a thing as predestination, then it follows irresistibly that we must embrace some doctrine of predestination."[43] It is not an option to say, "I don't believe in predestination." To do so denies biblical teaching. In a *Tabletalk* article that coincided with the book release, R. C. states plainly, "Predestination is a biblical concept. It is a biblical word. It was not invented by Calvin or Luther."[44] But as R. C. points out in *Chosen by God*, once we realize that the Bible teaches predestination, "the real struggle begins, the struggle to sort out accurately all that the Bible teaches about the matter."[45]

Next, R. C. recounts his own pilgrimage regarding this doctrine. He speaks of how he did not like the Reformed view: "I did not like it at all. I fought against it tooth and nail all the way through college."[46] This was back in 1957 and went through 1961. Then came seminary (1961–1964). R. C. recalls how he went through "painful stages" in learning and embracing this doctrine. Through the persistent, faithful teaching of Gerstner he

---

42 John Calvin, cited by R. C. Sproul in his Right Now Counts Forever column "Predestination: A Solemn Warning," *Tabletalk*, vol. 10, December 1986, 3.

43 R. C. Sproul, *Chosen by God* (Wheaton, IL: Tyndale, 1986), 3.

44 Sproul, "Predestination: A Solemn Warning," 3.

45 Sproul, *Chosen by God*, 3.

46 Sproul, *Chosen by God*, 3.

came to accept it. He was at a sort of intellectual truce with the doctrine. As R. C. put it, "OK, I believe this stuff, but I don't have to like it!"[47] But soon his heart followed his head: "Once I began to see the cogency of the doctrine and its broader implications, my eyes were opened to the graciousness of grace and to the grand comfort of God's sovereignty. I began to like the doctrine little by little. Until it burst upon my soul that the doctrine revealed the depth and the riches of the mercy of God."[48] R. C.'s own personal struggle likely afforded him both sympathy and patience as he endeavored to help others see it and embrace it.

R. C.'s exposition of predestination starts by observing, "What predestination means, in its most elementary form, is that our final destination, heaven or hell, is decided by God not only before we get there, but before we are even born."[49] This leads directly to the sovereignty of God. R. C. tells his readers of a little game he played once with students in a seminary class. He cited the Westminster Confession of Faith on the sovereignty of God:

> God, from all eternity, did, by the most wise and holy counsel of His own will, freely, and unchangeably ordain whatsoever comes to pass.

Then he asked for a show of hands of anyone who disagreed. Many hands went up. Then he asked, "Are there any convinced atheists in the room?" Not a single hand went up. R. C. followed with, "Everyone who raised his hand to the first question should have also raised his hand to the second question."[50] That was not well received. But R. C. pointed out that the sovereignty of God is not particularly Calvinist or Presbyterian. It belongs to theism; it is "a necessary tenet of theism."[51] As he would say, "If God is not sovereign, then God is not God."

47 Sproul, *Chosen by God*, 4.
48 Sproul, *Chosen by God*, 4–5.
49 Sproul, *Chosen by God*, 12.
50 Sproul, *Chosen by God*, 15.
51 Sproul, *Chosen by God*, 15.

Once R. C. makes a case in the book for sovereignty and predestination, he next answers several related questions. One is: Why doesn't God save all? R. C. replies, "I don't know. I have no idea why God saves some but not all. . . . One thing I do know. If it pleases God to save some and not all, there is nothing wrong with that."[52] R. C. is content to leave the matter there.

Another question is, What about human freedom? R. C. answers by pointing to the biblical teaching of our corrupt, sinful nature: "Our nature is so corrupt, the power of sin is so great, that unless God does a supernatural work in our souls we will never choose Christ."[53] Our wills turn us in the opposite direction from Christ. R. C. learned from Luther's *Bondage of the Will* and Edwards's *Freedom of the Will* the fundamental tenet of the Reformed faith: regeneration precedes faith. As R. C. explains, "We do not believe in order to be born again; we are born again in order that we may believe."

One final question R. C. seeks to answer is, Is God just? Here R. C. wades into the discussion of double predestination, the same subject he addressed in his essay on the book for Gerstner in 1976. R. C. speaks of double predestination, election to salvation and election to reprobation or damnation, as asymmetrical, as being a positive-negative relationship. In election, God actively chooses His elect. In the decree of reprobation, He passes over the nonelect. Augustine spoke of humanity as "Adam's sinful lump." Out of that lump, God saved some. This is different from how most normally think. Most tend to think that humanity is neutral, with God saving some and capriciously sending others to hell. R. C. counters with the view that all are lost. Then he says:

> This is how we must understand double predestination. God gives mercy to the elect by working faith in their hearts. He gives justice to the reprobate by leaving them in their own sin. There is no symmetry

52 Sproul, *Chosen by God*, 25.
53 Sproul, *Chosen by God*, 55.

here. One group receives mercy. The other group receives justice. No one is a victim of injustice. None can complain that there is unrighteousness in God.[54]

R. C. ends *Chosen by God* with a discussion of assurance. In the *Tabletalk* interview he did for the book's release, R. C. warmly concluded: "There's nothing that gives me more assurance of my salvation or more security in my faith than the doctrine of predestination. As I wrestle with that doctrine I can hear God saying to me, 'You are mine,' and there's tremendous comfort in that." He adds, "I hope my book attests to this."[55]

As the Deer

The year after R. C. published *Chosen by God*, he published *One Holy Passion: The Consuming Thirst to Know God*.[56] Here R. C. continues to offer expositions of the character of God. This book, however, addresses the attributes of God from the perspective of questions, the hard or complex questions, that people ask of God and of life. Many of the questions R. C. had himself.

The very first chapter recalls R. C.'s painful loss of his father while he was still a teenager. This left him angry and asking, "Who are you, God? And why do you do the things you do?"[57] R. C. found the answer in Moses's encounters with God. Next he asks, "Who made you, God?" This did not come from that place of pain and anger, but it did raise a sticky intellectual problem. If God made everything, because every effect has a cause, then . . . who or what made God? R. C. answers by discussing an often-neglected aspect of God's nature, the aseity of God.

54 Sproul, *Chosen by God*, 119.
55 Sproul, "Predestination: A Solemn Warning," 5.
56 Originally published by Thomas Nelson, this book was republished as *The Character of God: Discovering the God Who Is* (Ann Arbor, MI: Servant, 1987), and again under that title (Ventura, CA: Regal, 2004). It was republished again as *Enjoying God: Finding Hope in the Attributes of God* (Grand Rapids, MI: Baker, 2017).
57 R. C. Sproul, *One Holy Passion: The Consuming Thirst To Know God* (Nashville, TN: Thomas Nelson, 1987), 7.

This word, *aseity*, sent chills up and down his spine. Just months before he passed away, he was asked, if he were able to write one more book, what he would write about. Without hesitation, R. C. said he'd write a book on the aseity of God.[58] But back in 1987, at least he was able to write a chapter on the subject. *Aseity* means that "God exists by His own power. He alone is self-existent. Aseity, meaning 'self-existent,' is the characteristic that separates Him from all other things. God is the only one who can say, 'I am who I am.'"[59] We are not self-existent. R. C. notes, "Life is lived between two hospitals."[60]

So what do we learn from God's self-existence? Or of what practical use is the doctrine of the aseity of God? First, it is the answer to all our fears orbiting the fragility of life. We live and diminish and die. Yet God is eternal, and, through the eternal Son, death—and all of the frailty of being human—is conquered and vanquished. R. C. points to the comforting work and words of Christ: "Jesus is a savior with power, ultimate power, and He holds the power of being in His hands. His words, 'Do not be afraid,' are not empty words. I have nothing to fear from death."[61]

R. C. also points to how aseity relates to our salvation. God brought forth life by the power of His word. God also brings life from death. R. C. learned the doctrine of aseity from the Reformed classical tradition, to be sure, but he also learned it from Paul in the "crucial passage" of Acts 17:24–25 and 28:

The God who made the world and everything in it, being Lord of heaven and earth, does not live in temples made by man, nor is he served by human hands, as though he needed anything, since he himself gives to all mankind life and breath and everything. . . . For "In him we live and move and have our being."

58 Nichols with Sproul, personal interview, October 20, 2017.
59 Sproul, *One Holy Passion*, 16.
60 Sproul, *One Holy Passion*, 18.
61 Sproul, *One Holy Passion*, 22.

The key phrase is "as though he needed anything." As self-existent, God needs nothing. R. C. sees how God as self-existent answers the three main puzzles that have baffled philosophers and scientists: life, motion, and being.[62] Shelley's fictional Dr. Frankenstein thought he could create life. But only God gives life. "We move because He moves."[63] "We *are* because He *is*."[64] R. C. concludes, "We are awed by the grand difference between human beings and the Supreme Being."[65] The doctrine of aseity gave R. C. chills.

For each chapter of this book, R. C. chose a psalm, or at least a large portion of a psalm. It is simply inserted near the middle of each chapter. In one sense R. C.'s discussions on the attributes and character of God are but commentary on the psalms.

In 1988, for the fourth year in a row, R. C. published a book on the doctrine of God, *Pleasing God*.[66] This book draws a straight line back to *The Holiness of God* by linking sanctification—growing in holiness in the Christian life—to the character of God, namely His holiness.

The advertising copy on the inside jacket flap draws attention to the pressing question of the book: "How can imperfect man hope to please God?" One of the answers is by simply remembering that the Christian life is seeking God: "To seek God is a lifelong pursuit. The seeking after God is what Jonathan Edwards called 'the main business of the Christian life.'"[67]

R. C. was rather emphatic that while salvation is monergistic—the work of God alone—sanctification is a cooperative venture—the work of God and man. His book calls on Christians to take up their calling: "To be sanctified involves work. . . . I must work and God will work."[68]

62 Sproul, *One Holy Passion*, 25.
63 Sproul, *One Holy Passion*, 25.
64 Sproul, *One Holy Passion*, 25.
65 Sproul, *One Holy Passion*, 25.
66 R. C. Sproul, *Pleasing God* (Wheaton, IL: Tyndale, 1988).
67 Sproul, *Pleasing God*, 31.
68 Sproul, *Pleasing God*, 227.

That's R. C.'s counsel at the beginning of the book. He says the same thing at the end. R. C. cites Hebrews 12:28–29: "Therefore, since we are receiving a kingdom which cannot be shaken, let us have grace, by which we may serve God acceptably with reverence and godly fear. For our God is a consuming fire" (NKJV). R. C. offers these last sentences of the book: "It is for this consuming fire that we live. It is Him that we strive to please. It is for Him that we rise up again after repeated failures. It is He who is our destiny."[69]

Loving a Holy God

In 1988 Ligonier hosted its first national conference on the theme "Loving a Holy God." The speakers were J. I. Packer, Chuck Colson, Jerry Bridges, and R. C. Sproul. That first conference was held at the Hilton Orlando/Altamonte Springs, right alongside Interstate 4, a short drive from the Ligonier offices. The conference intended to address the questions: "How can we be drawn more fully in love with God who is holy, holy, holy?" and "What are the practical implications of how God's holiness affects your life?"[70]

One of the very practical implications concerns suffering. In February, right after he hosted the first national conference, R. C. filmed a video teaching series. This was nothing new for R. C. He had been teaching to the camera for well over a decade. But the location was new. The series was filmed at the MD Anderson Cancer Hospital in Houston, Texas. As he began the lectures, R. C. said, "I recognize that in the audience this evening, we have physicians; we have hospital staff and administration; we have distinguished clergy who are present. . . . But I'm directing these lectures to patients first of all, and, second, to all friends and to families of those people who have to face firsthand profound levels of pain and uncertainty and suffering and in many cases death itself."[71]

69 Sproul, *Pleasing God*, 234.
70 *Tabletalk*, vol. 11, December 1987, 6.
71 *Surprised by Suffering*, teaching series, lecture 1, "Suffering a Case Study," 1988.

R. C. took the patients and their friends and families to the drama of Job and to Christ. Ultimately, R. C. led them to God. As R. C. wrote in the book that accompanied the series and was published in the same year, we must "really live life believing that God is sovereign, and maintain our trust in Him even when it seems that life is spinning out of control."[72]

R. C. also found a way to connect the holiness of God and the doctrine of God to kids. His first children's book came out in 1996, *The King without a Shadow*. R. C.'s own grandson Ryan gets a starring role, as does Ryan's dog, "Sir Winston." (Yes, Winston was the dog's name.) Ryan asked the king, "Where do shadows come from?"[73] The king did not know, so he went on a quest, which led him to a prophet. The prophet told the king who had a shadow about the King who had no shadow. "He has no shadow because He is completely holy," said the prophet to the king. The king found the boy and he knighted the dog: "I dub you, Sir Winston of Wingfield North." Then the king told Ryan and the dog what he had learned about "the mysteries of the shadows."[74] He told Ryan, "Shadows come from the light. This Great King is Himself the light. His light is brighter than the sun itself." When the king told Ryan that the Great King is holy, Ryan asked, "What is this 'holy?'"

"To be holy means two things," answered the king with a shadow. "First, to be holy means to be greater than anything else in the whole world. It means that God is different from us. He is higher than high and deeper than deep. But that's not all. . . . He is called holy because he is pure." And then the king with a shadow added, "All men must bow before Him in His great majesty."

There is no other name in twentieth- and twenty-first-century Christianity more associated with the holiness of God than the name of R. C. Sproul. It's for good reason. This chapter has looked mostly at

72 R. C. Sproul, *Surprised by Suffering: The Role of Pain and Death in the Christian Life* (Wheaton, IL: Tyndale, 1988), 38.

73 R. C. Sproul, *The King without a Shadow*, ill. Liz Bonham (Elgin, IL: Chariot, 1996).

74 Sproul, *King without a Shadow*.

the four-year span from 1985 through 1989 and all the ways that R. C. taught and wrote on the holiness of God. Of course, this emphasis may be seen long before 1985. R. C.'s teaching stretches all the way back to 1967 and sermons on Uzzah, to 1970 and the Saranac Lake lectures, to the many, many times he lectured on holiness at the study center. The holiness of God comes up again and again in Ligonier conference themes, beginning in 1988 and continuing well into the twenty-first century.

As R. C. said of his college experience, "I had an awakening to the biblical concept of God that informed my whole life after that."[75]

---

75 Nichols with Sproul, personal interview, October 20, 2017.

8

STAND

The gospel is the veritable power of God to save.

R. C. SPROUL

IN HIS COPY OF Luther's *Three Treatises*, R. C.'s active underlining and margin notating escalated to the next level. As a seminarian and doctoral student, he was reading for an immediate and specific purpose: success in a course. But he was also having the first extensive and intense conversation with someone who, though separated by centuries, would be a good friend and a constant companion. R. C. said directly, "I always loved Luther."[1] The years of Luther's life between 1517 and 1521 overflowed with drama. R. C. found it fascinating. These years began with Luther posting the Ninety-Five Theses to the church door at Wittenberg and ended with Luther declaring, "Here I stand" at Worms. It is the stuff of legends. But for R. C., these moments are far more than historical curiosity. They shaped his theological identity and put steel in his spine.

RCS

R. C. had his work at Ligonier, his writing, his speaking, and his traveling. Some of that traveling was to Jackson, Mississippi, to teach as

1 "Sproul Memoirs," session 8, recorded 2014, Ligonier Ministries, Sanford, Florida.

adjunct professor at Reformed Theological Seminary (RTS). In 1982 he was appointed professor of theology, a post he held until 1989. He was traded from Jackson to Orlando and tasked with being the first academic dean. The first convocation service was held at the Maitland Sheraton in Maitland, Florida. Carl F. H. Henry spoke to a crowd of several hundred. Scott R. Swain, the current president of RTS Orlando, notes, "So instrumental was [R. C.] establishing the campus that some friends of the seminary on occasion would mistakenly refer to RTS as 'RCS.'"[2] Swain adds that RTS would seize recruiting opportunities provided by Ligonier National Conferences held on their home turf of Orlando. Ligonier also employed many RTS students and spouses over the years. RTS also used R. C. in much of its advertising. He was a draw. Many ministers not in Presbyterian denominations enrolled in RTS's doctor of ministry program with the sole purpose of studying under R. C.

R. C. forged many friendships during his time at RTS, both in Orlando and in Jackson. He also had unexpected encounters. Once while back in Jackson, he spent some time on the golf course with actor Gene Hackman. Hackman was in Jackson filming the 1988 movie *Mississippi Burning*, and he joined the same golf club at which R. C. played. Both were together when one of the club's employees shared his family's story of struggles in the segregated South. When the movie came out, R. C. and Vesta went to see it. At one point in the movie Hackman, in an ad-libbed scene, retold the exact story that he and R. C. had heard. R. C. could hardly believe that he was watching it take place on screen.

He forged friendships with the faculty. At Jackson he became close with John R. de Witt. De Witt left Jackson for the pulpit of Second Presbyterian Church in Memphis, Tennessee. The church had hoped to woo R. C. away from Ligonier, but R. C. said no and said that they would do very well to have de Witt. R. C. also enjoyed the students.

2   Scott R. Swain, "In Memoriam R. C. Sproul, Preacher and Teacher of a Thrice-Holy God," December 14, 2017, https://rts.edu/news/news-orlando/in-memoriam-r-c-sproul-preacher-and-teacher-of-a -thrice-holy-god/.

Vesta came to every class with him. John Wingard, who went on to get a PhD in philosophy and teach at Calvin College, Wheaton College, and Covenant College, remembers how R. C. would ask the students a question and none of them would know the answer. After a bit of time elapsed, R. C. would turn to Vesta, and she would provide the answer.

At Orlando his fellow faculty were Richard Pratt, an Old Testament professor; and his former Gordon colleague Roger Nicole. In 1991, philosopher Ronald Nash joined them. He was another of those tough-minded apologists in the classical tradition. And, again, R. C. enjoyed the students.

In addition to his work at RTS Orlando, he was busy traveling and writing. During one of his trips to Chicago in the late 1980s he was able to spend a significant amount of time with Mortimer Adler. They discussed classic texts, philosophy, and the writing craft. R. C. also made many trips to DC during these years. One time, he and Colson met with William F. Buckley. R. C. also got to know Jack Kemp. Kemp, a former NFL and Canadian Football League player before he turned to politics, kept a football in his office. He and R. C. tossed the football as they discussed politics, ethics, and theology. They got so wrapped up in a conversation once that an assistant was sent in to break up the game of catch, as the Soviet Ambassador had been kept waiting for some time.

R. C. got to know that bow tie–wearing Democratic senator from Illinois, Paul Simon, and had lunch with him. R. C. also got to know Donald Hodel, secretary of the interior in Ronald Reagan's Cabinet.

These Washington relationships stemmed from his longtime interest in ethics, his time on the board of Prison Fellowship, and R. C.'s involvement with the Value of the Person movement and his biography of Wayne Alderson. A copy of the Alderson book made its way into the hands of Richard Nixon. Nixon wrote R. C. to tell him he was taking the book on a vacation, and that he "shall read it with interest," and that he would "spread the good word."

The Alderson book was published in 1980. The decade of the 1980s saw a lot of books come from the pen of R. C. One of them was the book he published in 1989, *Surprised by Suffering*, that went along with the teaching series he filmed at the MD Anderson Cancer Center. In 1990 he published two books that, when taken with *Holiness of God*, rounded out his treatment of the Trinity. *The Glory of Christ* and *The Mystery of the Holy Spirit* were both published by Tyndale. That year he also published a book that was very important to him: *Abortion: A Rational Look at an Emotional Issue*. Published by NavPress, R. C. was truly saddened that this book did not sell well. He was sad not for selfish reasons but because he found that so few in the church wanted to talk about the heinous sin of abortion.

R. C.'s devotional writings on Romans that appeared in *Tabletalk* in 1989, and his devotionals through Luke, which appeared in 1990 *Tabletalk* issues, were published respectively as *Before the Face of God: Book I* in 1992 and *Before the Face of God: Book II* in 1993. And in 1993 he published *Not a Chance*. There's a backstory.

Cosmos By Chance

Back in a 1988 issue of *Tabletalk*, R. C. published a lengthy article on Carl Sagan, reviewing and answering Sagan's popular book *Cosmos* from 1980, which went along with the very popular science documentary *Cosmos: A Personal Journey*. R. C. had a high regard for Sagan. He was impressed by Sagan's academic credentials, but what impressed R. C. the most was the way Sagan so brilliantly and compellingly communicated. R. C. speaks of his being "profoundly impressed by [Sagan's] work. Not only does he display an uncanny level of erudition, but he couples it with a marvelous literary style. That he has turned his pen to fiction is a congruous extension of his abundant literary gifts."[3]

Even though Sagan is "the high priest of cosmological materialism," R. C. deeply respected him. Sagan was to science as R. C. was to theology.

3   *Tabletalk*, vol. 12, August 1985, 4.

R. C. Sproul and his parents, Mayre and Capt. Robert Cecil Sproul, 1945

R. C. Sproul wearing a Toronto Maple Leafs jacket given
by team members, Lake Muskoka, Ontario, Canada, 1949

R. C. Sproul, 1957

Wedding day, June 11, 1960, Pleasant Hills Community Church

The Sprouls' living room, the Ligonier Valley Study Center,
Stahlstown, Pennsylvania, early 1970s

John R. Stott's visit to the study center, November 1972

ARE YOU AND YOUR CHURCH READY FOR VIDEO?

Brochure produced by Ligonier, 1970s

Cassette tape of R. C. Sproul's teaching, 1972

Q & A session with R. C. Sproul and Chuck Colson
at the study center, late 1970s

TABLE TALK

VOL. 1 NO.4   A NEWSLETTER OF THE LIGONIER VALLEY STUDY CENTER   SEPTEMBER 1, 1977

Left to right: Alane Barron, Patty Temple, Pat Erickson, Carol and Bill White, R. C. and Vesta Sproul, Kathy and Stu Boehmig, Janice and Steve Gooder, Jackie Shelton, Art Lindsley, Marilyn and Tim Couch, Toni and Dave Fox. Not pictured Marcia Orr, Jack and Linda Rowley.

LIGONIER CELEBRATES SIXTH YEAR

August 1, 1977 marked the sixth anniversary of the opening of the Ligonier Valley Study Center. Begun as a result of the common vision of an interdenominational group of lay persons and clergy, the Center was designated to be a resource facility for the Christian community in Western Pennsylvania and it was expected that a resident study program would develop involving pastors and other Christian leaders from this locale. We have been pleasantly surprised to welcome people from all over the continent and overseas as well, and these have been a cross section of the Christian church involving students, adult couples, business people, housewives, pastors, missionaries, professional people and retired persons. Expecting that our on-site program would be the mainstay of our work, we have been amazed to see a multiplication of our ministry through audio and color video tape, and through the publication of books by R.C. Sproul. These beginning years have been exciting to say the least!

Our purpose initially was to provide Biblical and theological training that was more than what is normally offered in the local church, but less than what could be obtained in a formal academic program (which is often inaccessible to people because of the time and money commitment involved). This purpose has been fulfilled to a large extent, and in addition . . . we have been pleased that over 20 colleges and universities have accepted work done at Ligonier for academic credit, and the list keeps growing.

In view of the history and development of our ministry, and as a result of careful thinking and planning with respect to the future, we have recently stated our purpose as follows: **TO BE A RESOURCE CENTER FOR LIFE-LONG CHRISTIAN EDUCATION.** We firmly believe that God calls all of us to a lifetime of growing in knowledge of the things He has revealed about Himself. All of us, therefore, need to be involved in life-long Christian education. We are anxious to see what the next six years have in store as we address ourselves to this stated purpose.

In our first year of operation we received 169 resident students and our total lecture attendance was about 3,280 (accurate figures were not kept). This past year we took in nearly 800 resident students and total lecture attendance exceeded 18,000 . . . we began in faith having been promised financial help from three churches and a few dozen people. Today forty some churches underwrite 19% or our budget, over 400 individuals underwrite 41% of our budget. The balance is covered by student fees and some foundation grants. Over 60% of our program involves adults, the balance includes students who have not yet finished their preparation for their life's vocation. The number of people purchasing our tapes and renting our tapes through our loan library system is growing rapidly, and we know that many tapes going out are utilized by Sunday School classes and home Bible Study groups and shared liberally abroad so no accurate estimate of total exposure through tape can be made. How grateful we are for this record of growth as we celebrate our sixth birthday!

First-year issue of *Tabletalk*, featuring staff photo, September 1, 1977

SUMMIT REPORT

On October 26, 1978, at the Hyatt Regency O'Hare, ICBI convened its Summit Conference on biblical inerrancy. There were 268 participants on hand to take part in three days of rigorous meetings. The participants came from a variety of backgrounds and represented many diverse works and places. There was representation from 34 seminaries, 33 colleges and other schools, 41 churches, and 38 interdenominational Christian works. Eleven different countries were represented, including Africa and India. While our backgrounds were diverse, our goals were common. We all hold to the absolute authority, integrity, and full inerrancy of God's word, and we came together to forge out a statement which would state succinctly and clearly what we mean by biblical inerrancy. A remarkable spirit of unity and anticipation marked the Summit which culminated in signing the finished statement on Saturday. Those who were present were deeply moved and went from that place rejoicing in what God had done.

Lives were changed and hearts knitted together at this conference. Many participants commented on the significant impact the conference had on their lives. One such comment was made by David A. Barnes, Associate European Director, Greater Europe Mission: "Having been at many conferences on missions, evangelism and church affairs, I can say very simply that this conference has been the most significant of all for me coming at a moment which is strategic in my own personal ministry as well as in the History of the Church."

The conference had three major goals: 1) the authoritative preaching from God's Word; 2) grapling with problems concerning inerrancy; and 3) defining inerrancy.

SUMMIT SERMON SERIES

The preaching from God's Word on His Word took place during the six plenary sessions. Entitled *"Great Sermons on the Bible,"* the speakers and messages were as follows:

1. **Edmund P. Clowney**
   CHRIST IN ALL SCRIPTURE

Signing the Statement. left to right: James M. Boice, Edmund P. Clowney (standing) R. C. Sproul, James I. Packer, Earl D. Radmacher, Harold W. Hoehner.

2. **James I. Packer**
   A LAMP IN A DARK PLACE
3. **Robert D. Preus**
   SCRIPTURE: GOD'S WORD AND GOD'S POWER
4. **James M. Boice**
   THE MARKS OF THE CHURCH
5. **W. A. Criswell**
   WHAT HAPPENS WHEN I TEACH THE BIBLE AS LITERALLY TRUE
6. **R. C. Sproul**
   HATH GOD SAID

SUMMIT PAPERS

There were 14 major papers prepared for and presented at the Summit, addressing some of the key problem areas involving inerrancy. The papers were mailed to the participants prior to the Summit to give them adequate time to critique them. During the paper sessions at the Summit, each author presented a 20-minute summary of his paper, then answered questions and comments from the participant for the remaining 30 minutes of the session. The papers presented were as follows:

1. **John W. Wenham**
   "CHRIST'S VIEW OF SCRIPTURE"
2. **Edwin A. Blum**
   "THE APOSTLES' VIEW OF SCRIPTURE"
3. **Gleason L. Archer**
   "ALLEGED ERRORS AND DISCREPANCIES IN THE ORIGINAI MANUSCRIPTS OF THE BIBLE'
4. **J. Barton Payne**
   "HIGHER CRITICISM AND BIBLICAL INERRANCY"
5. **Walter C. Kaiser, Jr.**
   "LEGITIMATE HERMENEUTICS'
6. **Greg L. Bahnsen**
   "THE INERRANCY OF THE AUTOGRAPHA"

Continued Page 2

Signing of the Chicago Statement on Biblical Inerrancy, 1978

John Gerstner, 1980

The Ligonier Ministries Board, Dora Hillman and R. C. Sproul seated, 1982

In front of the camera, 1982

R. C. Sproul, 1982

At work, 1983

In the recording studio, 1983

R. C. and Vesta Sproul on the Martin and Katie Luther stools,
the Black Cloister, Wittenberg, Germany, 2009

Preaching at Saint Andrew's Chapel, Sanford, Florida, 2009

In the recording studio, 2011

At the chalkboard, 2012

Lunch with Reformation Bible College students, 2013

At the recording of *Glory to the Holy One*,
the Bastyr Chapel, Kenmore, Washington, 2014

Speaking at Ligonier National Conference, Orlando, Florida, 2014

R. C. and Vesta, 2014

Sagan communicated not so much to fellow scientists but to laypeople, to the common man. He was able to present complex ideas in a clear and simple way without being simplistic and without distortion. R. C. always saw that as the singular trait of a great teacher. You can oversimplify something, and you can certainly reduce complex ideas or arguments in a way that distorts. It was R. C.'s goal not to teach other professional theologians or not to write for other professional theologians or for the guild. R. C. loved theology, and he did not want it be an exclusive club. He wanted the laity to be part of the discussion. This was true from the day the Ligonier Valley Study Center first opened. It was true from his very first book. And it was true from the very first conference. R. C. saw this in Sagan. He admired it in Sagan—though he vehemently disagreed with Sagan.

R. C. sent Sagan a letter, and Sagan replied. This led to a time of correspondence between the two. R. C. kept pressing him on the one issue to which Sagan could not give an adequate account. What was there before the cosmos began? R. C. asked Sagan, "What happened before the Big Bang?" Sagan replied, "I don't want to go there."

All of this led to R. C.'s 1993 book *Not a Chance*. In his introduction to R. C. at the 1994 National Conference, Ravi Zacharias mentioned that what sets R. C. apart is the blending of philosophy and theology.[4] *Not a Chance* provided for that blend to address the history of science and scientists on the crucial question of the origin of the universe. In the process, R. C. circled back to the themes he so enjoyed: the cosmological argument; Aquinas's "Five Ways," especially the argument from necessity (necessary being); and the doctrine of God's self-existence (aseity) and eternality.[5] R. C., in the end, makes a direct argument against the naturalism of modern science. The theory holds that before the Big Bang

---

4   Ravi Zacharias, introduction of R. C. Sproul, "Who Is Our Commander?," Ligonier National Conference, Orlando, Florida, 1994.

5   R. C. Sproul, *Not a Chance: The Myth of Chance in Modern Science and Cosmology* (Grand Rapids, MI: Baker, 1993), see esp. pages 167–92.

there was nothing, which is to say that out of nothing, everything came. R. C. saw that as patently absurd. To hold such a view, he argued, not only jeopardizes theology but also logic and science itself.

In addition to the books and the RTS teaching, R. C. kept up a rigorous travel schedule.

2:53 a.m., September 22, 1993

In September of 1993, R. C. and Vesta traveled to Chattanooga to speak, then to Memphis. From Memphis they took the train to New Orleans, where they boarded the eastbound Sunset Limited for an overnight trip back to Florida. They were in a sleeper car, the very last of the eleven cars of the train. They had fallen asleep as the train raced across the bayous of Alabama at 70 mph. Moments before the train approached the bridge over Big Bayou Canot, a string of barges two across and three deep, in the fog, bumped into one of the railroad bridge supports, knocking the track slightly more than three feet out of line. The train hit the misalignment at 2:53 a.m. The first two locomotives flew 150 feet into the air, slamming deep into the muddy bank. When the first locomotive went into the ground, the force decoupled it from the second locomotive, which twisted and then exploded. Passengers who witnessed the immediate aftermath spoke of flames shooting 70 feet into the air. Four cars went into the bayou, two of them submerged in the 25 feet of water. The remaining five cars perched precariously on the bridge. Stewards helped the passengers, including R. C. and Vesta, disembark from those five cars on the bridge and make it safely to the back of the train. R. C. recalls what he saw:

> From our vantage point at the rear of the train, the scene before us was almost surrealistic. Dense fog mixed with clouds of smoke rose from the swamp. The pillar of flames was still visible on the right side of the train. I could see the ray of a boat's searchlight eerily piercing the fog and smoke, and I could make out the form of train cars protruding

from the water at a strange angle. I had no idea that more cars were submerged beneath them. Scores of people were milling around by the tracks, many with blankets. I don't know how many people had survived the water, but it was certainly more than fifty. None of us realized the full gravity of the moment. There were no shrieks of pain or panic among the survivors. There was no realization that so many people had been killed. Those who perished died in the first minutes after the crash, entrapped in the submerged cars.[6]

Five of the eighteen crew were killed. Forty-two of the 202 passengers were killed. It was, and remains, the deadliest crash in the history of Amtrak. When the Sprouls arrived back home in Orlando, there was a camera crew and reporters waiting for them. They asked R. C., "Why do you think your life was spared?" R. C. said he didn't know, and added, "We have certainly experienced afresh the tender mercy of God and we are profoundly grateful for His providential care."[7] R. C. recalled the train wreck in his 1996 book on the doctrine of providence, *The Invisible Hand*. He ended that book with these words: "The Providence of God is our fortress, our shield, and our very great reward. It is what provides courage and perseverance for His saints."[8] All of life comes back to the doctrine of God.

"Evangelicals and Catholics Together"

In addition to the books and speaking around the country, R. C. was planning and speaking at Ligonier conferences. The First Ligonier National Conference was held in 1988. In those early years, the usual suspects showing up on the speaker list were Chuck Colson and J. I. Packer. These were all friends of R. C.'s. These friendships were about to be tested.

The clouds started to form in the friendship with Colson in 1991, when Colson sent R. C. the manuscript for his book *The Body: Being Light in*

6 R. C. Sproul, *The Invisible Hand: Do All Things Really Work for Good?* (Dallas: Word, 1996), 151–52.
7 Sproul, *The Invisible Hand*, 154–55.
8 Sproul, *The Invisible Hand*, 210.

Darkness. Colson had made it a practice to send all his manuscripts to R. C. for theological review. R. C. was concerned, based on the draft, that Colson "did not quite understand the issues with Roman Catholic theology."[9] R. C. even sent Colson some tapes of a teaching series he had done on Roman Catholicism. Colson listened to the tapes, but he made no changes to the manuscript. It was the last manuscript he sent to R. C.

At about the same time, Colson had forged a friendship with John Richard Neuhaus. Neuhaus was a Lutheran minister who had gained significant attention through his 1984 book, *The Naked Public Square*. The old New England town square had a church on one side and the town hall on the other, the point being that religion and the institutional church played a significant role in public life. Secularism and strict separationists of church and state denuded the public square by exiling religion from public life. Neuhaus advocated for a robust religious presence in civil society. A civil society absolutely depends on it.

In 1990 Neuhaus left the Lutheran Church for the Roman Catholic Church. He continued his activist work on such issues as bioethics, euthanasia, and abortion, very critical issues in the 1990s in Washington DC and across the nation. Colson found Neuhaus to be a brilliant cobelligerent. Francis Schaeffer had used that term, *cobelligerent*, in the previous decade. *Cobelligerency* means, as the adage expresses, the enemy of my enemy is my friend. The enemy here is the worldview and ethic of secularism and naturalism. Schaeffer's 1979 book, coauthored with C. Everett Koop, *Whatever Happened to the Human Race?*, gained significant attention and gave cause for people to reach out to Schaeffer from all points on the theological compass. As Schaeffer battled against euthanasia and abortion and for human dignity and pro-life issues, he found common cause with many Roman Catholic theologians. They, with Aquinas firmly behind them, stressed natural law theory and were rather active around Washington DC on these very same issues. Francis

---

9 "Sproul Memoirs," session 7, recorded 2013, Ligonier Ministries, Sanford, Florida.

Schaeffer felt that the stakes were so high for culture on these natural-law, or common-grace, issues that he could join forces with them.

This was first-wave cobelligerency. There was no discussion of issues of soteric or saving grace; only the discussion of common-grace issues. Schaeffer knew where he stood on the doctrine of salvation, and he knew where Roman Catholicism stood—God had used him to convert many Roman Catholics to the discovery of justification by faith alone. But strictly in matters of common grace, evangelicals and Roman Catholics could be cobelligerents. In fact, the fuller context of Schaeffer's coining of the term was "cobelligerents, not allies." You can campaign on a single issue, like abortion, without having to say anything about any other issue. That's how Schaeffer preferred it.

The second wave of cobelligerency went past common grace and began to think not in terms of cobelligerents, but, to use Schaeffer's language, as allies. This is the Colson-Neuhaus wave that eventuated in the document "Evangelicals and Catholics Together" (ECT), unveiled on March 29, 1994. The document was primarily the work of Colson and Neuhaus, and of the two, Neuhuas was the significantly more trained theologian. Prominent Roman Catholics also involved in drafting the final version include Peter Kreeft, Michael Novak, George Weigel, and Avery Dulles. The Evangelical side included J. I. Packer, Bill Bright, and Os Guinness—all with varying degrees of association with R. C.

R. C., however, did not see this coming. Just prior to the release of ECT, R. C. said that the evangelical church is in a crisis, and "we're in a war," meaning the culture war, which was making inroads in the church. R. C. then added, "And nothing encourages me more than to be with men and women of valor. When the battle gets bloody, I want Jim Packer . . . in my foxhole."[10] During the question and answer session, someone asked R. C. if he and Packer ever disagreed. R. C. couldn't think of a single time, so he replied no.

10 Zacharias, "Who Is Our Commander?"

R. C. was in his makeshift office in the locker room of the country club he belonged to. As an early riser, he would get in a quick round of golf just as the sun was coming up; then he'd write in the locker room, where he occupied a full corner and four lockers containing his books. His secretary could reach him on the pay phone. A lot of his books from the mid-1980s onward were written from his locker room office. Eventually the club remodeled the locker room and effectively evicted R. C. He then went to Steak 'n Shake, open 24 hours a day, to write. He sketched book outlines, lecture ideas, even letters, on the back of Steak 'n Shake paper place mats. But back in March of 1994, R. C. was still using his locker room office.

Joel Belz of *World* magazine was ready to break the story of ECT. He wanted to get R. C.'s take on the document. Mentioning that it was the work of Colson and Neuhaus, Belz called R. C.'s secretary, who gave him the pay phone number. Belz read some of the key passages from ECT over the phone to R. C. It was the first R. C. had heard of it. "I was shocked," he said. Then he added, "That's a betrayal of the Reformation. Worse than that, that's a betrayal of the gospel and a betrayal of Christ."[11]

R. C. called Colson that afternoon. Colson told him that Packer had reviewed it, found it acceptable, and signed it. That was enough for Colson. R. C. then called Packer and relayed to Packer the deficiencies with the statement. R. C. recalls that Packer responded by telling R. C., "Yes, I see the problem. Perhaps I shouldn't have signed it." R. C. wrote it down and told Packer that he would relay that to Colson. R. C. then called Colson back and read the comments that Packer had just made to him. Colson was not pleased.

James Montgomery Boice, who had helped to establish the Alliance of Confessing Evangelicals (ACE), of which Packer was a council member, called for a meeting with Packer to discuss justification and specifically Packer's view of ECT in light of ACE's stance. Packer told Boice in that

11 "Sproul Memoirs," session 9, recorded 2014, Ligonier Ministries, Sanford, Florida.

meeting that justification by faith is the small print of the gospel. Boice said no to that, saying instead that it is the bold print of the gospel.[12] After the meeting, Packer was no longer a council member of ACE.

These ruptures were capturing significant attention. Packer wrote a two-part editorial in the pages of *Christianity Today* magazine in December of 1994, under the title "Why I Signed It."

A closed-door meeting was called, held in the office of D. James Kennedy at Coral Ridge Presbyterian Church in Fort Lauderdale, Florida. Present were R. C., John MacArthur, Michael Horton, John Ankerberg, and Kennedy as nonsigners and critics of ECT, and Bill Bright, Chuck Colson, and Packer as its advocates. Joseph Stowell and John Woodbridge attended as moderators. Colson started the meeting by stressing the need for unity, noting the importance of staying together as brothers. R. C. noted Colson's belief in the possibility of unity between evangelicals and Roman Catholics, as championed by ECT. R. C. did not share that belief, stating the significance of the difference, a difference which makes the question of unity a difficult one.

R. C. then engaged Packer on the question of justification by faith alone, stating that it is essential to the gospel, while Packer claimed it is central. R. C. said "essential"; Packer said "central." All sitting around the table affirmed justification by faith, but not all would say it is essential.

Then the conversation turned to imputation. Again, R. C., MacArthur, and Horton were of one mind on the position that imputation is essential to the doctrine of justification by faith, versus the Roman Catholic understanding of infusion. ECT left imputation out of the conversation about the gospel, which R. C. said cannot be done. In the end, they disagreed on all these points but still regarded each other as brothers. It was reported, however, that they had reconciled all their differences. R. C. described the whole affair as the most difficult time in his life. He had truly enjoyed his friendship with Colson and genuinely

---

12 R. C. Sproul recounts this conversation in *Faith Alone: The Evangelical Doctrine of Justification* (Grand Rapids, MI: Baker, 1995), 183.

appreciated his foxhole companion Packer, but ECT cost those two friendships.

At the same time, R. C. was reconsidering his time and position at Orlando's Reformed Theological Seminary, given the pace and pressure of work at Ligonier. By 1994 the RTS Orlando campus was five years old and thriving. He felt that it was time to move. He told the then-president of RTS that he would step away from his professor role but wanted to continue teaching one or two one-week doctor of ministry courses. The RTS president asked R. C. if it had to do with ECT. The other faculty at RTS had not signed ECT, but they had not come out in opposition to it either.

By 1994 RTS had a good relationship with Campus Crusade, which had moved its headquarters to Orlando and relied on RTS for training for many staff. Bill Bright, head of Campus Crusade, was a visible and vocal participant in ECT, which complicated things. Additionally, faculty and administration at RTS did not like to see the rift between R. C. and Packer, and they were concerned about its effects on the broader Reformed community. R. C. assured the RTS president that the decision to step away was not prompted by ECT. Of course, RTS's reluctance to criticize ECT did not help R. C. find extra resolve to stay on. But, again, he assured the president that the decision was independent of the controversy. When the president announced to RTS students and faculty that R. C. would be stepping away, he told them that it was because of ECT.[13]

The Missing Doctrine

R. C. believed then, and over the years his belief only grew stronger and deeper, that ECT was a grave error that caused serious damage to the mission of the gospel and had a negative impact on the American evangelical church—the effects of which erupted, again, during the New Perspective on Paul controversy. The rupture in friendships was one thing;

13 "Sproul Memoirs," session 9.

injury to the gospel was another, and this was what truly saddened R. C. He countered by writing a book, *Faith Alone: The Evangelical Doctrine of Justification.* R. C. notes that ECT declared, "Evangelicals and Catholics are brothers and sisters in Christ. We have not chosen one another, just as we have not chosen Christ. He has chosen us, and he has chosen us to be his together."[14] R. C. observes, "It is this assertion, so central to ECT, that provokes serious concern about Evangelicals who endorse this document and concern about their commitment to the essential character of justification by faith alone."[15]

R. C. also calls attention to this statement and the subsequent list from ECT:

> We note some of the differences and disagreements that must be addressed more fully and candidly in order to strengthen between us a relationship of trust in obedience to truth. Among points of difference in doctrine, worship, practice, and piety that are frequently thought to divide us are these:
>
> - The church as an integral part of the Gospel or the church as a communal consequence of the Gospel.
> - The church as visible communion or invisible fellowship of true believers.
> - The sole authority of Scripture (*sola scriptura*) or Scripture as authoritatively interpreted in the church.
> - The "soul freedom" of the individual Christian or the magisterium (teaching authority) of the community.
> - The church as local congregation or universal communion.
> - Ministry ordered in apostolic succession or the priesthood of all believers.
> - Sacraments and ordinances as symbols of grace or means of grace.
> - The Lord's Supper as eucharistic sacrifice or memorial meal.

14 "Evangelicals and Catholics Together: The Christian Mission in the Third Millennium," 1994.
15 Sproul, *Faith Alone*, 31.

- Remembrance of Mary and the saints or devotion to Mary and the saints.
- Baptism as sacrament of regeneration or testimony to regeneration.

The curious thing about the list is that justification is missing. R. C. notes, "The list nowhere mentions justification by faith alone. Indeed, justification is not included at all (unless it is hinted at in the veiled issue of sacerdotalism)."[16]

R. C. then notices this:

> The cause of Christ is the cause and mission of the church, which is, first of all, to proclaim the Good News that "God was in Christ reconciling the world to himself, not counting their trespasses against them, and entrusting to us the message of reconciliation" (2 Corinthians 5). To proclaim this Gospel and to sustain the community of faith, worship, and discipleship that is gathered by this Gospel is the first and chief responsibility of the church. All other tasks and responsibilities of the church are derived from and directed toward the mission of the Gospel.[17]

"The glaring problem remains," observes R. C., "What is the Gospel?" He continues, "If Rome denies *sola fide* and if *sola fide* is an essential element of the gospel, then no matter what the authors' intentions, ECT involves a tacit betrayal of the gospel."[18] R. C. further writes, "Charles Colson is convinced that evangelicals who participated in drafting ECT gave nothing away and did not compromise the gospel. Others, including myself, believe that the document seriously compromises the gospel and negotiates away the very heart of historical Evangelicalism."[19] R. C. then adds, "The light of the biblical gospel is more important than historical alliances. It is far more important than any manifestation of cobelligerency

16 Sproul, *Faith Alone*, 41.
17 "Evangelicals and Catholics Together."
18 Sproul, *Faith Alone*, 44.
19 Sproul, *Faith Alone*, 47.

on social and political matters. The gospel is the veritable power to save."[20] Near the end of the book, R. C. says that as a result of ECT, "old alliances have crumbled and former allies have become opponents."[21] There is a great deal that lies behind these sentences.

Imputationists

A particular point that is missing in this discussion from the larger missing doctrine of justification by faith is imputation. R. C. loved that Mike Horton used the analogy of chocolate chip cookies to explain the importance of imputation. Horton said if you have all the ingredients for chocolate chip cookies but leave out the chocolate chips, then you don't have chocolate chip cookies. Imputation is to the doctrine of salvation what chocolate chips are to chocolate chip cookies. The crucial difference between the Reformation view of justification by faith and the Roman Catholic view has everything to do with two things. First, the word *sola*; second, the difference between imputation and infusion. To help us understand infusion, R. C. takes us back to the Council of Trent, which he studied in depth with Gerstner while in seminary. R. C. notes that chapter 16 of Trent declares:

> For since Christ Jesus Himself, as the head into the members and as the vine into the branches (John 15:1f), continually infuses strength into those justified, which strength always precedes, accompanies and follows their good works, and without which they could not in any manner be pleasing and meritorious before God, we must believe that nothing further is wanting to those justified to prevent them from being considered to have, by those very works that have been done in God, fully satisfied the divine law according to the state of this life and to have truly merited eternal life.[22]

20 Sproul, *Faith Alone*, 48.
21 Sproul, *Faith Alone*, 183.
22 Cited in Sproul, *Faith Alone*, 125.

The idea is that we are "meritorious," righteous before God, by both justification and infusion. Christ's strength is infused, it fills us, and then we are enabled to do good works. This is salvation by cooperation. God works and God infuses us to do good works. Salvation is by faith *and* works, not by faith *alone*.

Infusion is about cooperation. Imputation, on the other hand, is the work of one. Imputation is an accounting term. It means to put on one's account. There is actually a double imputation. Our sin is imputed to Christ. He takes on our sin, debt and penalty. Ultimately, our penalty is the wrath of God. The wrath of God is poured out upon Christ instead of upon us. Christ bears the awful brunt of the most severe punishment fathomable. Then Christ gives us his righteousness. Luther spoke of righteousness as "alien righteousness," as outside of us. It is *extra nos*, outside or beyond us. Francis Turretin, a true favorite theologian of R. C.'s, put it this way:

> The gospel teaches that what could not be found in us and was to be sought in another, could be found nowhere else than in Christ, the God-man (*theanthropo*); who taking upon himself the office of surety most fully satisfied the justice of God by his perfect obedience and thus brought to us an everlasting righteousness by which alone we can be justified before God; in order that covered and clothed with that garment as though it were of our firstborn (like Jacob), we may obtain under it the eternal blessing of our heavenly Father.[23]

This is what Trent Canon 11 has to say about imputation: "If anyone says that men are justified either by the sole imputation of the justice of Christ or by the sole remission of sins . . . let him be anathema." Trent cursed those who would cling to Christ's righteousness alone for salvation. The imputed righteousness of Christ is the ground of our salvation. On that statement Roman Catholics and evangelicals are not together, and that statement is the gospel.

23 Cited in Sproul, *Faith Alone*, 103.

R. C. points out near the end of the book that the issue is not whether "there are saved Christians in the Roman Catholic Church, believers who cling to the biblical Christ, who believe the biblical gospel, and trust solely in Christ for their salvation," for "all agree that there are."[24]

The issue is the content of the gospel. What is the gospel that is preached and set down in confessional standards? On that, a wide gulf exists between Roman Catholicism and evangelicalism in the vein of the Reformation. In the wake of that closed-door meeting in Kennedy's office, Michael Horton suggested the term *imputationist*. The term *evangelicalism* had become rather elastic and inclusive, as had the term *Christian*. *Imputationist* points to the heart of the theological definition of those who seek to proclaim a biblically faithful gospel.

J. I. Packer's biographer, Leland Ryken, suggests that Packer's involvement in ECT was due to his "ecumenism."[25] Ryken also observes that ECT was not the first time Packer found himself on the other side of a divide. In 1970 he and D. Martyn Lloyd-Jones divided over Packer's Anglo-Catholic ecumenical efforts and Packer's contribution to the book *Growing into Union.*

Those opposed to ECT were just as committed to the unity of the church as those who were for it. The question was, what is unity centered upon? The Nicene Creed speaks of the "one, holy, catholic, apostolic church." That last word, *apostolic*, is a reference to the teaching of the apostles, which is to say, the content of the gospel—what Paul calls the "good deposit" in 2 Timothy 1–2. The *depositum fide* (deposit of faith) was to be taught, handed down, guarded, and contended for (Jude 4).[26]

This contending for the "faith once for all delivered to the saints" has played out in many church controversies over the centuries. In the early church, the controversies and heresies centered on the person of Christ:

24 Sproul, *Faith Alone*, 185–86.
25 Leland Ryken, *J. I. Packer: An Evangelical Life* (Wheaton, IL: Crossway, 2015), 408.
26 The footnote in the *Reformation Study Bible* at Jude 3 relays, "Here 'faith' indicates the doctrinal content of the message taught by the apostles and held in common by all Christians. . . . Christianity includes an authoritative body of belief given by God to the church through the apostles."

His true humanity, His true deity, and the unity of His person in two natures. Once the church wrangled with these doctrines at the Nicene (325), Constantinopolitan (381), and Chalcedonian (451) Councils, the orthodox view emerged. After the Chalcedonian Creed (after 451, that is), affirming that Christ is truly man and truly God, two natures in one person (the hypostatic union), meant you were biblically faithful and orthodox. To deny the Chalcedonian formula meant you were outside the bounds of unity of the true church. Or in the words of the early church, you were a heretic.

Nicea and Chalcedon were clarifying moments on the Bible's teaching—the "whole counsel of God"—on the person of Christ. The Reformation was such a clarifying moment as well. Theologians speak of the formal principle and the material principle of the Reformation; both were the divide between the Roman Catholic Church and those who "protested." The formal principle deals with the question of authority. The Reformers planted the flag on *sola Scriptura*, Scripture alone as the church's authority. Rome responded at Trent formally, but also in the debates with Luther, by affirming *scriptura et tradition*, Scripture and tradition, as the authority. The material principle concerns the gospel. The Reformers heralded *sola fide*, faith alone. Rome responded with *fide et opera*, faith and works. To put a fine point on it, the Reformers are defined by the word *sola*, whereas Rome is defined by *et*. But there is a wide gulf between those two words and formulations.

As those who live post-Chalcedon are defined as part of the true church by affirming the Chalcedonian Creed, so, too, those who live post-Reformation must also take a stand either with or against *sola Scriptura*, *sola fide, sola gratia, solus Christus*, and *soli Deo gloria*. R. C., and the others who stood with him on this battlefield, believed that unity must be around the gospel—around the person and work of Christ—as defined by the ancient creeds and the *solas* of the Reformation. R. C. took this to be the litmus test for the biblically faithful proclamation of the gospel, the faithful teaching of the whole counsel of God. To deny the ancient creeds or the *solas* is to betray the gospel; to downplay the *solas*, or to skirt them, is equally a betrayal.[27]

R. C. was glad to come alongside Jim Boice and others in writing and promoting the Cambridge Declaration in April 1996. As an effort to "recover the historic Christian faith," this document was written because:

> Today the light of the Reformation has been significantly dimmed. The consequence is that the word "evangelical" has become so inclusive as to have lost its meaning. We face the peril of losing the unity it has taken centuries to achieve. Because of this crisis and because of our love of Christ, his gospel and his church, we endeavor to assert anew our commitment to the central truths of the Reformation and of historic evangelicalism. These truths we affirm not because of their role in our traditions, but because we believe that they are central to the Bible.[28]

The Cambridge Declaration is a reaffirmation of the Reformation *solas*. The document refers to *sola fide* as "the chief article," declaring:

> Justification is by grace alone through faith alone because of Christ alone. This is the article by which the church stands or falls. Today this article is often ignored, distorted or sometimes even denied by leaders, scholars and pastors who claim to be evangelical. Although fallen human nature has always recoiled from recognizing its need for Christ's imputed righteousness, modernity greatly fuels the fires of this discontent with the biblical Gospel. We have allowed this discontent to dictate the nature of our ministry and what it is we are preaching. . . .
>
> We reaffirm that justification is by grace alone through faith alone because of Christ alone. In justification Christ's righteousness is imputed to us as the only possible satisfaction of God's perfect justice.

27 When R. C. founded Reformation Bible College, he wrote vows for the board members and faculty to recite and subscribe to on an annual basis. One of the vows is to affirm ancient creeds (Apostles', Nicene, and Chalcedonian creeds), the five *solas* of the Reformation, and the consensus of the Reformed confessions.

28 "The Cambridge Declaration," April 20, 1996, Alliance of Confessing Evangelicals.

We deny that justification rests on any merit to be found in us, or upon the grounds of an infusion of Christ's righteousness in us, or that an institution claiming to be a church that denies or condemns *sola fide* can be recognized as a legitimate church.[29]

The Cambridge Declaration was prompted by ECT and other developments in the American evangelical church. It was the product of a group of men who cared deeply about theology and the theological identity of the church. Sometimes there is an assumption that those driven by theology are less concerned with unity. That is not true of R. C., Boice, MacArthur, and others who took a stand against ECT.

It was not as though one side of ECT was for unity and one side was for division. Each side defined unity differently. There was no doubt R. C. thought that ECT had everything to do with the Reformation debates. In fact, he saw ECT as a "same song, second verse" of some of those debates. He devoted a chapter of *Faith Alone* to Luther, retracing his journey from the Wittenberg door to Worms.

The Wild Boar

Martin Luther made the 500-kilometer trek from Wittenberg to Worms by wagon in 1521. As he passed through Saxony's towns and hamlets on the journey, he received a hero's welcome. That changed when he entered Worms on April 6. It would be Luther *contra mundum*. His friends pleaded with Luther not to go, as they did not trust the outcome. R. C. said, "You know what he replied? 'If there are as many devils as there are red tiles on the roofs of those buildings,' he said, 'I am going to go.'"[30] R. C. added, "If you have ever been over there, you would see that every house roof was made with red tiles."[31]

Luther appeared at the Diet of Worms before Charles V and other dignitaries, papal legates and church officials, and the host of demons

29 "Cambridge Declaration."
30 "R. C. Sproul and Bainton's *Here I Stand*," *Open Book* podcast, May 17, 2018, season 1, episode 10.
31 Sproul, "R. C. Sproul and Bainton's *Here I Stand*."

on April 16 and 17, 1521. It was on the seventeenth that he delivered his famous "Here I Stand" speech. What led Luther to this point in time and to this place?

R. C. goes back to 1505 and the thunderstorm that sent Luther into the monastery. R. C. points out: "Luther suffered uncommon anguish as he sought desperately for peace in his soul."[32] Luther used the German word *anfechtungen* to express these deep soul anxieties and struggles. Luther thought that God had unleashed this lightning storm with the express purpose of taking his life. R. C. notes, "In terror he cried out, "St. Anne help me! I will become a monk.""[33] As Roland Bainton observed tongue-in-cheek in one of R. C.'s favorite books, *Here I Stand*, God kept his end of the bargain, and Luther kept his. In the monastery, "five years later Luther suffered another spiritual crisis. His personal odyssey of faith reached its nadir during his pilgrimage to Rome" in 1510.[34] To call it a nadir was an intentional irony. As a devout monk, the pilgrimage to Rome should have been his zenith. Instead it was the opposite.

When Luther arrived in the Holy City, he headed straight to the Scala Sancta, the sacred stairs supposedly leading to the praetorium of Pontius Pilate, relocated to Rome by Constantine the Great as a gift to his pious mother. Pilgrims ascended and descended on their knees, muttering the Lord's Prayer and Hail Marys as they went. When Luther reached the top of the stairs, he uttered, "Who knows if all this is true?"[35] Luther was utterly disillusioned. Then came the events of 1517, the painting of the Sistine Chapel by Michelangelo, the indulgence sale by Tetzel (in order to pay for the Sistine Chapel painting, among many other things), and the showdown with Pope Leo X. In between the 1510 trip to Rome and 1517, Luther was lecturing on Psalms, Roman, Galatians, and Hebrews, then back to Romans again.

32 Sproul, *Faith Alone*, 56.
33 Sproul, *Faith Alone*, 56.
34 Sproul, *Faith Alone*, 56.
35 Martin Luther, cited in Sproul, *Faith Alone*, 56.

R. C. observes, "His preparation for these lectures was formative for his thinking on justification."[36]

R. C. cites this extended selection from Luther to show what great difficulty attended Luther's "discovery" of justification by faith:

> I greatly longed to understand Paul's Epistle to the Romans and nothing stood in the way but that one expression, "the justice of God," because I took it to mean that justice whereby God is just and deals justly in punishing the unjust. My situation was that, although an impeccable monk. I stood before God as a sinner troubled in conscience, and I had no confidence that my merit would assuage him. Therefore I did not love a just and angry God but rather hated and murmured against him. Yet I clung to the dear Paul and had a great yearning to know what he meant.
>
> Night and day I pondered until I saw the connection between the justice of God and the statement that "the just shall live by his faith." Then I grasped that the justice of God is that righteousness by which through grace and sheer mercy God justifies us through faith. Thereupon I felt myself to be reborn and to have gone through open doors to paradise. The whole of Scripture took on a new meaning, and whereas before the "justice of God" had filled me with hate, now it became to me inexpressibly sweet in greater love. This passage of Paul became to me a gate to heaven.[37]

R. C. points out how this discovery and reformed way of thinking about the righteousness of God and about how one obtains it "collided head-on" with the Roman Catholic Church. Tetzel's unprecedented indulgence sale, with the full blessing and imprimatur of Pope Leo X, was, as psychologists would say, the presenting problem. R. C. called it a "crass peddling."[38] The indulgence sale was nothing less than selling forgiveness

---

36 Sproul, *Faith Alone*, 56.
37 Martin Luther, cited in Sproul, *Faith Alone*, 56–57.
38 Sproul, *Faith Alone*, 60.

of sins. Luther could not stand by and watch his church commit such a theological atrocity. He wrote up ninety-five theses for distribution, in Latin, intending a debate with the theologians of the church. He posted the document on the doors of the Castle Church in Wittenberg, likely the most famous doors in all of history.

In the process of challenging Tetzel's indulgence sale, the Ninety-Five Theses raised all sorts of questions regarding Roman Catholic dogma and practice. The Ninety-Five Theses also garnered a lot of readers. It was quickly translated into German and, through the printing press, was "circulated across the entire German nation within barely two weeks."[39]

Luther's original posting of the theses occurred on October 31, 1517, and it triggered a series of events. In April of 1518 Luther presented another set of theses at Heidelberg. In October of 1518 Luther debated Cardinal Cajetan. Then he debated Johann Eck in the disputation at Leipzig in 1519. In the fall of 1520 he wrote his *Three Treatises*. R. C.'s copy is heavily marked. In the margin of the short but powerful *Christian Liberty*, R. C. wrote this note: "discovery of inability." Luther wrote, "Faith alone, without works, justifies, frees, and saves. Here we must point out that the entire Scripture of God is divided into two parts: commandments and promises. . . . [The commandments] are intended to teach man to know himself. That through them he may recognize his inability to do good, and may despair of his own ability."[40]

These sentences, heavily underlined by R. C., present Luther's idea that the law is a "schoolmaster" that points us to Christ. To put it existentially, as Luther does, the law makes us despair over our inability. Therefore, we need a righteousness *extra nos*, outside of us. This stresses, again, the necessity of the doctrine of imputation. Luther was the original imputationist.

In the Papal Bull condemning Luther, Leo X called Luther "a wild boar," trampling underfoot the gospel and threatening the church. Pure irony. Luther was condemned by the church for preaching the gospel.

---

39 Sproul, *Faith Alone*, 61.
40 Martin Luther, *Three Treatises* (Philadelphia: Fortress Press, 1960), 282, using R. C.'s personal copy.

This all came to a head at Worms. On April 6 Luther made his first appearance. He was told to renounce his books and recant his teaching. Luther had hoped for a debate, but instead he was on trial. He asked for time to consider. He was given one day. R. C. picks up the story: "That evening, alone in his room, Luther poured out his heart in prayer. His prayer reveals the soul of a terrified man prostrate before his God, desperately seeking assurance and courage to do the right thing. It was Luther's private Gethsemane."[41] R. C. further notes, "Luther came to Worms in fear and trembling. There was boldness and courage to be sure. But it was a courage required by the piercing fear that haunted the man."[42] R. C. admired Luther, intrigued by this mixture of fear and courage in him. He longed to see the same in himself.

The next day arrived, April 17, 1521. Luther was asked a single question: Will you recant? (*Revoco* in Latin.) In so many lectures and sermons, this word reverberated from R. C. in his deepest voice. To that single question, Luther delivered his famous speech:

> Since your majesty and your lordships ask for a plain answer, I will give you one without horns or teeth. Unless I am convinced by Scriptures or by right reason, for I trust neither in popes, nor in councils, since they have often erred and contradicted themselves—unless I am thus convinced. I neither can nor will recant anything, since it is neither right nor safe to act against conscience. God help me. Amen.[43]

Other versions end with, "Here I stand. I can do no other. God help me. Amen."[44]

Vesta vividly remembers the time R. C. and she led a Ligonier study tour through Luther's Germany. At Worms, the group went to the place where the 1521 diet was held. The building no longer stands, but a plaque

41 Sproul, *Faith Alone*, 53.
42 Sproul, *Faith Alone*, 52.
43 Sproul, *Faith Alone*, 54–55.
44 See Gordon Rupp, *Luther's Progress to the Diet of Worms* (New York: Harper & Row, 1964), 96–97.

on the ground commemorates the spot. R. C. stepped up and from memory recited the speech. It was one of those moments where everyone present realized the full significance of that place and time in the sixteenth century and in the twentieth century as well, as R. C. took his stand on many occasions and in many situations for the uncompromised gospel. Luther was no mere historical figure for R. C. He was as much a mentor as Dr. Gregory or Dr. Gerstner. He was as much a friend as Jim Boice or John MacArthur. R. C. loved Luther, "the wild boar," and he especially appreciated that Worms did not bring him down. As R. C. notes, "The wild boar was loose and nothing would stop him."[45]

New Geneva

R. C. realized how much sway dispensationalism held over the twentieth-century church and also how quickly it spread. As he looked at that, he realized that of the factors that caused the fast and wide spread, "first and foremost was the *Scofield Reference Bible*."[46] This prompted R. C. to see that a study Bible would be a strategic tool to propagate the Reformed faith, "to help influence people in their basic education."[47] While the *Scofield Reference Bible* was the motivation, it was not the model. For the model, R. C. looked back (again) to the Reformers, this time to Calvin's Geneva. As British and Scottish refugees flooded into Geneva during the reign of Bloody Mary (1553–1558), Calvin encouraged them to find some labor and industry while in exile. A number of scholars began work on a new Bible translation. This Bible would come to be groundbreaking for two reasons. First, it was the first English Bible to use verse divisions. The *Stephanus Greek Text* (1546) used verse divisions, but no other English Bible had. Second, the Geneva Bible had annotations at the bottom of the page and sometimes running up the margins. These were study notes.

45 Rupp, *Luther's Progress to the Diet of Worms*, 64.
46 R. C. Sproul, "Remarks on the Fifth Anniversary of Reformation Bible College," 2015.
47 Sproul, "Remarks on the Fifth Anniversary."

The *Geneva Bible* was, in effect, the first study Bible. The New Testament was published in 1557 and the complete Bible in 1560. Though in English and not French, it is called the *Geneva Bible* in honor of the Reformation city where those English scholars labored. It was the Bible of the Puritans, the preferred but not exclusive text for Shakespeare. It was the Bible that the Pilgrims and the New England Puritans had. It was more popular, for some decades at least, than the King James Version of 1611. It had influence.

R. C. had assembled a fine collection of rare books; among them is a 1609 edition of the *Geneva Bible*. In 1995 R. C. served as the general editor for the *New Geneva Study Bible*, in the New King James Version, published by Thomas Nelson. The *New Geneva Study Bible* had extensive notes, lengthy book introductions, and a significant number of short theological articles, many of the latter penned by J. I. Packer. The notes came from a veritable who's who of Reformed biblical scholars from the major Reformed seminaries and colleges. James Boice, Edmund Clowney, Roger Nicole, and Packer served as associate editors.

During the next year, 1996, R. C. released two books aimed at a youth audience, *Ultimate Issues* and *Choosing My Religion*. He also filmed teaching series, again aimed at youth, to go along with the books. They emphasized apologetics, doctrine, and the gospel.

R. C.'s Contribution to the Christian Tradition

Going back to 1973 and extending through the 1980s, R. C. was at the very center of the inerrancy controversy, and, with the help of others, he was leading the charge. ICBI and the Chicago Statement followed the long tradition of linking inerrancy to inspiration. That is to say, the Bible is true because it is God's word. In 1984, R. C. released *Classical Apologetics*. The "classical" in classical apologetics is a reference to both the classical arguments for the existence of God and to the classical theist tradition. R. C.'s name is inextricably linked to the position of

classical apologetics, which is to say that R. C. has taken his place in
the long line of classical theists, stretching back to and including Augustine, Anselm, Aquinas, Luther, Calvin, Turretin, Edwards, Hodge,
and Warfield.

If God tarries and church history continues, the book of R. C.'s that
will likely take the prominent place among church history's classic texts
is *The Holiness of God* from 1985. As demonstrated earlier in chapter 7,
that book set off a whole chain of books on the doctrine of God. If there
was only one thing that R. C. could teach people about who God is, it
would be that God is holy.

Because God is holy, and we are not, we need a righteousness that
is *extra nos*. We need the righteousness of an acceptable substitute who
can not only endure the cup of God's wrath but also meet the absolute
standard of God's pure righteousness. That is what R. C. saw at stake in
the controversies of the 1990s, chief among them being the "Evangelicals
and Catholics Together" document. R. C. is as equally associated with the
five *solas* of the Reformation as he is with inerrancy, as he is with classical
apologetics and classical theism, and as he is with shining a spotlight on
the holiness of God.

All of these emphases and contributions to the church and the Christian tradition circle back to that main driving question that propelled
R. C. to write all those books, speak at all those conferences, and record
all those teaching series: people, in the church and in the culture, need
to know who God is.

Roland Bainton ends his magisterial biography of Luther by connecting the *solas* to the person of God. Bainton writes:

> The God of Luther, as the God of Moses, was the God who inhabits
> the storm clouds and rides on the wings of the wind. At his nod the
> earth trembles, and the people before him are as a drop in the bucket.
> He is a God of majesty and power, inscrutable, terrifying, devastating,
> and consuming in his anger. Yet the All Terrible is the All Merciful too.

"Like as a father pitieth his children, so the Lord . . ." But how shall we know this? In Christ, only in Christ.[48]

In addition to these theological contributions, there are also the contributions of the institutions R. C. founded and helmed. Of course, chief among them is Ligonier Ministries, christened on August 1, 1971. But as the second millennium approached, R. C. would be involved in founding two more institutions, a church and a college.

---

48 Roland Bainton, *Here I Stand: A Life of Martin Luther* (New York: Abingdon-Cokesbury Press, 1950), 385–86.

9

HOLY SPACE, HOLY TIME

Then, in 1997, God did something that I never anticipated.

R. C. SPROUL

DURING THE FINAL DAYS of March 1996, R. C. and Vesta traveled
back to Ligonier for the funeral service of John Gerstner. Gerstner died
on March 24 at the age of eighty-one. Four days later, the service was
held at Pioneer Presbyterian Church in Ligonier, Pennsylvania. David
Kenyon was pastor at the time, the brother of Wynn Kenyon, whose
ordination case served as the catalyst for R. C. to transfer his credentials
to the PCA. Both David and Wynn participated in the service, as did
David Williams. Williams had gone to Pittsburgh Theological Seminary
in order to be a minister. He was unconverted until he met his professor,
Dr. Gerstner, who led him to Christ. R. C. gave a testimonial to the ministry of his beloved mentor. You might recall that R. C. called Gerstner his
"lifeline" through his three years at the predominantly liberal Pittsburgh
Theological Seminary. R. C. started his memoriam by lamenting, "Our
captain has fallen." Of all the relationships R. C. had with mentors and
colleagues, the relationship with Gerstner stands a cut above. They had
their similarities. They had their differences. R. C. growled. Gerstner
growled more. Both were deeply passionate and compassionate. Both
thought Edwards was well worth reading. Both witnessed, up close and

personal, the duplicity and deleteriousness of liberalism. Both labored for the purity of the church and of her worship. Both were committed to theological education. Both loved the local church and "the holy catholic church," in the words of the Apostles' Creed.

While in the Ligonier Valley together—what a *place* that valley had to be to sustain the two of them—they both were at Pioneer Presbyterian Church. Imagine having to preach to R. C. only to find that, when you took your eyes from him, they could end up locked on those of John Gerstner.

When the Sprouls went to Orlando, they were at Orangewood Presbyterian Church. In 1991 they were part of a group that planted St. Paul's Presbyterian (PCA) in Winter Park, Florida. R. C. wrote a play for the new church, *Saint Paul's Play*. In his typical crisp cursive on yellow paper, the play has five acts, complete with stage directions. Paul and Luke are the main characters, alongside a supporting cast. It starts with Luke recalling the adventure he and Paul had in Ephesus. It ends with Paul writing his second letter to Timothy. The curtain falls on Paul, while Luke is left standing on stage for these last lines:

> I was with him that day. Soon afterward the Emperor Nero had Paul executed by beheading with the sword. Today the Apostle Paul is adorned with a crown of righteousness, which crown will surely be given to all who love the appearing of Christ. The Just shall live by faith.
>
> [House lights dim. Luke Exits. Lights come back on.][1]

At the same time he wrote a play, R. C. was appearing in front of a small audience for his teaching sessions, usually teaching eight times a week. These sessions became episodes for teaching series produced by Ligonier and for the radio broadcast *Renewing Your Mind*. Airing for the first time in 1994, there was a uniqueness to *Renewing Your Mind* in

---

1 R. C. Sproul, "Saint Paul's Play," unpublished manuscript, 1994.

the field of Christian radio. Not only was R. C. Calvinist and Reformed, not only did he talk about Aristotle and Aquinas, not only did he use a lot of Latin, but he also used real chalk on a real chalkboard. He even developed a sort of Zoro-like signature move. He would emphatically dot i's and cross t's. And he emphatically ended a sentence with a period. And there were times, like a perfect storm, when he had an "i" to dot, a "t" to cross, and a period to drill into the board. You could hear the dot, slash, DOT. Zoro with a piece of chalk leaving his telltale mark.

It simply sounded different, what R. C. was saying, how he was saying it, and how he was writing it with chalk. It was theater of the mind.

Church Planter

To help him, there was a live audience of about thirty people in the recording studio. There was also a lectern with some notes that he never looked at. And there was the aforementioned chalkboard. R. C. was spending a lot of time in this studio. He was producing teaching series that were both released on *Renewing Your Mind* and produced as teaching series with study guides. In 1997 Ligonier released the rather ambitious *Dust to Glory*. At fifty-seven lectures, this series offers "a panorama of biblical truth." R. C. thought of it as the most important series Ligonier produced. It walks through the Bible, starting with the creation of man, from a handful of dust, in the original creation to the transformation and glorification in the new heavens and the new earth. It spans from Genesis to Revelation and hits all points in between. As R. C. says in the last lines of the fifty-seventh lecture, "Dust to glory, that's the story." R. C. presents this series in such a way that the listener or viewer can connect all the individual episodes of the drama of redemption to the big picture; the listener or viewer can see how all sixty-six books of the Bible fit together.

Some of this same audience were regular visitors to the Sproul home for a Bible study. A group of families within that audience wanted to start a church. They approached R. C., wanting him to be a pastor. He recalls saying to them, "I have my day job."[2] And it was quite a day job. While Ligonier had various presidents, directors, and administrators over the years, R. C. was serving as president at this time, in 1997, and was, of course, the primary teacher. The group persisted. They sent R. C. a letter:

> We the undersigned, along with twelve other families, seek to establish a church in the northwest section of metropolitan Orlando which is faithful to the Westminster Confession of Faith and Reformed theology. We intend to emphasize God-centered worship, dynamic biblical preaching, and the joy of Christian fellowship.
>
> With these distinctives in mind, we are convinced that you are the best man to preside as senior preaching minister. After much prayer and counsel, we are hereby issuing you a call to that post.

The letter is signed by Guy Rizzo, David Buchman, Chuck Tovey, and Walter Kerr. As they point out in the letter, Saint Andrew's Chapel and R. C. were a great fit. R. C. accepted and took the post.

R. C., looking back on this moment years later, said it this way: "Then in 1997, God did something I never anticipated: he placed me in the position of preaching weekly as a leader of a congregation of His people—St. Andrew's in Sanford, Florida."[3]

R. C. noted that "when God called me into full-time Christian ministry, he called me to the academy."[4] He served the people of God from behind the lectern mostly. Then God called him to stand behind the pulpit weekly. It became a true joy for him. "I have come to love the task of the local minister," he testified.[5] R. C. became a church planter.

Saint Andrew's Chapel first met in the recording studio. R. C. called it a chapel because it was small, and R. C. anticipated that it would remain small. Vesta pointed out that Saint Andrew's came from Andrew

---

2 "Sproul Memoirs," session 10, recorded 2015, Ligonier Ministries, Sanford, Florida.
3 R. C. Sproul, *Romans: St. Andrew's Expositional Commentary* (Wheaton, IL: Crossway, 2009), 11.
4 Sproul, *Romans*, 11.
5 Sproul, *Romans*, 11.

the apostle—not from the fabled St. Andrew's golf course in Scotland. Though not as prominent as the other apostles, Vesta explained why his name was chosen: "Andrew was always bringing people to Christ. That's why we wanted to name it Saint Andrew's."[6] Andrew brought his brother, Peter, to Christ, and of all the disciples, the boy with loaves and fish approached Andrew.

The studio contained church attendees for about a month. Then they met in a theater. Next, they were offered a large space of a private school in Sanford. They were there for two years. Visitors thought they recognized somebody in the choir. It was Vesta. She was as happy singing as R. C. was preaching. Outgrowing the Page School, they purchased a parcel of land off Orange Boulevard in Sanford, Florida, broke ground, began to build, and dedicated the building in 2001. Outside is masonry with such architectural features as arches and columns. Inside, a stained wood ceiling and beams come to a center peak over a stained-glass rose window. The chandeliers add to the Gothic structure. Soon enough they outgrew that sanctuary and went to two services. One of the members, Jack, had been led to Christ by his neighbor, Gary, an "Andrew" of St. Andrew's. Jack joined the church and helped serve cookies during the fellowship hour. Saint Andrew's made it a practice from the early days of offering coffee and tea and cookies for the fellowship time in between services. Of course, they would have chocolate chip cookies. Jack gave R. C. his quota, sometimes sneaking in an extra.

Even with two services, they outgrew the sanctuary and facilities. They learned from Seminole County that they had maximized the impervious surface footprint for the property for their site. They were denied a permit for an expansion. They were not allowed, R. C. recalled, "to add a single brick."[7] Meanwhile, on the other side of Orange Boulevard, bordering Wayside Avenue, a new property became available. It had two private residences on adjacent parcels. An undeveloped portion of the land would

6 Stephen Nichols with Vesta Sproul, personal interview, September 5, 2018.
7 "Sproul Memoirs," session 10.

become the site of Saint Andrew's Chapel; the large Spanish-Mediterranean, "Florida style" home would house the administrative offices for Ligonier Ministries. Two satellite buildings would also hold Ligonier staff. All that needed to be done now was to build a church building.

Oaken Doors under a Gothic Arch

A cathedral rose out of the dirt and sand in central Florida. It has a steeple and a bell tower, with a carillon. It has a cloister walk, both in keeping with the cathedral Gothic style and for protection from the Florida rains. It has quadrafoils and arches, pillars, chevettes, and columns. It has buttresses and pinnacles. The front doors are made of oak and installed under a Gothic arch. "The door was made of heavy oak with a Gothic arch," reads a sentence from the early pages of *The Holiness of God*, as R. C. recalls his midnight trek and entering the chapel of Westminster College.[8] There is the narthex, with stained-glass windows on the west wall. Your eyes are immediately drawn to a large wooden case displaying a Torah scroll. Nearly four hundred years old, its meticulous handwritten text is opened to Exodus 20, the Ten Commandments. The Torah scroll was a gift to R. C. for the church, but they needed a proper place to display it. The new narthex was such a place. Before that, it had been in a box under the Sprouls' bed. It had a note on it warning thieves that it was of no monetary value, as they would surely be caught if they tried to steal it.

It is opened to Exodus 20 purposefully; the entrance is on the west side purposefully. You soon realize that nearly everything in the building and the building itself is purposeful. The narthex is kept dark before services, and you pass by the Law. Then you come into the sanctuary. The nave is flanked by aisles, set off by piers and arches, topped by the triforium, which is topped by the clerestory. Cruciform shape, your eyes are drawn down the center of the nave to the large wooden pulpit, then

8 R. C. Sproul, *The Holiness of God* (1985; repr., Carol Stream, IL: Tyndale, 1998), 4.

to the stained glass above it, then upward still to the towering ceiling. The morning light filters through the stained glass. Out of the darkness of the narthex you come into the light of the nave. *Post tenebras lux.* Visitors pause to take it all in.

The north and south transepts each have a rose stained-glass window, one with a throne and the other with a crown and scepter, symbolizing the reign of Christ. The apse, on the east wall behind the choir and platform, has five stained-glass windows. Paul takes the center, flanked by Matthew and Mark and by Luke and John. There's a pipe organ. The floors are brick and stone. The large wooden pulpit has stairs with a slight spiral in the back for the pastor's ascent.

Everything about the physical building of Saint Andrew's Chapel is medieval Gothic, except for two things. A prominent pulpit instead of a prominent altar is one. And on the center of the pulpit is a carved "Luther Rose," which is the other exception. This was Luther's symbol. It may also be found on the carved frames around the pipes mounted on the choir walls. Saint Andrew's Chapel is the meeting of medieval Gothic with Reformation theology and Reformation preaching. R. C. himself was stunned by the place every Sunday. "I can't believe God did this," he would say.

R. C. said, only partly tongue-in-cheek, "There are other architectural styles than Gothic, but I'm not sure why."

The church sign says "Saint Andrew's Chapel, A Reformed Congregation." A note on the church website explains:

Saint Andrew's was founded in 1997 as an independent congregation in the Reformed tradition. As such, Saint Andrew's is not affiliated with a particular denomination. That is not to say, however, that we are non-denominational or inter-denominational. On the contrary, Saint Andrew's is an independent congregation on account of our desire to remain steadfast in the Reformed tradition without the influence of denominational governance. Nevertheless, our pastors are ordained ministers in the Presbyterian Church in America (PCA).

R. C. had his PCA ministerial credentials the entire time he pastored an independent church. It was not strictly his decision. The group that wanted to start the church and (kindly) cajoled R. C. into being their pastor met with representatives from the presbytery. That group felt that the representatives, at the time, were less interested in the confessional and doctrinal position of the church and more interested in its business plan and vision. This gave them pause. They reported back to R. C. In the end, they decided not to join the PCA but to remain independent.

Even with the large sanctuary, a second service was added to accommodate the growing congregation. When asked why he thought so many people came to Saint Andrew's, R. C. replied, "I think one of the main things is that we have a classic worship service, fighting against the flow of contemporary worship that's become the norm, more or less, in our day. We have a classic liturgy and a lot of people are drawn to that aspect of our worship."[9]

Threshold

On the front of the weekly bulletin at Saint Andrew's are these words: "We cross the threshold of the secular to the sacred, from the common to the uncommon, from the profane to the holy." The word *threshold* is an interesting one. Physically, literally, it is the strip of metal or wood or some other material at the bottom of a doorway. You cross it to enter a building, room, or space. It also has a more profound meaning, used for momentous occasions: "We have reached a threshold," one would say. To cross that kind of threshold means entering into a significant new "space." R. C. uses this latter meaning as he writes in *The Holiness of God*, "We seek a threshold that will lead us over the border for the profane to the sacred."[10] He continues, "Even within the confines of a closed universe, people seek some place that will serve as a point of access to the transcendent. We feel an aching void that screams to be filled by

9 "Sproul Memoirs," session 10.
10 Sproul, *Holiness of God*, 249.

the holy. We long for holy space."[11] Moses at the burning bush, Jacob's "ladder," and all those altars erected by all those Old Testament saints are thresholds, gateways to the sacred.[12]

Then R. C. turns his attention to church architecture and this notion of *threshold*. He speaks of church architectural styles that are functional or aimed at the comfort of the audience. He senses that. "What is often lost in these functional church designs is the profound sense of *threshold*."[13] R. C. pointed out that "the first people filled with the Holy Spirit were artisans and craftsmen who built and adorned the temple so the people could worship God in the beauty of His holiness."[14]

R. C. speaks of all of this as sacred space. In a simply beautiful line he writes, "Each of our lives is marked by sacred sites that we cherish in our memories."[15] These are "holy spaces." There is also "holy time."

Place and time have always been important to R. C., to his own self-understanding, to his analysis of the times, and to his analysis of the church and of the culture. His *Tabletalk* column title is "Right Now Counts Forever," patently aimed at the secular worldview of the "here and now." He connects the concepts of space and time to that other most important subject to him, holiness. Consequently, he ends his classic text *The Holiness of God* with the chapter "Holy Space and Holy Time."

Holy space is the sanctuary. Holy time is the Lord's Day. R. C. notes how God first established the seventh day, the Sabbath, as holy, as set apart. It is curious to note that as part of the programmatic dismissal of all thing religious, in the wake of the French Revolution authorities attempted to have a ten-day week. It was an effort to remove the trace of a Lord's Day. It failed miserably. As R. C. notes, even the most profane of people recognize the need for a break for the rhythm of the week.

11 Sproul, *Holiness of God*, 249.
12 Sproul, *Holiness of God*, 249–55.
13 Sproul, *Holiness of God*, 256.
14 R. C. Sproul, sermon on Luke 21:1–22, "The Destruction of Jerusalem," Saint Andrew's Chapel, Sanford, Florida.
15 Sproul, *Holiness of God*, 258.

R. C. more happily notes, "Believers observe sacred time in the context of worship."[16]

R. C. devoted his "Right Now Counts Forever" column in the December 1991 *Tabletalk* issue to worship. He discusses how we should be instructed by the Old Testament patterns for our worship today. He advocates for form and liturgy, all the while acknowledging the danger of formalism and liturgicalism. He counters by saying the antidote is not to abandon the externals, the form, or the liturgy, but to "communicate the content they are designed to convey, there must be constant instruction so that people understand their meaning." Then he ends with this:

> We need a reformation of worship, a new discovery of the meaning of classical forms. I cannot be casual about worshipping God. God stripped of transcendence is no God at all. There is such a thing as the Holy. The Holy is sacred. It is uncommon. It is not always user-friendly. But it is relevant. It provokes adoration, which is the essence of godly worship.[17]

As important as it was to stress the holy, the experience of the holy at and in church, it was also important to R. C. that the people of Saint Andrew's be friendly. He recalled how a minister friend of his, upon visiting Saint Andrew's, remarked to R. C. that it "was formal and friendly." R. C. labored to overcome the feeling of coldness that is sometimes associated with more formal and liturgical worship. He explained, "We want to be warm and friendly as we can while at the same time we maintain a high liturgy reflective of our view of God."[18]

The holy invades the profane in sacred space and sacred time. Saint Andrew's Chapel, dedicated in 2009, is the manifestation of the vision laid out in the last chapter of the classic book from 1985.

16 Sproul, *Holiness of God*, 262.
17 R. C. Sproul, "Worship: A Tale of Two Friends," *Tabletalk*, vol. 15, December 1991, 6.
18 Stephen Nichols with R. C. Sproul, personal interview, April 7, 2017.

"Preach the Drama"

Worship, including the design of the sanctuary—the *place*—is a hallmark of Saint Andrew's. So also is the emphasis on preaching, the centerpiece of the sacred time spent on the Lord's Day. R. C. preaching at Saint Andrew's was like Calvin preaching at St. Pierre's in Geneva or like Luther preaching at the *MarienKirche* in Wittenberg or Edwards preaching at First Church, Northampton, Massachusetts. You can read Calvin's *Institutes*, and you can read Luther's *Bondage of the Will*, and you can read Edwards's *Freedom of the Will* (and R. C. would say, "You *ought* to read those books"), but if you want to know the heart of Luther or Calvin or Edwards—if you want to hear and see them applying their theology—then read their sermons.

For the *Open Book* podcast, one of the ten or so books R. C. selected from his personal library that impacted him was John Calvin's *Sermons on Galatians* and his *Sermons on Ephesians*. The Galatians sermon volume was actually not on his library shelves; it was on his desk. R. C. was preaching through Galatians at the time and using Calvin as he went through Paul's epistle of Christian liberty. R. C. said, "The greatest theologians in history were pastors." He named his usual suspects—Augustine, Anselm, Luther, Calvin, Edwards—adding, "These were the great geniuses of the theological world. They were all pastors. . . . When I was studying them, I realized they were all world-class scholars, but they were also battlefield theologians. They took their message to the people."[19] Through their sermons that have been published and translated, these battlefield theologians are still taking the message to the people.

Near the end of his life, R. C. was asked what he would like to be if he could go back and live over again and do something different. He said he'd like to be a ballplayer. When he wrote his novel, however, the main character was a preacher. He could have written himself into any number

19 "R. C. Sproul and Calvin's Galatians and Ephesians Sermons," *Open Book* podcast, June 30, 2017, season 1, episode 4.

of scenarios. He chose to write himself into the pulpit. Serving the people of God, the church, was R. C.'s singular purpose and mission in life.

In 1996 Ligonier Ministries celebrated its twenty-fifth anniversary. The August issue of *Tabletalk* celebrated the past and looked forward to what, Lord willing, came next. R. C. devoted his "Right Now Counts Forever" column in that issue to answering the question "Why Ligonier?" R. C. took that question to mean, what is the ultimate purpose for Ligonier, which R. C. always saw as "to help strengthen the church by providing resources for its people."[20] He ends his column:

> [Ligonier] exists to help the church and serve the church. Its job is to help equip the saints for ministry. Our current purpose statement reads: "To help awaken as many people as possible to the holiness of God in all its fullness." One cannot be awakened without seeing the church as the people of God who are summoned to worship Him, serve Him, and obey Him. To worship God means chiefly to join with the corporate body. To serve and obey Him is to serve and obey Him by serving His church.[21]

As that articulates Ligonier's purpose, so it captures the purpose of R. C. Though he is known mainly for his service to a parachurch ministry, he experienced a season of great joy as he spent twenty years (1997–2017) in a local church ministry, pastoring the congregation and preaching the Word at Saint Andrew's Chapel. R. C. testified, "I am eternally grateful to God that he saw fit to place me in this new ministry, the ministry of a preacher."[22]

In one of his personal notebooks from the early 1970s, he wrote out a list called "Keys to Church Renewal." Number one was "<u>Preaching</u>," which he double-underlined. Then he added ". . . God's way." Throughout his ministry at Saint Andrew's R. C. emphasized preaching.

---

20 R. C. Sproul, "Why Ligonier?" *Tabletalk*, vol. 20, August 1996, 7.

21 Sproul, "Why Ligonier?," 7.

22 R.C. Sproul, "Series Preface," in *Romans: St. Andrew's Expositional Commentary* (Wheaton, IL: Crossway, 2009), 11.

From early on in his preaching there, R. C. decided he would preach through biblical books. The early church used the expression *lectio continua*, meaning continuous lectures or expositions, to refer to this approach to studying and preaching the Bible. R. C. notes, "This method of preaching verse by verse through books of the Bible (rather than choosing a new topic each week) has been attested throughout church history as the one approach that ensures believers hear the full counsel of God. Therefore I began preaching lengthy series of messages at Saint Andrew's, eventually working my way through several biblical books."[23]

One of his earlier series was on John, then came Acts, Romans, Mark, Philippians, Matthew, 1 and 2 Peter, 1 and 2 Samuel, Luke, and Ephesians. He started preaching on Galatians in 2015. He told the congregation that he prayed God would give him the strength to finish the series, and he added, "Then I prayed for it to be the longest sermon series on the book of Galatians."

R. C. published some of these sermon series as the St. Andrew's Expositional Commentary Series. The volumes on Romans and John were published in 2009, Acts in 2010, Mark and 1–2 Peter in 2011, and Matthew in 2013. When preachers, especially those starting out, asked R. C. for advice on what to preach, R. C. would say, "Preach books." He added, make sure your congregation knows the Gospels: "You can't give the people too much Jesus." Then he would add, "Be sure to Romanize your people." He also reminded pastors that "the power of the Word is cumulative."[24] It takes time to grow, but, over time, the consistent preaching of the Word will have not only an immediate effect, but also a cumulative effect.

On an unseasonably cold, for Florida, January night in 2014, R. C. told a group of pastors, gathered at Saint Andrew's for a question-and-answer session on preaching, "When I get discouraged, and I do, I tell myself,

---

23 R. C. Sproul, "R. C. Sproul on the St. Andrew's Expositional Commentary Series," Ligonier, March 31, 2010, https://www.ligonier.org/blog/rc-sproul-st-andrews-expositional-commentary-series/.

24 R. C. Sproul, Question and Answer Session, January 29, 2014, Saint Andrew's Chapel, Sanford, Florida.

it's not my job to convict. It's my job to preach the Word and to trust that God will honor His Word."[25]

While R. C. had taught these books before, or taught from them, the experience of preaching them was different from teaching them. He explains, "I knew that I was responsible as a preacher to clearly explain God's Word to them and to show them how they ought to live in light of it."[26] He aimed for understanding and transformation when he preached. And he would preach the text. He explained, though, that "I focused on the key themes and ideas that comprised the 'big picture' of each passage I covered." He stuck to the biblical text because the biblical text is the word of God. He observed, "I think the greatest weakness in the church today is that almost no one believes that God invests his power in the Bible. Everyone is looking for power in a program, in a technique, in anything and everything—except where God has placed it: His Word."[27] He said plainly in a sermon on Romans 1:8–17, "The foolishness of preaching is the method God has chosen to save the world. This is why Paul said he was not ashamed. He wanted to preach the gospel because it is the power of God to salvation."[28]

Not only does the Word of God have power; it also has drama. There's a connection between the power and the drama. Preaching on Matthew 6:13, R. C. observed that the Greek word for power is *dynamis*: "From that word we get the English word *dynamite*. When you hear the Word, and the Spirit takes it to you, it explodes in your soul."[29]

The fact that the Word of God is the power of God is no excuse for a minister not to exert time and energy honing the craft of preaching. In seminary, the course on preaching is called "homiletics." When R. C. taught homiletics, he labored to convey two points that mattered greatly to him.

---

25 Sproul, Question and Answer Session, January 29, 2014.

26 Sproul, "R. C. Sproul on the St. Andrew's Expositional Commentary Series."

27 R. C. Sproul, *The Prayer of The Lord* (Orlando, FL: Reformation Trust, 2009), 101.

28 Sproul, *Romans*, 33.

29 R. C. Sproul, *Matthew: St. Andrew's Expositional Commentary Series* (Wheaton, IL: Crossway, 2013), 176.

First, do not preach from a manuscript. R. C. would sometimes write a sermon outline. He would take a 3x5 card and turn it lengthwise and write out a list of single words or phrases. This was his outline. Sometimes he wrote it out and left it in the pastor's robe room or on the table by his chair on the platform. Of course, it helps that he had a mind like a full file cabinet, and he knew where every folder was, and he knew what was on every sheet of paper. He had read broadly and studied deeply, poring over the biblical text in his old well-worn *Thompson Chain-Reference Bible* and over his underlined, asterisked, and annotated copies of the great classic theological texts. He had familiarity with the theological concepts he encountered in the biblical texts he preached. But it was early in his own preaching that he forsook manuscripting a sermon, and he was glad that he had.

The second thing that mattered to him and that he told his students was this: "Find the drama in the text, then preach the drama. Preaching is an art form. The medium is words. The argument for that is the Bible itself. The Bible is full of beautiful, compelling, stunning, persuasive drama. Our Lord frequently told stories, R. C. observed.

He offered his own five-step process for sermon preparation:

1. Read and read and read the text.
2. Look for the drama in the text.
3. Check the commentaries for interpretive or controversial issues.
4. Think about it all week.
5. Preach it.[30]

The fifth point is important. R. C. was a speaker in real time, never "canned." He sometimes repeated sermons, especially at the various conferences. Many times conference hosts or pastors at churches where R. C. filled the pulpit asked him to preach on Uzzah or on Abraham's test of sacrificing Isaac or on Isaiah 6. But he was fully in the moment when he preached. It was fresh to him, no matter how many times he had

30 Sproul, Question and Answer Session, January 29, 2014.

preached it or how many times he had told the same Luther anecdote or personal anecdote. When he preached, he *preached it.*

As for the other steps, R. C. explained, "My normal procedure in sermon preparation is to look at the text carefully, look at it in the Greek, look at it in the Latin, and then consult four or five commentaries to see what insights I might gain from others who have studied the text."[31] He adds that if he engaged a thorny issue in the text, he would examine at least ten commentaries.

When he moved from study and preparation to delivery, R. C. was a fan of concision. He always appreciated "Occam's razor." You need not multiply entities. He pulled from a wide variety of illustrations. Philosophers, classic movies and sometimes more recent ones, historical events, the Reformers, music, economics, current affairs—these all showed up in R. C.'s sermons. He used humor. He opened a sermon once by saying that he'd changed the text as it was printed in the bulletin. He said, "I asked the clergy," meaning the associate pastors at Saint Andrew's while they were in the robe room, "do you know why I am changing the text this morning? They said, 'No.' I said, 'because I can.'" As he placed the handful of baptismal water over the head of Noah his great-grandson, Noah started to cry. R. C. quipped, "Noah, you of all people should not be afraid of a little water." It was an endearing humor.

Speakers can talk on a subject, but communicators connect with an audience. R. C. pierced through a crowd and connected with the individual. Listening to R. C. preach, you could feel like he was talking directly, personally, to you. And you sensed that he was pleading with you. He wanted you to do something about whatever it was he was saying—or, rather, whatever it was the text was saying. "Don't listen to the Word," he would say, "Press in to the Word." "We are saved for works. We are not to waste our lives for a second," he exhorted. In a sermon on Palm Sunday on Zechariah 9, "Behold Your King," R. C. spoke of so

31 Sproul, *Prayer of the Lord*, 97.

many seeking after "a tarnished kingdom, kingdoms that had gone to rust." Then comes a King, riding on a donkey, bringing joy.

He could turn a phrase. He understood that words have timbre, and together they have melody, harmony. He was a master of pace and of gestures. He would say, "It has been said that it is a sin to bore people from the pulpit."[32] It is the Word of God that makes preaching a high and holy calling. R. C. was a communicator.

"Please, God, Not Jim"

From 1997 through 2000, R. C. was busy preaching every Sunday at Saint Andrew's, producing teaching series for *Renewing Your Mind*, writing books, and running Ligonier. Vesta's mom also moved in with them, and they provided caregivers for her. Around this time, they purchased a second home on the eastern side of Lake Monroe in Florida. They called it "the Ranch." It provided a place for the Sprouls, and the grandkids, to get away. Also, ahead of Y2K, R. C. wanted to be prepared. The Ranch was self-sustaining, with a windmill to generate power, chickens, a garden, and of course the lake—which did mean that alligators would wander on the property from time to time.

On April 21, 2000, Jim Boice heard the news from his doctors that he had very aggressive liver cancer. In eight weeks, it took his life. He died on June 15. The memorial service was held the next week. R. C. said at the service, "Here we had a valiant warrior, militant for the church in our age." When R. C. received the news of Jim's cancer diagnosis, he spent some time that morning writing a letter to his friend. He wrote out the letter longhand and then gave it to his faithful secretary, Maureen Buchman, to type. Boice was a friend, a colleague, a brother-in-arms. R. C. knew he could count on Boice. They first met, as R. C. recalls in the letter, in either 1968 or 1969. Boice's first year at Tenth Presbyterian Church was 1968. They were in the trenches together through the International

32 Nichols with Sproul, personal interview, April 7, 2017.

Council on Biblical Inerrancy—including navigating some of the interesting personalities on the council—and they were in the trenches through the "Evangelicals and Catholics Together" controversy.

Through the 1980s and 1990s R. C. often played up his Columbo impersonation. He could pull it off rather well. Boice was more prep school. They were teased as the Oscar and Felix of the Reformed world. R. C. kept a photo in his office of a straight-faced Boice standing in the austere pulpit at Tenth while R. C. is giving him a kiss on the cheek, with his trademark mischievous grin. They laughed together on many occasions. They watched each other's kids grow up. Their wives, Vesta and Linda, were and are friends—both widows now.

The letter R. C. wrote to Boice is reproduced in full below. With both titans having now passed, it seems appropriate that the letter be given a public viewing. Most people see the platform figures, and they see the friendships, the camaraderie, from a distance. This letter gives a close-up. It has R. C.'s warmth; it's profoundly theological, and it has a touch of humor as R. C. refers to Donald Grey Barnhouse, who occupied the pulpit decades before Boice:

> My Dear Jim,
>
> I remember the day (but not the year) that I first met you. My friend Tim Couch was visiting us in Oreland while I was working at Conwell School of Theology at Temple. It was 1968 or 1969. Tim was effusive in telling us about this friend from Stony Brook who was the new pastor at 10th Church. Nothing would do but that he would take us there to meet you.
>
> I consider that day a providential moment of intersection that would have an enormous impact on my life. I believe that on that day I was introduced to true greatness. I met a man who is a champion in the things of God and who would be for me an encouragement, an inspiration, a leader, statesman, and a valiant warrior.
>
> I am deeply grateful to God for gifting His church in our time with you. I know that you can take no credit for the gifts and talents He

bestowed upon you. But I have watched what you have done with those gifts for over thirty years. You have used them with uncommon discipline, with undaunted courage, with a rare sense of humility, and with a quiet but fierce passion for truth.

I know that apart from an extraordinary act of providence . . . your days among us are numbered. It doesn't surprise me to hear that you are using them to finish a book and write hymns. Of course that's what you would be doing.

Before you leave us I want you to know something for sure, that I am confident that you already know to some degree. It is this: I love you deeply, Jim. I love you profoundly with a singular affection. When I heard of your illness it was as if a menacing giant grabbed my heart and tried to squeeze the life out of it. I was confused and frightened. I cried out, "Please God, not Jim—not my beloved 'Jimmy,' I can't take that."

But that prayer, as we both know, is utterly selfish on my part. Now my prayer is that you would be borne swiftly on angels' wings into the immediate presence of Jesus. That you would see the light of His countenance and behold the fullness of the beatific vision. That you would enter into your abiding rest, far removed from the cares of this world—that you would hear Him say, "Come, My beloved, inherit the kingdom the Father prepared for you from the foundation of the world." I suspect also, that when you see Him He may smile and say, "But after all, Jim, it is Dr. Barnhouse's Church!"

If I don't see you before you depart let me bid you farewell. Wait for me over there. I will do what I can to keep your work going here—your books, etc. Love to Linda and the girls.

I love you,

R. C.

Violin

In 2001 the *Pittsburgh Tribune-Review* ran a story on the "Populist Reformer," the "dynamic theologian," who "started it all in Stahlstown." A side column ran along with the article on Sproul's take on the Steelers. The author notes, "When western Pennsylvanians hear such complex doctrines as predestination and topics like divine vocation described with reference to the Steelers, they may believe they've found true religion." The author of the article was so impressed that he added, "He is almost as apt at expounding on the trials and travails of [quarterback] Kordell Stewart and the Steelers' offense as he is on the five points of Calvinism." That's R. C. the sports commentator. As for R. C. the "populist reformer" and "dynamic theologian," the article picks up on R. C.'s humor, noting that he scrawls a Greek word on a chalkboard, then says, "Euripedes? My tailor says, 'Euripides, Eumenides.'"[33]

The article points out the counterintuitiveness of R. C.'s teaching ministry: "Sproul's success largely has been accomplished with him telling people what they do not want to hear. . . . Sproul espouses such doctrines as original sin and total depravity, which fly in the face of American individualism and modern culture's emphasis on self-esteem."[34] In his 1997 book *Grace Unknown: The Heart of Reformed Theology*, R. C. observes, "Reformed theology is first and foremost theocentric rather than anthropocentric." He quickly adds, "This God-centeredness by no means denigrates the value of human beings." R. C. explains, 'I have argued that Reformed theology has the highest possible view of humanity. Because we have such a lofty view of God, we care so much about the one created in His image. . . . Reformed theology maintains a high view of the worth and dignity of human beings."[35]

R. C. stressed that being in the image of God has two immediate implications. One is the aforementioned value, worth, and dignity of every human being. The second concerns what theologians refer to as the communicable attributes of God. The incommunicable attributes—God's

33 Lee Wolverton, "Populist Reformer," *Tribune-Review*, December 2, 2001.
34 Wolverton, "Populist Reformer."
35 R. C. Sproul, *Grace Unknown: The Heart of Reformed Theology* (Grand Rapids, MI: Baker, 1997), 25.

aseity, infinity, eternality, perfection, the "omnis" (omnipotence, omniscience, omnipresence)—these are all exclusive to God. But some of God's attributes are communicable in that, to a degree, human beings can possess and manifest them. The communicable attributes include love, goodness, justice, truth, and beauty, among others. Socrates, through Plato, spoke of the pursuit of the good, of living "the examined life," and pursuing truth, goodness, and beauty. This philosophical quest is ultimately theological and can be traced back to the garden as the Creator made man in His image, and so we possess and manifest those shimmering communicable attributes of God. R. C. said, "The full-orbed Christian experience and the church must have all three—truth, goodness, and beauty."[36]

This was part of the reason R. C. so zealously pursued the Value of the Person movement in the 1970s and 1980s. Pursuing goodness and justice is extremely worthwhile. It's why the abandonment of truth was something worth pushing back against. It is why theocentric Reformed theology, as R. C. argued, has the highest view of man of any theology, philosophy, ideology, or worldview. It also explains why R. C. was so enraptured by beauty—the beauty of nature, the beauty of good literature, the beauty of the paintings of the Dutch masters, and the beauty of the sound of the violin.

In 2002 R. C., along with Saint Andrew's Chapel, founded the Saint Andrew's Conservatory of Music. It is likely that he founded the conservatory so that he could learn to play the violin. R. C. loved music, understood music, and wanted intensely to play the violin. He had taken piano lessons when he was young, and he played piano throughout his life. While speaking at a conference in San Diego, he bumped into an old friend, also an accomplished piano teacher, who hosted a televised piano teaching series. The two of them found a piano in a choir rehearsal room. R. C. said to him, "Teach me some things about the piano," adding how

36 Stephen Nichols with R. C. and Vesta Sproul, personal interview, September 26, 2013.

he loved to play and loved to learn new little things and techniques.[37] R. C. wanted to learn a new big thing—how to play the violin.

One of the early conservatory faculty members was Olga Kolpakova. Russian born, she received her MM in violin from the Kiev Tchaikovsky Conservatory and played for eight years with the Kiev Chamber Orchestra. R. C. more than once jokingly remarked that he learned more Russian from Olga than violin. He learned, "Nyet, nyet, nyet," from his accomplished teacher. She would show him how to hold the bow or how to play a note. He didn't quite get it right. Or, more often than not, he, by his own admission, lacked patience. He wanted to run before he learned to walk. So his master teacher would say, "Nyet."

We should explore, however, to see if there's also more to the story. In a sermon R. C. delivered on Acts, he offered himself as an illustration: "When I took violin lessons, my teacher would ask, 'Did you practice this week?' I'd say, 'Yes, teacher.' But she did not take my word for it. She would take my hand and run her fingers across the tips of my fingers to see if they were calloused."[38] They were not always calloused.

But R. C. persisted. At one point he made progress. Olga said, "Bravo." He replied, "Not 'Bravissimo'?" Her answer? "Nyet." R. C. was sixty-three years old when he picked up the violin. That alone should qualify for a "Bravo." Olga played, and continues to do so, every Sunday morning at Saint Andrew's Chapel as a member and conductor of the Saint Andrew's Sinfonia. As R. C. sat in the pulpit chair waiting to preach, you could see how enraptured he was watching her play, effortlessly, gracefully, beautifully.

That he was not always faithful practicing his violin lessons might be forgiven when you consider all that he was doing in the 2000s.

From Plato to Paul

From June 12–22, 2003, R. C. led a Ligonier tour through the ancient city-states of Greece. They billed it as the "From Plato to Paul" tour. R. C.

---

37 Sproul, *Prayer of the Lord*, 1.
38 R. C. Sproul, *Acts: St. Andrew's Expositional Commentary Series* (Wheaton, IL: Crossway, 2010).

had been leading tours for Ligonier since the 1980s. There were Holy Land Tours, tours of Britain and Scotland, and tours through Luther's Germany and to Calvin's Geneva. R. C. and Vesta thoroughly enjoyed these tours. He loved visiting these "sacred" sites that were scenes of moments of great courage. These were the battlefields in the defending of and contending for the faith over the centuries. R. C. would preach from the pulpit at St. Pierre's in Geneva, or from pulpits where Luther preached. R. C. and Vesta also enjoyed time with the people on the tours. Friendships were forged over meals together. Ligonier also hosted Caribbean study cruises. This was one of the means that Ligonier, which reached tens of thousands each year, could have a more up-close and personal impact.

In addition to the tours, Ligonier kept up a robust pace of conferences, spinning off regional conferences around the major event of the national conference. In those years, it was typical for R. C. to speak three times at the national conference and participate in question-and-answer sessions. R. C. also was in demand for other conferences across the country.

Books continued to flow from R. C.'s pen onto yellow pads and onto printing presses. Each year saw two or three new books from R. C., along with two or three previously published books updated, repackaged, and republished. Some highlights from 2000 until 2005 include: *The Consequences of Ideas* (2000); *What's in the Bible* (2001); *Loved by God* (2001); *Saved from What?* (2002); *The Dark Side of Islam* (2003); *Defending Your Faith* (2003); and *Scripture Alone* (2005). R. C. continued his practice of handwriting, in cursive, his manuscripts on yellow note pads. He went through a lot of yellow notepads. Many of these drafts are impeccable. There were no false starts, cross outs, and edits. For some books, like *Saved from What?*, chapters appear as if they were written in one sitting, sentences and paragraphs flowing seamlessly from the start of the chapter to the end. Even footnotes were assembled in a dutiful line at the end of these manuscript pages. His mind was like a bear trap holding onto all that he had studied and read. And he continued producing teaching series and *Renewing Your Mind* episodes.

Around 2005, however, R. C. needed to make adjustments to his schedule. He had had a stroke. It actually took some time to realize that he had had one, and then afterward, even while he appeared fully recovered, there were some lasting aftereffects. Before the stroke he could have occasional bouts of dizziness. From 2005 on, however, he experienced severe dizziness that could spiral to vertigo. Also, he experienced fatigue. Family and Ligonier colleagues began to realize that R. C.'s physical space and time needed to be protected. If people approached from the left, for instance, it could trigger the dizziness. At Ligonier conferences, R. C. had to pace himself between book signings, question-and-answer sessions, and lectures—as well as all the backstage meetings and speaker moments. Few people realized the extent of his physical struggles from the mid 2000s until the time of his death. He always made it look effortless, and when it came time to speak, the old athlete put on the game face. There was work yet to be done.

The 35th General Assembly

Way back in 1982, New Testament scholar James D. G. Dunn coined a term: the "New Perspective" on Paul. It was made popular in the late 1990s and through the first decade of the 2000s by N. T. Wright, who went by Tom Wright when he published popular-level books. It made a quick and precipitous inroad among American evangelicalism and even in American Reformed circles. The "old" perspective was that of Luther and the Reformation. The issue was, again, the doctrine of justification by faith alone. Many evangelicals wondered how the new perspective, so patently wrong, could find such a warm and welcome reception. R. C. did not wonder. He saw this as a direct result of "Evangelicals and Catholics Together." The connection is that ECT caused the view that justification by faith alone, and the discussion of imputation, is not essential to the doctrine of salvation. This had the effect of weakening what was a previously held "shibboleth" of being an evangelical, one who believes in and proclaims the gospel.

Wright changed the phrase "the righteousness of God" to "God's covenant faithfulness." Compare the ESV with Wright's translation, *The New Testament for Everyone*, of 2 Corinthians 5:21:

ESV: For our sake he made him to be sin who knew no sin, so that in him we might become the righteousness of God.

NTE: The Messiah did not know sin, but God made him to be sin on our behalf, so that in him we might embody God's faithfulness to the covenant.

While the New Perspective on Paul was ricocheting through evangelical circles, it manifested as the Federal Vision movement in Reformed circles. It had caused a tempest in the Presbyterian Church in America, R. C.'s denomination. A study committee was appointed, and their findings were brought to the thirty-fifth General Assembly for a debate. The General Assembly met from June 12–14, 2007, in Memphis, Tennessee. R. C. attended.

As it was brought to the floor by the moderator for debate, various teaching and ruling elders lined up at the microphones to speak on the motion. Eventually, those in the lines noticed R. C. waiting his turn. They stepped out of line and returned to their seats, and so R. C. found himself at the microphone, delivering this floor speech:

Yes, R. C. Sproul, Central Florida Presbytery, speaking against the motion. I think we're all aware of Luther's evaluation of the doctrine of justification where he says it was the article upon which the church stands or falls. Calvin added to that, "It's the hinge upon which everything turns." And in our day, we've had an unprecedented attack on the Reformation understanding of *Sola Fide*, particularly at the point of the denial of imputation, which, if you look at the declarations, you see is front and center of this report. And I believe, fathers and brethren, that the Kingdom of God is not at stake here, but I think the purity of the PCA is, and I don't understand—I just can't fathom—the hesitancy about this matter. Too much is at stake, this is the *gospel* we're talking about, gentlemen. And if the Westminster Confession does not already give us a faithful exposition of the gospel, at what point can we trust our Confession? And it seems to me to add these people to the committee, whom our previous committee, fulfilling their mandate to examine whether their views weren't conforming to our confession, is like asking in a courtroom to have the accused become members of the jury. It just doesn't make any sense to me.

Applause

Moderator: Gentlemen.

R. C.: Shame on you, fathers and brothers, you're not allowed to do what you just did.

Moderator: What he said.

R. C.: I apologize for the outburst of unseemly, but righteous, applause.

Moderator: Well, I was outgunned on that one.

And that was the end of the discussion. Presbyterians live to do things "decently and in order," especially at a General Assembly. But R. C. helped all those gathered to recognize what was at stake. As a result of the study committee's report, many at the General Assembly, and R. C.'s applause-generating floor speech, the PCA ruled the Federal Vision and the New Perspective on Paul to be out of bounds in the denomination.

As with ECT, the controversy around the New Perspective on Paul and the Federal Vision underscored the importance of the doctrine of justification by faith and of imputation. Without *sola fide*, there is no gospel. Without the doctrine of the imputation of Christ's righteousness, there is no *sola fide*. R. C. would say that imputation was the "rock of stumbling" in the Protestant Reformation in the sixteenth century, and it remains the rock of stumbling in every century since. "If there was any single word that was responsible," R. C. observed, "it is this word of imputation." R. C. was present—and he made sure he was accounted for—at the controversy over this word at the end of the twentieth century, namely

ECT in 1994, and the controversy at the beginning of the twenty-first century, the New Perspective and the Federal Vision.[39]

R. C. had an additional tempest awaiting him at the end of 2007. D. James Kennedy died on September 5, 2007. Not only was he pastor of Coral Ridge Presbyterian Church and host of the *Truths That Transform* radio program; he also founded Knox Theological Seminary in 1989. Knox met at and was under the auspices of (until 2013) Coral Ridge Presbyterian Church. Dr. Kennedy was the president. At one point, he attempted to woo R. C. to take on the presidency. They had a lot in common, and R. C. enjoyed the time with Kennedy. In his earlier days, Kennedy was an Arthur Murray ballroom dance instructor. R. C. could always count on Kennedy to help refine his own moves. So when Kennedy asked R. C. to preside over Knox, R. C. considered it. He wrote out a list of pros and cons. The cons won. Additionally, Vesta was helping R. C. continue to make wise and good decisions about his own priorities in light of the flow of the many opportunities that came his way.

While he declined the presidency, R. C. taught at Knox and served on the board. After Kennedy's death, R. C. was interim chairman of the board. At the time, a controversy that had been brewing among the faculty erupted. When R. C. saw Anne Kennedy, Dr. Kennedy's widow, at a meeting, she looked visibly affected by it all. She told R. C. she had mourned her husband's death; now she was mourning the death of the seminary.

Theological education had been a part of R. C.'s life since 1960, as either a student or professor or dean or visiting lecturer. Lay theological education was his passion, but formal theological education was not too far from the center. From those European Reformation tours in the 2000s, R. C. could not shake an idea that kept returning. It was an idea that would come to fruition in 2011.

---

39 R. C. Sproul, "Counted Righteous in Christ," Ligonier National Conference, 2008, Orlando, Florida.

10

A NEW REFORMATION

*Between the influence of the graduates of the small
university at Wittenberg and the graduates of the small
Academy of Geneva, the world was changed.*

R.C. SPROUL

R. C. WOULD SAY, "I do not even have to close my eyes. I can see it."
He had in mind a moment in Geneva during one of the Ligonier tours,
when he was standing in front of the Reformation Wall. Stretching 100
meters in length, the center of this monument displays four much larger-
than-life statues of John Calvin, William Farel, Theodore Beza, and John
Knox. They look as if they are about to step forward, these titans dressed
in clerical robes, Bibles in hand. Murals and more statues flank the four
stalwart Reformers on the left and the right. The wall is built into the
rampart that climbs up to the old city of Geneva. Beyond the towering
figures and the Old City wall, you see the stones that once formed the
building that was the Academy of Geneva.

Calvin started the Geneva Academy (now the University of Geneva)
in 1559. The roots of the academy at Geneva stretch back to Calvin's
time in Strasbourg. Martin Bucer preached in German at the cathedral,
while Calvin pastored two congregations of French-speaking refugees.
Calvin himself was a refugee, exiled from Geneva. But that's another story.

While in Strasbourg, Calvin offered theological instruction in his home. Students would gather around as he taught the Bible and theology—not at all unlike the early days of the Ligonier Valley Study Center.

The city of Geneva invited Calvin back, and so he returned. Calvin plied his efforts to preaching and bringing about educational and moral reform. The establishment of the academy was integral to his desire not only for the Genovese but for his greater aspirations and goals for the longevity and spread of the influence of the Reformation. The academy at Geneva trained an army of ministers who went into France and established a network of underground churches. Students came from all over Europe and points east toward Russia. They were trained by Calvin, and off they went, taking the theology of the Reformation with them. Some stayed in Geneva and took up trades. Others filled pulpits in the Swiss city-states.

That's what R. C. saw in his mind's eye. He did not even have to close his eyes to see it.

Calvin was not the only Reformer committed to theological education. When Luther went to Wittenberg to take up his position as a professor in 1508, the University of Wittenberg was only six years old. Frederick the Wise, the university's founder, was determined to make his brand-new university one of the finest in Germany, if not Europe. Luther was his anchor scholar. This was a decade before Luther posted the Ninety-Five Theses, but his abilities as a scholar and as a communicator—a true teacher—were evident. After the posting of the Ninety-Five Theses and the Diet of Worms, students flocked to Wittenberg from across the compass points. Luther trained them all and sent them back to their cities and lands, and they, like Calvin's students, took Reformation theology with them. Frederick the Wise founded it, but it was Luther's university.

The schools at Wittenberg and Geneva were like Reformation theology flywheels, their influence spreading far and wide and deep. Luther and Calvin were interested in reforming not simply their respective cities of Wittenberg and Geneva; they were interested in the message spreading.

Likewise, they were not content that the gospel be discovered for their generation alone. They were equally concerned about the next generation. They were teachers training the next generation of teachers. R. C. observed, "Between the influence of the graduates of this small university at Wittenberg and the graduates of the small Academy of Geneva, the world was changed."[1]

When R. C. said that he saw the academy at Geneva, this is what he meant. He saw Calvin's vision of a place for theological education. It further impressed R. C. that neither Calvin's academy nor Luther's university were large or had great numbers of students, especially compared to the masses of students at major universities today. R. C. likened it to the difference in training a small group of elite special forces and the training of the larger regular army. He also liked to frame it in a reference to one of the great epic filmmakers from his childhood: "This is not Cecil B. DeMille's 'cast of thousands.'" He had a vision for a small, intimate college that would train students in the Reformed classical tradition. He sent out a memo and called a meeting of some of the Ligonier staff. The result of that was Reformation Bible College (RBC), which opened its doors for the first time in the fall of 2011. There were fifty students. In every way, the college reflected R. C., as seen in the name, the seal, the curriculum, and even the size.

Reformation Bible College

Starting a Bible college was not a cutting-edge enterprise in 2011. R. C. had missed the curve by about a century. The first Bible college, though at the beginning they were one- and two-year institutes, was Moody Bible Institute in Chicago, founded in 1886. Next came the Boston Missionary Training Institute, founded in 1889. That institution would change its name to Gordon College, where R. C. taught from 1966–1968. After these, a host of Bible institutes sprang up across the nation and in Canada.

---

1   R. C. Sproul, "Remarks on the Fifth Anniversary of Reformation Bible College," September 2, 2016, Sanford, Florida.

In the 1950s, many of these institutions became four-year-degree granting colleges, changing their names from institute to college. In the 1980s and on, many of them also transformed into liberal arts colleges, greatly reducing the number of Bible and theology credits and dropping the word *Bible* from their names. The number of Bible colleges has been in decline since that time.

Back at the beginning, the rise of the Bible institute/college movement coincided with the spread of dispensationalism. R. C. observed two significant catalysts contributing to the quick spread of dispensationalism. First was the Scofield Bible. R. C. observed that it "took off and became a staple of education for evangelical Christians in America." The second catalyst was the proliferation of Bible institutes. Again, R. C. observed, "In a very short period of time these schools graduated enough people with enough influence to change the whole landscape of evangelicalism."[2]

R. C. recalled, "I had a dream that somehow we would be able to produce a Reformed study Bible."[3] As mentioned in chapter 8, that dream came true with the publication of the *New Geneva Study Bible* in 1995. But in reality, all his efforts at Ligonier were about disseminating the Reformed faith not only through the study Bible but through all the books, teaching series, broadcasts, tours, and conferences. As R. C. continued to reflect on all of these efforts, he observed, "The crown jewel of the vision was, for me, to start a Bible college." He notes, "I was involved as the founding dean of RTS seminary here in Orlando, and Vesta and I were founding board members for the Geneva School (Orlando, Florida). That was part of our overall picture of what we wanted to accomplish. But the ultimate thing was to start a Bible college that would not be large, but would be influential."[4]

That Reformation Bible College was a *Bible* college was intentional. Bible and theology credits would dominate the curriculum. It was also

2 Sproul, "Remarks on the Fifth Anniversary."
3 Sproul, "Remarks on the Fifth Anniversary."
4 Sproul, "Remarks on the Fifth Anniversary."

intentional that it was a *college*. R. C. taught undergraduates, graduates, and doctoral students. It seemed that undergraduates were his favorites. He had found from experience that undergraduates are more responsive both in the classroom and outside of the classroom. His syllabus for his contemporary theology course at Gordon for the fall semester of 1967 includes this note under office hours:

> The Professor is available for consultation regarding academic prob-
> lems. Also, the Professor is always available to spend time with the
> student on a personal basis regarding spiritual or other problems. The
> student is to feel completely free in making such appointments with
> the Professor. Also. I would like to personally invite any student, who
> so wishes, to make appointments to visit me in my home. My home
> telephone number is 468-3458. Address: 14 Woodside Road, South
> Hamilton (Off Linden).

He then informs them how class discussions will go:

> I enjoy a casual and informal atmosphere in the classroom. Free-wheel-
> ing debate and questioning is welcomed. It is hoped that no student
> will ever hesitate to ask questions in class. Questions from the student
> is the only barometer (outside of exams) by which the professor can
> measure the degree of understanding the class has attained. My only
> request is that students retain their dignity at all times and exhibit a
> high degree of courtesy within the classroom.

Of course, R. C. was concerned with communicating content, but as these syllabus remarks show, he wanted to make sure that students were understanding what they were learning and that they were connecting what they were learning to their lives. He cared about them.

R. C. made a distinction between "learners" and "disciples." Disciples and learners both learn. But unlike learners, disciples obey. Disciples are committed to following commands, which they have to know first. R. C. remembered that when they started the Ligonier Valley Study Center in

1971, he wanted disciples, not learners. He once told a Ligonier gathering, "You do not graduate. You are a lifelong disciple." He added that disciples, having been persuaded by the truth of Christianity, obey and live by the truth claims of Christianity. He saw the aim of his teaching through Ligonier to produce knowledgeable and articulate Christians who are passionate for the truth and desire to live it. Discipleship ultimately calls people to obedience to Christ. Initially, Ligonier carried out that teaching in a life-on-life context at the study center. Many, but certainly not all, who showed up at the study center were college students. As the ministry grew, the teaching and discipleship took other forms and means. R. C. saw the opportunity that Reformation Bible College presented for a return to the roots of Ligonier.[5] *FaithTalk*, the magazine for WTLN, the Christian radio station in Orlando, ran an article on the opening of RBC. The article observes:

> Reformation Bible College is the encapsulation of everything Ligonier Ministries and Dr. R. C. Sproul have valued and advocated for the past 40 years. It is a natural outgrowth of Ligonier's decades of teaching Christians to think deeply, critically, and obediently about every aspect of faith.[6]

When Ligonier Ministries left the Stahlstown campus, someone took with them a carved wooden sign for the Ligonier Valley Study Center—with a distinct 1970s-looking font. It was in storage for years. When the college opened its first building in 2011, that wooden sign was prominently displayed in the lobby. With RBC, Ligonier was once again investing in life-on-life discipleship of college students. When he founded the college, R. C. wanted it to be a place of rigorous learning, and a place of discipleship.

The final word to look at in the name is the first word: *Reformation*. There has likely been no other person who introduced more people to

---

5   R. C. Sproul, "Disciple," Reformation Circle Event, October 22, 2016.
6   "What Is Reformation Bible College All About?" *FaithTalk* (Winter 2011): 18–19.

Martin Luther, the five *solas*, and the Reformation than R. C. What he truly admired and loved about the Reformers was the whole package of their content, their convictions, and their courage. And they were communicators. R. C. saw the Reformation, from the human plane, coming about through a handful of theologians "who had rediscovered the gospel and had an energetic vision and zeal for the gospel."[7] Of course, the leaders of this small handful were Luther and Calvin. R. C. continued, "They were both first-rate scholars, but in addition they had an uncanny ability to take their case to the people. They were battlefield theologians, and they understood that they were in a spiritual war. They not only instructed; they also mobilized troops for battle."[8] When R. C. looked to the Reformers he saw examples of those who knew the faith, defended the faith, and contended for the faith. That was what R. C. wanted for the college.

Post Tenebras Lux

In one of R. C.'s private notebooks is a long list of Latin phrases. Among them:

soli Deo gloria	glory to God alone
Deus pro nobis	God for us
judex aeternus	eternal judge
ex lex	apart from the law
fides viva	living faith
fides caritate formata	faith formed by love
simul justis et peccator	simultaneously just and sinner
finitum non capax infiniti	the finite cannot contain the infinite

And more. He used these Latin phrases and Latin words all the time. Latin was the language of the theologians as late as the middle of the

---

7 Sproul, "Remarks on the Fifth Anniversary."
8 Sproul, "Remarks on the Fifth Anniversary."

nineteenth century. R. C. liked the precision the Latin terms brought to theological discussion. He also liked the drama contained in some of the phrases. That's true of *post tenebras lux*, "after darkness, light." It is the motto of the city of Geneva. It can be seen etched ubiquitously around the Old City. The idea of light as a metaphor for salvation is from the pages of Scripture itself. As a Reformation motto, it serves to underscore the reason for the Reformation in the first place. The Roman Catholic Church had drifted and apostatized from the true *depositum fide*, the true tradition of the deposit of faith, taught by Jesus to the apostles, inscripturated in the Gospels and the Epistles comprising the New Testament, and then taught to a succession of *faithful* men. The Roman Catholic Church (R. C. preferred to call it the "Roman Communion") over the centuries steadily diverged from the orthodox tradition and obscured the very gospel that was to be at the heart of the church's mission and identity.

In *Are We Together?: A Protestant Analyzes Roman Catholicism*, published in 2012, R. C. observes, going back to the Council of Trent, that Rome affirmed Scripture and tradition as the authority in the church. In Roman Catholicism, then, there are two sources of authority.[9] After looking at the foundation of authority, R. C. in his book turns to the question of justification, the church, the sacraments, the papacy, and Mary. Rome had drifted from the biblical teaching on all of these in the sixteenth century. The result? The church was not a place of light but of darkness. The Reformation was a rediscovery, a rediscovery of the Word of God and, consequently, a rediscovery of the gospel. *Post tenebras lux*, after darkness, light.

R. C. used the phrase for the seal and original logo for RBC. The logo also included three pillars or columns. The pillars evoked classical architecture, which reflected the classical approach of the curriculum and the college's emphasis on Reformed classical theism. That there are three pillars represents the three core principles of history, truth, and faith.

---

9   R. C. Sproul, *Are We Together?: A Protestant Analyzes Roman Catholicism* (Sanford, FL: Reformation Trust, 2012), 24–28.

Incidentally, this was not the only logo R. C. designed. Of course, he contributed to the idea for the Ligonier logo. Also, while he was a board member at Colson's Prison Fellowship, R. C. suggested the bruised or bent reed from Isaiah 42:3 for their logo.

RBC's curriculum was designed by R. C. Sproul and reflects his emphases. It is a rigorous theological education that focuses on Scripture in context of the historic Christian faith, as expressed in the consensus of the Reformed confessions. The curriculum offers a full survey of seven courses of systematic theology, seven courses of Bible survey, and seven courses of the great works. Courses in biblical theology, hermeneutics, church history, and, of course, apologetics and philosophy round off the curriculum. While R. C. served as chancellor, the syllabi for the various courses were sent to him for review. One of the courses to which he always gave extra attention was modern philosophy. He thought of it as *one* of the most important courses. You sense why when you look back to his book *The Consequences of Ideas*, published in 2000. The subtitle of that book is *Understanding the Concepts That Shaped Our World*. R. C. saw that book as one of his most important contributions. It surveys the great philosophers of history, from the pre-Socratics, Plato, and Aristotle right on through philosophers of the twentieth century. Very important along the way is his discussion of the views from Descartes through Kant. The shadows of those philosophers are cast over all aspects of modern life, including law, ethics, religion, science, knowledge, and truth. Those thinkers and their ideas had grave consequences, or to use a favorite and descriptive word of R. C.'s, they had and continue to have ghastly consequences.

In a marketing piece for the college, R. C. once said, "Grounding college students in what is good, true, and beautiful through Scripture is one of the most effective ways we can seize tomorrow's ground for Christ today." That quote both sums up the curriculum and the educational outcomes for his college.

There was little doubt about how much the college mattered to R. C. He pushed for it when conventional wisdom would have paused.

Of course, he always did like to "zig" while others would "zag." He was teaching on Christian radio stations about Aristotle and the four different causes—and connecting that directly to the gospel and theology. The Ligonier Valley Study Center was an outlier. While starting the college may have been unconventional, it was certainly not out of character for R. C.

The college also gave him great joy. He invited me to speak at the 2012 convocation, and during the convocation we were sitting together in the narthex of Saint Andrew's. He was watching the bagpiper ready his "war costume" and the pipes. He leaned over to me and said, "Isn't it nice they call them 'pipers' and not 'bags'?" Then the students lined up for the formal procession. R. C. beamed as he looked at them. He seemed to come alive, gaining an extra measure of energy simply by seeing them. What excited him most was the potential of this small group of knowledgeable and articulate Christians.

The Declension Narrative

In his 2014 book *Everyone's a Theologian*, R. C. recalls being invited to a well-known Christian university to address the administration and faculty in an address titled "What Is a Christian College or University?" Prior to giving his address, the dean gave him a tour. Like the apostle Paul, who took note of an inscription as he walked around the city of Athens, R. C. "noticed this inscription on a set of office doors: 'Department of Religion.'" He asked the faculty during the address if it had always been called the "Department of Religion." R. C. writes, "An older faculty member replied that years ago the department had been called the 'Department of Theology.'"[10] R. C. proceeded to explain the difference, noting that religion has traditionally come under the broader category of sociology or anthropology in the university whereas theology is the study of God: "There is a big difference between studying

10 R. C. Sproul, *Everyone's a Theologian: An Introduction to Systematic Theology* (Sanford: FL: Reformation Trust, 2014), 3.

human apprehensions of religion and studying the nature and character of God Himself. The first is purely natural in its orientation. The second is supernatural, dealing with what lies above and beyond the things of this world."[11]

So R. C. then answered the question that was put to him:

Question: What is a true Christian college or university?
Answer: A true Christian college or university is committed to the premise that the ultimate truth is the truth of God, and that He is the foundation and source of all other truth. Everything we learn—economics, philosophy, biology, mathematics—has to be understood in light of the overarching reality of the character of God.[12]

The "declension narrative" is the story of apostasy. Sadly, church history is littered with declension narratives; chief among them rank colleges and universities. Typically, as the academy goes, so goes the church and so goes the culture. As R. C.'s book title declares, ideas have consequences.[13]

R. C. enjoyed the study of the history of education. Primarily it teaches a cautionary tale. Harvard, founded in 1636, had in two generations drifted from its moorings, allowing "latitudinarianism." The latitude concerned subscription to the Westminster Confession of Faith (1647) and the Cambridge Platform (1648). The Reverend Timothy Edwards, a Harvard alum, decided to send his son Jonathan to the newly established Yale (1703) instead of risking sending him to Harvard. By the 1750s Yale had drifted, and Princeton emerged as a pillar of orthodoxy. Eventually, the study of divinity was moved from Princeton University to Princeton Theological Seminary, established in 1812. Three generations later, J. Gresham Machen left Princeton to found Westminster Theological Seminary. Western Theological Seminary, which became Pittsburgh Theological Seminary, was a bastion of theological orthodoxy

11 Sproul, *Everyone's a Theologian*, 3.
12 Sproul, *Everyone's a Theologian*, 3–4.
13 R. C. Sproul, *Consequences of Ideas* (Wheaton, IL: Crossway, 2000).

in the 1880s and into the early decades of the twentieth century. When R. C. arrived on the Pittsburgh Theological Seminary campus in 1961, he was one of a handful of conservative students, a few Daniels in a den full of lions.

This is the declension narrative. R. C. knew it too well.

He also saw the declension narrative play out in denominations such as his own PCUSA. This is why R. C. cared such a great deal for theological precision over "studied ambiguity." Studied ambiguity allows for latitude, allows for people to apply different meanings to the same word. R. C. saw this dynamic at work in ECT in 1994. He saw it again in the Manhattan Declaration: A Call of Christian Conscience in 2009. R. C. writes this of the Manhattan Declaration:

> The Manhattan Declaration says, "Christians are heirs of a 200-year tradition of proclaiming God's Word." But who are the Christians it is speaking about? The document refers to "[Greek] Orthodox, Catholic, and Evangelical Christians." Furthermore, it calls Christians to unite in "the gospel," "the gospel of costly grace," and "the gospel of our Lord and Savior Jesus Christ," and it says it is our duty to proclaim this gospel "both in season and out of season." This document confuses the gospel and obscures the distinction between who is and who is not a Christian. I do not believe that the Roman Catholic and Orthodox churches are preaching the same gospel that evangelicals preach.
>
> For these reasons I could not sign the Manhattan Declaration.[14]

R. C. built in many safeguards, as many as he could, to make it very hard for future administration and faculty to drift away from Reformation Bible College's convictions. He prayed deeply. He wrote intense faculty, administration, and board vows that must be signed and verbally affirmed annually, and he wanted the college to be small. He wanted it to

---

14 Sproul, *Are We Together?*, 5.

be small so that students would know each other and could care for each other. He also wanted it to be small so that there would be a small faculty. R. C. had observed how larger faculties at other Christian colleges and seminaries allowed for factions and led to less control and supervision. He wanted a small faculty that was committed to the theology and the vision and mission. He wanted as many safeguards as could be to keep his college from falling prey to the declension narrative.

Keeping it small did not mean that R. C. did not have high expectations, for he did. Among the giants from the past who influenced R. C. was J. Gresham Machen. While R. C. mentioned Aquinas, Luther, Calvin, and Edwards far more than Machen, Machen's impact was profound, especially on the college. Machen was consistently there at the center of the storm taking a stand for truth and orthodoxy. His biographer and colleague, Ned Stonehouse, called him "Valiant-for-Truth," from Bunyan's *Pilgrim's Progress*. When Machen left Princeton Theological Seminary, only a handful of students went with him. The first graduating class was just over a dozen students. Yet that initial class and the small classes from those early days had a tremendous impact on the church. R. C. speaks of sitting down and writing on a piece of paper "one hundred people whom I knew were leaders of the Reformed faith in America." Of the list of one hundred names, R. C. "could trace the roots of ninety-nine of them, at one way or another, back to Westminster Theological Seminary that was founded by Machen."[15] Machen was a battlefield theologian who produced a generation of battlefield theologians. That certainly inspired R. C., who was honored to be awarded an honorary doctor of divinity degree from Westminster Theological Seminary, conferred on May 24, 2012.

The official purpose statement for RBC encapsulates R. C.'s aspirations for the graduates of the college: "The purpose of Reformation Bible College is to produce knowledgeable and articulate students

15 Sproul, "Remarks on the Fifth Anniversary."

who embrace God in His holiness as taught in the Reformed classical tradition."

Awakening

While applying his efforts to founding and starting RBC in the years 2011 to 2014, R. C. continued his schedule of preaching at Saint Andrew's as well as writing, speaking, and providing leadership at Ligonier. In the fall of 2014, R. C. and Vesta led a Ligonier study tour that covered the roots of American Christianity. The tour started in Boston and navigated through New England, on down to Princeton, with a special moment of a visit to Jonathan Edwards's grave, and then on to Philadelphia. One of the sites visited in New England was Old South Church, Newburyport, Massachusetts. The church was established in 1740, when George Whitefield first visited the town. One of the people converted by Whitefield's preaching was Jonathan Parsons, a minister at First Church, Newburyport. After his conversion, his own church no longer wanted him. He, along with others converted during Whitefield's preaching, established Old South Church. They built a respectable meetinghouse in 1756; the bell was cast by Paul Revere & Son from Boston.

Whitefield returned in 1770. He preached on Saturday, September 29. After he preached, a crowd followed him to the home where he stayed. They insisted he preach to them. He stood on the stairs and preached to those who filled the room and spilled out the door and on to the yard. He preached until the candle he was holding went out. He retired to bed. He died at six o'clock the next morning, Sunday, September 30, 1770. The funeral was held on October 2. A crowd, estimated at eight thousand, overflowed the sanctuary and the adjacent streets. In life and in death, people flocked to Whitefield. Whitefield was buried under the pulpit of Old South Church.

There was no speaking time scheduled during the visit to the church. We were going to tour the building, see the grave, board the bus, and move on to the next site. For a moment, though, the group was sitting in the pews, and R. C. went forward and climbed into the pulpit. He began to preach an impromptu sermon. He started with a joke. Legend has it, R. C. said, that just before Whitefield left the gathered crowd to retire for the evening, he turned to them and said that a preacher would come someday from Orlando, Florida, to preach here, but, Whitefield thundered, "over my dead body!"

Turning on a dime, R. C. quoted Matthew 16:13–17 and launched into a sermon. He spoke of Jonathan Edwards and his sermon "A Divine and Supernatural Light" from the same biblical text in Matthew. The knowledge of who Christ is, truly, and of what Christ did, truly, is not known by natural means, but by supernatural means. Edwards was one who had the personal experience of awakening, and he labored to preach the gospel so that others might be awakened. R. C. then spoke of the difference between great expositors or great teachers and "anointed preachers." R. C. noted that such anointed preachers are rare jewels of church history. Into this category he placed Martyn Lloyd-Jones, Charles Haddon Spurgeon, Jonathan Edwards, and George Whitefield. R. C. noted how he had read many sermons from each one of these. He noted that they had very similar subject matter and nearly identical concerns. They all had personally experienced the same transformative, supernatural visitation. That is what they preached. He also noted that although they stood alone in their own time and place, they were not discouraged or dissuaded. They were not concerned about being politically correct but with being theologically correct, preaching to please God, not to please man. They all took costly stands and were valiant in their defense of the uncompromised gospel. R. C. talked of these men as if he knew them.

This "anointed preaching," R. C. said, was the animus behind the Great Awakening. He said there was no voice powerful enough to wake the dead. No human voice. But a divine voice, heard through the impassioned preaching of the Word, could wake the dead. All of those men preached for conversion, a "monergistic, immediate visitation of the Holy Spirit," which accompanies the faithful preaching of the gospel. God has decreed His Word to have the power to bring life from death, to bring dead men to life.

R. C. continued, gaining strength sentence by sentence: "Every generation needs to recover anew the Word of God and rely on its power afresh." People need the new birth. They need to see the light of the gospel, no longer blind and in darkness. People need to come awake.

After R. C. finished, he turned to the few stairs to the side of the pulpit and descended. For a few moments no one moved.[16]

After that, R. C. talked about awakening a great deal. He testified how it caused him to preach differently, to be more fervent in his appeal to repent and believe. The Ligonier National Conference theme for 2015 was "After Darkness, Light." R. C. offered this sentence to go along with the theme: "God's people must cry out for His revival and a restoration of the light." He spoke that year on Isaiah 6, "Holy, Holy, Holy." He mentioned the Edwards sermon, then he proceeded:

> Following that was what is called in New England and American history—"The Great Awakening," where person after person after person was awakened by God the Holy Spirit. And that awakening by God the Holy Spirit moved them from darkness into light by the divine and supernatural light, not the light of an incandescent bulb, not the light of a candle, not the light of the sun or the light of the moon. Those are natural lights. This light that brings awakening is supernatural and it is divine. Immediately imparted to the soul.
>
> You know, every single day without fail, I pray for awakening for Saint Andrew's where I pastor, for the church in America, and for the church around the world because a new darkness has fallen over the landscape of the countries where we live. And that huge shadow has in many ways covered the church, and we are returning to our natural state which is the darkness.

16 R. C. Sproul, Old South Church, Newburyport, Massachusetts, September 26, 2014, from notes taken by Stephen J. Nichols. In the middle of R. C.'s sermon, Chris Larson and I looked at each other and both realized that we wished we could have recorded this impromptu sermon.

R. C. then showed the connection to Isaiah 6, the text he had preached on so many times:

> We hate, by nature; we hate the light and we love the darkness because our deeds are evil. We want to live in a state of hiddenness before God, even though the glory of God fills the earth. We flee from it, we hide from it and prefer the shadows where we're safe over the light that exposes us and causes us to say "Woe is me."
>
> But Isaiah in his misery, crying about his filthy mouth, was driven to repentance that had a price tag to it. God dealt with that filthy mouth. He directed the angel to go to the altar and to take a burning coal, a hot coal, with a tong from the altar and bring it over and put it on the lips—one of the most sensitive part of the human body—of his prophet that is trembling beneath Him.
>
> Not to torture him, not to destroy him, not to punish him, but to cauterize his lips, to cleanse them, to heal them. And then while his lips are sizzling in the flesh he hears the voice of Adonai, "Whom shall we send? Who will go for us?"
>
> And notice Isaiah doesn't say, "Here I am over here," indicating his location. It's not "Here I am," but "Here am I, send me." That's how people respond when their lips have been cleansed by a Holy God. That's how people respond when a divine and supernatural light has invaded their souls and quickened them from spiritual death to spiritual life.

Then R. C. weaves Edwards back in:

> Now, when Edwards is preaching that sermon on Matthew 16 he tries to expand on the significance of that divine and supernatural light, what it brings into the life of a person. What is it that the Holy Spirit does when He visited us with this supernatural, immediate light from God?
>
> He says the first thing that regeneration does, or the quickening, or the visitation of the Holy Spirit does is to show us the truth of the Word of God. . . . And when the Word is proclaimed the Spirit will

take it and use it to pierce your heart and to pierce your soul, so that now you say, "I see it. I get it."

When you are visited by that divine and supernatural light, your eyes are opened. And you come out of the darkness, and you see the light of the Word of God that lights every man that comes into the world. And you see it in its truthfulness.

But Edwards went beyond that, and he said the divine and supernatural light is not something that simply convinces you of the truth. But it shows you two other things about the truth and about God. This supernatural, immediate, work of the Holy Spirit upon your soul shows you the beauty of the truth. . . .

That truth overwhelms us with its beauty. Every word that comes forth from the mouth of God, even those words that drive us to say, "Woe is me," are words filled with beauty because they come to us from the author of beauty.

And then Edwards goes even further in his analysis of this divine and supernatural light when he says not only does the Spirit immediately awaken us to the truth of God and of his Word, and the beauty of God and of his Word, but he says it persuades us of the glory of God, coming from the Hebrew that means weightiness, substance, that which is magnificent, majestic, high and lifted up. Out of the darkness, light, the light of truth, the light of beauty and the light of the glory of God, who is holy, holy, holy.[17]

Awakening leads to knowing, adoring, worshiping, and the desire to express God's beauty, holiness, and glory in song. There is biblical precedent, namely the Psalms. There is also precedent in church history.

Glory to the Holy One

Writing hymns was a part of Martin Luther's reforming efforts from almost the beginning. Luther wrote, "Next to the Word of God, music

---

17 R. C. Sproul, "Holy, Holy, Holy," 2015 Ligonier National Conference, Orlando, Florida.

deserves the highest praise."[18] Luther wrote his first hymn in 1523. After that first hymn, Luther recognized the need for the reform of the church's singing. The church's theology, preaching, and liturgy—all were in need of a total and comprehensive reform. Luther wrote a letter announcing his attentions and asking for help:

> I am planning, according to the examples of the prophets and the ancient fathers, to create vernacular psalms, that is hymns, for the common folk so that the Word of God remain with the people through singing. Therefore, we are looking everywhere for poets.[19]

By 1524 the first German hymnal came off the printing press. It had eight hymns, four by Luther and two each by two additional "poets" that Luther had found. By the end of his life, Luther wrote thirty-eight hymns, chief among them "A Mighty Fortress," Luther's meditation on Psalm 46. Luther, an accomplished musician, wrote many tunes in addition to penning the lyrics for his hymns. He also collaborated with Johann Walter, Frederick the Wise's composer at Wittenberg and at Torgau. The result of the collaboration transformed the worship of Germany and later inspired Isaac Watts, in the 1700s, and the hymnody and liturgy of the Anglo-speaking world.

R. C. wrote his first hymn in 1991, "Glory to the Holy One." It appeared in the back of the second edition of *The Holiness of God*, released in 1998. The hymn is a meditation on Isaiah 6, the refrain echoing the words of the prophet:

> "Holy, Holy, Holy"
> Cried the seraph throng
> Glory to the Holy One
> Join in heaven's song.[20]

---

18 Martin Luther, *Luther's Works*, vol. 53, *Liturgy and Hymns*, ed. Ulrich S. Leopold and Helmut T. Lehmann (Philadelphia: Fortress Press, 1984), 323.

19 Martin Luther, "December 1523," *The Annotated Luther*. vol. 4, *Pastoral Writings*, ed. Mary Jane Haemig (Minneapolis: Fortress, 2016), 153.

20 The original lyric had "Is the angel's song," as the last line. R. C. changed it from a declaration to a call to action: "Join in heaven's song."

R. C. wrote another hymn, both the lyrics and the tune, "Come, Thou Savior, Spread Thy Table," in 1992. This hymn celebrates the Lord's Supper. In his foreword to Keith Mathison's *Given for You: Reclaiming Calvin's Doctrine of the Lord's Supper*, R. C. wrote of the importance of Communion noting, "I am convinced that where the sacrament of the Lord's Supper is taken lightly the people of God are sorely impoverished. Without both Word and Sacrament, we face a spiritual famine."[21] R. C. speaks of the Lord's Supper being in eclipse. He hoped Mathison's book would shine light on it. He had similar hopes for his hymn. The hymn's first verse calls upon Christ to come and "feed Thy helpless, starving sheep." And so the refrain:

Jesus, Jesus, we adore Thee,
Gift of heaven's Bread;
Jesus, Jesus, we adore Thee,
Keep our spirits fed.

Other hymns followed, including "Clothed in Righteousness," the college hymn for RBC. Then in 2014 R. C. began a collaboration with Jeff Lippencott. Lippencott is an extremely gifted and award-winning composer with multiple awards from the American Society of Composers, Authors, and Publishers (ASCAP) and Broadcast Music, Inc. (BMI) and Emmy nominations. He was drawn to R. C.'s theology and impressed by R. C.'s lyrical ability. Lippencott had scored movies and television shows and had a host of projects on his resume. At Chris Larson's suggestion, the two decided to work together to see what might come of it. The result was two hymn CD projects: *Glory to the Holy One*, released in 2015; and *Saints of Zion*, released in 2017.

The typical procedure was for R. C. to write lyrics and then for Lippencott to write the music. That was the case, except for "Highland Hymn." Jeff had written and composed the tune and on a visit to R. C.'s home played it for him and Vesta. R. C. went to his desk and ten min-

---

21 R. C. Sproul, 'Foreword," in Keith Mathison, *Given for You: Reclaiming Calvin's Doctrine of the Lord's Supper* (Phillipsburg, NJ: P&R, 2002), x.

utes later produced a piece of paper with the lyrics fully written out. The beginnings of the recorded hymn have the faint sounds of uilleann pipes rising like the mists over the Scottish Highlands. The song is epic, like the theme of a movie. The lyrics celebrate the great truth of the beatific vision beautifully described in 1 John 3:1–3, one of R. C. and Vesta's favorite biblical passages. The hymn crescendos, "We shall see Him face to face on that day." Lippencott observed that this hymn is the arc of the story of the project as a whole. Vesta said, "It's our favorite."

In keeping with Luther's example of "A Mighty Fortress" as a meditation on Psalm 46, R. C. wrote "The Secret Place" based on Psalm 91. On August 25, 2014, a private debut was held at Ligonier to listen through the recorded project ahead of its 2015 release. About twenty or so gathered around the Sprouls and the Lippencotts. After each hymn, Jeff and R. C. offered their comments, recalling the writing of the hymn or some moment from the recording. But after "The Secret Place" was heard, no one spoke. Replete with imagery, the song depicts the security of dwelling in "the shadow of our mighty King." The hushed tones of the choir and the final single piano key strokes bring the contemplative hymn to the end. Beauty hangs in the air.

The CD was released at the 2015 Ligonier National Conference. A debut concert was held at Saint Andrew's Chapel on Wednesday, February 18, 2015. The night before, a full dress concert with a full orchestra and full choir was performed to an empty sanctuary, except for the video and sound crew, and except for a couple seated on the end of the pew in the center aisle, four rows back. It was R. C. and Vesta. As the concert began, he put his arm around her. They sat in joyful silence for the entire performance. Seeing that, one might think that R. C. went to all these lengths to write and produce a hymn album just so he could take his sweetheart on a date to a private concert. Maybe he did.

Shortly after that, R. C. suffered another stroke. He was out from the pulpit and from his daily visits to Ligonier for the next several months. He recovered, but the stroke, coupled with previous strokes and the COPD, took its toll. Few knew how much of a struggle it was for R. C. to preach or lecture. But he soldiered on. There was still work to do.

R. C. had great concerns for the lack of precision and the shallowness of thought about the person and work of Christ in the contemporary church. Who Christ is and what he did are the gospel, and the proclamation of the gospel is the very heart and center of the church's mission. That led to the writing and release of The Word Made Flesh: The Ligonier Statement on Christology. It draws from both the ancient creeds and the contributions of the Reformers in putting forth the biblical teaching of the person and work of Christ.

> We confess the mystery and wonder
> of God made flesh
> and rejoice in our great salvation
> through Jesus Christ our Lord.

> With the Father and the Holy Spirit,
> the Son created all things,
> sustains all things,
> and makes all things new.
> Truly God,
> He became truly man,
> two natures in one person.

> He was born of the Virgin Mary
> and lived among us.
> Crucified, dead, and buried,
> He rose on the third day,
> ascended to heaven,
> and will come again
> in glory and judgment.

> For us,
> He kept the Law,

atoned for sin,
and satisfied God's wrath.
He took our filthy rags
and gave us
His righteous robe.

He is our Prophet, Priest, and King,
building His church,
interceding for us,
and reigning over all things.

Jesus Christ is Lord;
we praise His holy Name forever.
Amen.

The statement was principally written by R. C. Sproul and Stephen Nichols, with collaboration from the Ligonier teaching fellows and Chris Larson. The statement also includes twenty-six articles of affirmation and denial. R. C. wrote many of them. The Ligonier teaching fellows also contributed. The whole series of articles was edited and revised by Drs. Keith Mathison and John Tweeddale of RBC and by the editorial team at Ligonier Ministries.

There was a poetry to this project. At the beginning of R. C.'s public ministry he had been a catalyst for and a major writing contributor to the Chicago Statement on Biblical Inerrancy and the main writer of the accompanying articles of affirmations and denials. In the twilight years of his ministry, R. C. was there to serve the church as a catalyst for the Christology Statement.[22]

When Jeff Lippencott first saw the statement, he immediately set to work on a composition, which resulted in "The Word Made Flesh: A Christology Hymn." It would be released on the second hymn collaboration

---

22 See Stephen Nichols and R. C. Sproul, "The Word Made Flesh: The Ligonier Statement on Christology," 2016 Ligonier National Conference, Orlando, Florida, for a conversation between the two of us on the writing, content, and hopes for the statement.

project between R. C. and Lippencott, *Saints of Zion*. That project also includes "Psalm of the Shepherd" on Psalm 23. As R. C. dealt with his infirmities, he found great daily comfort in reading through and praying Psalm 23. At the 2016 Ligonier National Conference, R. C. said:

> A couple of weeks ago, somebody was asking me about some of the health issues I had to deal with this past year, and I said that I found myself ending my prayers reciting and praying the 23rd Psalm. I mean how basic is that? It's elementary. "The Lord is my Shepherd; I shall not want." And you go from there to the green pastures and the still waters and being led in paths of righteousness for His name's sake. You go through that glorious psalm and what it means, existentially and personally, that every Christian has a Savior who has purchased for us everlasting life—It just doesn't get any better than that, does it?[23]

Transitions

From the time R. C. turned sixty, in 1999, the board discussed succession planning for Ligonier Ministries. The first decision to make was whether Ligonier was exclusively tied to R. C. or to the teaching and theology that R. C. taught and defended. Would Ligonier come to an end with the passing of R. C.? Or, God willing, would it continue? The board determined that while R. C.'s personality was a huge part of the ministry, Ligonier Ministries was committed to the body of teaching that R. C. so compellingly communicated. The board was committed to carrying on the mission and bringing that teaching to the next and successive generations, God willing. Once that question was settled, the next question involved how, or more accurately, who? Who would succeed R. C.?

When the Ligonier Valley Study Center first started, it was a teaching fellowship. R. C. was the hub of the wheel, but he was not alone. There were other teachers. The board decided to revisit that model. Ligonier's

---

23 Nichols and Sproul, "The Word Made Flesh."

president, Chris Larson, also points out that "the board knew it would be impossible to find one man to whom the torch could be passed. The reality is that Dr. Sproul is a unique gift from the Lord."[24] This realization called the board to search "for men who were trustworthy, able-in-their-field, and wise."[25] They announced the four Ligonier teaching fellows as Drs. Robert Godfrey, Sinclair Ferguson, Steven Lawson, and R. C. Sproul Jr. Larson added, "These four men will serve as advisors to Dr. Sproul, the board, and senior leadership, and will be active teachers in all the ministries at Ligonier."[26] Dr. Stephen J. Nichols was added as a teaching fellow in May of 2013. In November of 2015, Drs. R. Albert Mohler Jr. and Derek W. H. Thomas were added. Dr. Burk Parsons was added in March of 2017.

When the first four teaching fellows were added, the Ligonier website banner changed from "The Teaching Ministry of R. C. Sproul" to "The Teaching Fellowship of R. C. Sproul." The teaching fellows were R. C.'s foxhole buddies in the final years of his life. He respected the gifts and the courage of each one. He had known them personally and had known the ministry of each. He appreciated their record of faithfulness and integrity. It also mattered to him deeply that the teaching fellows were committed to the Reformed faith, willing to defend it, and courageous to contend for it. He wanted "battlefield theologians" and communicators—all the qualities he so admired in his beloved Reformers.

To refrain from naming a single successor is itself a bold move. Few ministries or Christian organizations have attempted such a venture. It is rather unprecedented. The teaching fellowship was part of the succession plan. At Ligonier, Chris Larson was serving as president, and in the years leading up to R. C.'s death, R. C. turned over the day-to-day running of the ministry to Larson. R. C. then gave his own title, CEO, to Larson.

---

24 Chris Larson, "The New Teaching Fellows of Ligonier Ministries," May 12, 2010, https://www .ligonier.org/blog/new-teaching-fellows-ligonier-ministries/.

25 Larson, "New Teaching Fellows of Ligonier."

26 Larson, "New Teaching Fellows of Ligonier."

R. C. retained his position as chairman of the board. At Reformation Bible College, the board appointed Stephen Nichols to serve as the second president in 2014, while R. C. was appointed chancellor and kept a seat on the board. At Saint Andrew's, R. C. and the elders made Burk Parsons copastor. Before he died, the session, with R. C.'s full blessing, had announced that at R. C.'s passing Dr. Parsons would be installed as the senior minister.

The succession planning, which began in the early 2000s, was put in place through the 2010s. Vesta remains actively involved in the ministry, as she has all her life. She holds the title of cofounder. She is in the office daily, her red pen (or sometimes blue pen or sometimes pencil) traces over every printed word that comes forth from Ligonier. R. C.'s daughter, Sherrie Sproul Dorotiak, serves Ligonier as a senior advancement officer. Having grown up with *Tabletalk*, she knows rather well her father's theology, and also managed to pick up his sense of humor, his laugh, and his love for people.

On December 12, 2016, Ligonier issued the following statement: "Last Friday, the board of directors of Ligonier Ministries and Reformation Bible College received and affirmed the resignation of Dr. R. C. Sproul Jr. He is stepping away from his duties at the ministry and the college for personal reasons."[27]

These were the transitions that occurred in the 2010s, setting the stage for what would be R. C.'s final year, 2017, the five hundredth anniversary of the Reformation.

The Legacy Of Luther

R. C.'s very first publication was the article on Luther in the *Gordon Review* in 1968. One of the final projects he worked on was a book of essays on Martin Luther published by Ligonier's own Reformation Trust. R. C. had the last word in the book of essays. He entitled his chapter

---

27 "A Statement Concerning Dr. R. C. Sproul Jr.," December 12, 2016, https://www.ligonier.org/updates /rc-sproul-jr/.

"Luther and the Life of the Pastor-Theologian." R. C. points out how the Ninety-Five Theses, while intended for scholarly debate, were provoked by pastoral concerns. The indulgence sale of Tetzel resulted in a "travesty of false forgiveness" that "forced Luther not only to question the matter of indulgences but the whole salvific system of the church."[28] Then follows the Ninety-Five Theses. As R. C. put it, "The Reformation was now afoot."[29]

Luther was thirty-three years old when he posted the Ninety-Five Theses. He would live another twenty-nine years, dying at the age of sixty-two. In the sixteenth century, life expectancy was just under forty. Those who survived into their sixties tended to have gout, intestinal parasites, hearing and vision loss, arthritis, and other ailments. Luther had them all. He wrote to a friend one month before he died, "I am writing as an old man, decrepit, sluggish, tired, cold, and now also one-eyed."[30] Luther was feeling the strain of the years and of the struggles.

As 2017 began, R. C. too was feeling the strain of the years. His chronic obstructive pulmonary disease (COPD) was taking its toll. The effects of COPD impacted his sleep, which impacted his health. The winter and spring were difficult. At the Ligonier National Conference in March of 2017, with the theme "The Next 500 Years," R. C. participated in a question-and-answer session on the first day. He was fatigued afterward and unable to give his lecture, which was scheduled for Saturday as the closing of the conference. The spirit was willing, but the body was weak. As the summer came, however, R. C. increased in strength and good health. He was golfing again, for the first time in years. Those who knew him well commented that he looked and sounded in better health during the last summer and early fall of 2017 than he had for the last several years. He did not miss one Sunday of preaching during that time. In the

28 R. C. Sproul, "Luther and the Life of the Pastor-Theologian," in *The Legacy of Luther*, ed. R. C. Sproul and Stephen J. Nichols (Sanford, FL: Reformation Trust, 2016), 280–81.
29 Sproul, "Luther and the Life of the Pastor-Theologian," 281.
30 Martin Luther to Jacob Probst, January 17, 1546, in *Luther's Works*, vol. 50, *Letters 3*, ed. Gottfried G. Knodel and Helmut T. Lehmann (Philadelphia: Fortress Press, 1975), 284.

middle of an interview, his phone rang. It was the pro shop at the country club, letting him know that his driver had come in.

All of this was leading up to the month of October of 2017, the month within the year that held the five hundredth anniversary of the very day Martin Luther posted his Ninety-Five Theses. R. C. had all the anticipation of a kid at Christmas.

As October 2017 approached, R. C. was truly excited about the celebration coming at the end of the month. October 31, 2017, marked the five hundredth anniversary of Luther's posting of the Ninety-Five Theses. A spotlight was shown on the Reformation, a subject that had been dear to R. C. for five decades. When R. C. published *The Holiness of God* in 1985, he dedicated it to his, at that time, two grandchildren:

> To Kaki and Ryan
> and to their generation,
> that they may live during a
> a new reformation

R. C. hoped back then that the rediscovery of the centrality of the holiness of God would lead to a new Reformation. He longed for that. R. C. never studied the past like one would visit a museum. The past was not historical curiosity. For him the past served to catapult him to the future. He studied the Reformation and awakenings of the past because he longed to see a new Reformation and a new awakening. As Ligonier planned the 2017 national conference, which took place in early March, R. C. made sure it was not only about looking back. The conference theme was "The Next 500 Years." It was all about looking ahead. The five hundredth anniversary was a time to celebrate the past, but it was also a time to plan and pray for the future.

What those around him did not know was that the months of October and November would be his last. They would contain his last Reformation Circle event, a time he always cherished. His friend Max Maclean offered a dramatic retelling of the early Luther. R. C. spoke on the pivotal moments that led up to the Diet of Worms. At the same hotel, Ravi Zacharias was hosting an event for his ministry. The two apologists and friends were able to share some time together.

A Beggar Who Found Bread

October also was the month of R. C.'s last Ligonier conference, the Reformation 500 Celebration. It was held in Saint Andrew's Chapel and was livestreamed. R. C. spoke last on the topic "What Is the Gospel?" He started by drawing attention to aspects of the gospel: the objective content of the gospel and the subjective appropriation of the gospel. As for the objective content, R. C. said:

> The objective gospel simply is this: it's Jesus. Who He is, and what He has done. His life of perfect obedience, sinless-ness, His substitutionary atonement, His resurrection, His ascension into Heaven, His promise of His return.[31]

When you turn to the question of the subjective appropriation of the gospel, that is where the sixteenth-century controversy raged. The question was, How does the life of obedience of Christ and how does the work of the death of Christ and its benefits get appropriated by us? R. C. put a sharper point on it: "At the very heart of the dispute in the 16th century was this question: What is the instrumental cause of our justification? What is the means by which our salvation and our justification take place?" He continued, "Rome was very clear in their definition of what the instrumental cause of justification was. They found the instrumental cause of justification in the sacraments—two most importantly . . . the sacrament of Baptism and then the sacrament of Penance."[32]

R. C. then explained the Reformation's response:

31 R. C. Sproul, "What Is the Gospel?," October 30, 2017, Reformation 500 Celebration, Sanford, Florida.
32 Sproul, "What Is the Gospel?"

When Luther came to his understanding of justification by faith alone, the affirmation of the Reformers was this: that the instrumental cause of justification is not found in the sacraments; it's found in faith. Faith is the instrument, indeed the sole instrument, by which people are justified. And that was the battle. That was the fight between Rome and the Reformers.[33]

R. C. added, "Justification by faith simply means that the instrument of our justification is that with faith and by faith and through faith, we are linked to Jesus so that all that He is, and all that He has done, is given to us. Justification is by Christ alone. *Solus Christus*."[34]

That conference was also R. C.'s last question-and-answer session. These sessions were legendary among Ligonier conferences and a favorite for attendees. Chris Larson moderated the session, which included Ligonier teaching fellows and R. C. Larson asked, "In your assessment, what one personal quality or characteristic made Luther such an effective instrument in God's hands to reform the church? R. C. answered:

He was a beggar who found where he could get bread. And told everybody who would listen to him. How can a man stand against the whole world like he did? And the only way to understand that is you have to get back into his personal struggle with his lack of assurance of salvation with his violent search for justification in the presence of a Holy God, and visit with him in his utter despair. See, Luther understood who Luther was. And that's our problem. We don't understand who God is, and we don't understand who we are. It's like Isaiah in chapter 6, when he saw the Lord, "high and lifted up." He all of a sudden says, "Whoa, wait a minute. Woe is me. I've got a dirty mouth, and I'm not alone. I live with a whole people of unclean lips." So that was an awakening to his sin. You didn't have to teach Luther that he was a sinner. He was a brilliant student of jurisprudence, of the law. He read the law of

33 Sproul, "What Is the Gospel?"
34 Sproul, "What Is the Gospel?"

God. He examined himself in the light of the law of God, and he was helpless to save himself. And when he tasted the gospel, his soul was set on fire. And he said, I'm not going to give this up for anybody in the whole world. I have tasted the fruit of the gospel. And if all of the devils in hell oppose me, I will say to them, "Here I stand."[35]

On That Day

After that event and month, R. C. looked forward to what was coming next. The college was busy with a building project, which would house a library, faculty office suite, classrooms, student commons, and a capacious main hall. R. C. was thinking about the 2018 national conference, the theme of which was "Awakening." R. C. had selected it. He was thinking about the talk he would give. He was thinking about the books he wanted to write. He was talking to anyone in earshot of the importance of the doctrine of God and some of the current discussions swirling around that subject.

He preached every Sunday in November. He chipped away at golf and some writing projects. He was busy studying Hebrews, the biblical book he was preaching through, and reading biographies. He was working on a puzzle. As November ended, R. C. got a cold. On Wednesday and Thursday his condition worsened. He was taken to the hospital on Saturday, December 2. As he remained in the hospital, doctors were unable to get R. C. to successfully breathe on his own.

On December 14, Vesta, Sherrie and her husband, Dennis, and some grandchildren were gathered around his bed and in the room. They were listening to the *Glory to the Holy One* CD. The "Highland Hymn" came on. R. C. was not able to speak, not able to squeeze the hands that were clutching his. But they could see tiny movements as if R. C. was in there, listening but not able to respond. The "Highland Hymn" moved into the final verse:

---

35 R. C. Sproul, from Question and Answer Session, Reformation 500 Celebration, October 30, 2017, Sanford, Florida.

The beatific glory view
That now our souls still long to see
Will make us all at once anew
And like Him forever be.

Then the refrain one final time:

Lutes will sing
Pipers play
When we see Him face to face
On that day.

With the final note, R. C. Sproul drew his last breath.

11

DOXOLOGY

Theology leads to God.

THOMAS AQUINAS

THE FINAL EVENTS OF R. C.'s life seem as if they were scripted. His final Ligonier conference was on Luther and the Reformation. His final question-and-answer session ended with an answer that included Luther, the gospel, Isaiah 6, God's holiness, and the words, "Here I stand." His final two sermons expound the glory of Christ and the greatness of salvation (see chapter 12). His final sentence of his final sermon calls for awakening. His final breath drawn as "The Highland Hymn" concluded on the CD player in the hospital room. Pure poetry.

That uncanny finality extended to the day after he died and the episode broadcast on *Renewing Your Mind* on December 15, 2017. That week *Renewing Your Mind* was running the last five teaching episodes from the epic teaching series *Foundations*. The last episode, number sixty, is "The Believer's Final Rest." Here's how Lee Webb, host of *Renewing Your Mind*, introduced the broadcast:

> It is by God's providence that we are airing this program today on The Believer's Final Rest. This program has been on our broadcast schedule for several months. And when we scheduled it, we had no idea that

we would be sharing with you the sad news that our founder and dear friend Dr. R. C. Sproul has gone home to be with the Lord. . . . We are mourning his loss here at Ligonier, but what a comfort to know that Dr. Sproul is today—right now—enjoying the presence of Christ. Face to face. He is enjoying the very reality that he teaches in this lesson.[1]

Many were saddened by the news of R. C.'s passing. They were mourning the loss of their teacher. But even at his death, he was teaching his beloved Ligonier students, teaching them how to react and how to respond to his own death.

In the course of the episode, R. C. quotes 1 John 3:1–3:

Behold what manner of love the Father has bestowed on us that we should be called children of God! Therefore the world does not know us, because it did not know Him. Beloved, now we are children of God; and it has not yet been revealed what we shall be, but we know that when He is revealed, we shall be like Him, for we shall see Him as He is. And everyone who has this hope in Him purifies himself, just as He is pure. (NKJV)

Then R. C. expounds:

This text I think is one of the most important eschatological texts, if not the most important eschatological text, in all of the New Testament because what it promises the believer is the zenith of the felicity that we will enjoy in heaven, which is found in what is called technically in theology the "visio Dei," or the beatific vision. The first phrase, "visio Dei," simply means "the vision of God," which vision is called the beatific vision.

Why? Well, you may not be familiar with the term "beatific," but you are familiar with the term "beatitude." The beatitudes are those sayings that are recorded in the Sermon on the Mount when Jesus begins each of the beatitudes with the prophetic oracle of blessing. "Blessed are the

---

1   Lee Webb, Introduction, "The Believer's Final Rest," *Renewing Your Mind* radio broadcast, December 15, 2017.

poor. Blessed are the peacemakers and those who hunger and thirst after righteousness and so on." That is a promise of blessedness, a degree of happiness that transcends any pleasure or any kind of earthly happiness—when God gives blessedness to the soul of a person, that is the supreme level of joy and fulfillment and of happiness that any creature can ever receive. And this blessedness is what is in view here when we talk about the beatific vision: a vision that is so wonderful, a vision that is so fulfilling that the vision itself brings with it the fullness of the blessing.[2]

R. C. longed for this "delight of our souls," as Jonathan Edwards put it. We will see God "aglow with unvarnished, unveiled radiance."[3] R. C. closed with these words:

> For all eternity, God has established this place, which is the end and the destiny of all of His people. It doesn't get any better than that, and again, every aspiration, every hope, every joy that we look forward to will be there and then some in this wonderful place. Our greatest moment will be the moment that we walk through the door and leave this world of tears and of sorrow, this valley of death, and enter into the presence of the Lamb.

The day before this aired, R. C. walked through the door from the here and now to eternity, and he entered his rest. The teacher was dead; long live the teaching. That is on earth. In heaven, R. C. has joined the seraphim, worshiping the one who sits on the throne and the Lamb upon the glassy sea. He is still proclaiming the holiness of God.

"O Rare"

On the grave of Ben Johnson (1572–1637) in Westminster Abbey is etched simply, "O Rare." That could be said of R. C. John MacArthur

---

2 "The Believer's Final Rest."
3 "The Believer's Final Rest."

eulogized R. C. as a friend, as a defender of the faith, and as "this era's greatest Reformer."[4] In the pages of *World* magazine Joel Belz noted:

> R. C. Sproul was an enormously gifted scholar-communicator whose nuanced approach drove us all to a deeper commitment to the truth of the gospel. Who cannot revel in Sproul's magnificent grasp of Scripture—as well as his compelling teaching style? He was as carefully bounded by the Scripture as any preacher most of us have ever heard, although within those bounds he was also a fully liberated Renaissance man. It's a combination I don't expect to see ever again in my lifetime.[5]

R. C. was also eulogized in *USA Today*, the *Washington Post*, and his beloved hometown's *Pittsburgh Post-Gazette*. He was eulogized and remembered across major Christian news outlets, magazines, and blog posts. Crossway, publisher of a number of his books, asked people to share their response to the prompt: "I am grateful for R. C. Sproul because . . ." In a few days they had over seventeen thousand responses from all over the world. They published fifty of them on their website on December 19, 2017.[6] Here's a sampling:

> "He demystified theology for me." From someone in Ghana

> "He helped me have a more biblical view of God." From someone in Ohio

> "His ministry has taught me how to love God." From someone in New Mexico

> "His unrelenting pursuit of preaching the inerrant Bible and the doctrines of grace . . ." From someone in China

> "His clarity. Even the tough stuff! Amazing!" From someone in Northern Ireland

4 John MacArthur, "Eulogy," R. C. Sproul memorial service, December 20, 2017, Sanford, Florida.
5 Joel Belz, "Sensible Teacher," *World* magazine, January 20, 2018, 4.
6 "50 reasons We're Thankful for R. C. Sproul," December 19, 2017, Crossway, https://www.crossway.org/articles/50-reasons-were-thankful-for-r-c-sproul/.

"He was faithful to the end." From someone in Scotland

R. C. wrote over one hundred books, produced hundreds of hours of teaching series, and left behind a vault of sermons. He is quoted at the end of a vampire movie starring Christopher Walken (*The Addiction*, 1995). The quote: "We are not sinners because we sin, but we sin because we are sinners." One of his quotes appeared in *Bartlett's Familiar Quotations*: "Sin is cosmic treason."[7] Another of his quotes should have been, "There is no maverick molecule."

He is thanked in the liner notes of a Van Halen album. He was also mentioned by Alice Cooper, in a 2010 *Good Morning America* concert in the streets of New York City, as one of Cooper's influences and teachers. "Vince," as R. C. called him by his real name, read R. C.'s books and once attended a Ligonier conference in San Diego. After the conference, Cooper saw R. C. waiting to start a round of golf, as was he. They were not scheduled to golf together, but Cooper asked R. C. if he'd like to golf with him. The shock rocker and the theologian golfing.

It was the way R. C. combined things that made him so rare. The way he combined complex ideas with clear teaching. The way he combined philosophy with theology. The way he could weave in Aristotle with the presentation of the gospel. At a Ligonier Christmas gathering, he delivered a lecture on the history of science that ended by drawing all eyes to the incarnate one lying in a manger. He combined a mischievous sense of humor with a somber view of God. He knew what it was to tremble and rejoice. His circle of friends included the platform speakers of the Reformed and evangelical world and, by R. C.'s own description, the "heathens" with whom he played golf and ate lunch at the golf club. Both sets of friends spoke of the "gaping hole" left when R. C. died.

"O rare," he was.

---

7 In *Bartlett's Familiar Quotations: A Collection of Passages, Phrases, and Proverbs Traced to Their Sources in Ancient and Modern Literature*, 17th ed. (Boston: Little, Brown, 2002).

People were drawn to the teaching. R. C. wanted people to have a vison of who God is. He did not want people to have a vision of who R. C. was. Nevertheless, the man behind the teaching is important. In considering his legacy, we first consider the man.

The Man

Knowing R. C. the person involves understanding the role of family in his life, his sense of humor and love of laughter, his passion, his compassion and caring nature, and his hobbies. From the time he was little and waiting at the top of McClellan Drive to wave in the relatives coming for a dinner or a holiday, R. C. loved family. At the Ligonier Valley Study Center, R. C. not only invited students into the classroom; he invited them into his family, to his dinner table. In fact, even the "classroom," in those early days, was his living room. He loved his family and was generous and kind. Vesta said how people over the years would thank her for sharing R. C. with them. She said that the family never felt like he was shared. She said that when she or the kids needed him, he was there. Of course, his traveling schedule meant missing birthdays and some of those milestone moments in a kid's life. R. C.'s daughter, Sherrie, put it simply: "I had such a kind, fun, loving dad who was absolutely crazy about me."[8]

R. C.'s sense of humor is legendary. Al Mohler loved to speak at conferences with R. C. Not only did he enjoy hearing R. C. and catching up with his friend; Mohler knew that R. C.'s presence at the speaker dinner meant the time would be far more enjoyable, with exponentially more laughter and jokes. Steven Lawson called R. C. "the king of the one-liners." Others tried to keep up with him but couldn't. His sense of humor was known not only to his circle of friends and associates but also to all the students who watched him over the years. He joked, and he loved to hear jokes. He teased, and he loved to be teased. R. C. would

---

8   Sherrie Sproul Dorotiak, "A Unique Perspective," *Tabletalk*, Special Issue, 2018, 13.

want us to see the theological reason. Only one who has had their sins forgiven and has escaped the wrath of God can know true joy in life.

As evident as R. C.'s sense of humor, so evident was his passion. Whether it was his passion for God and holiness, or his work, or his family, R. C. was like Luther, full tilt. Like Samuel Taylor Coleridge's ancient mariner, who felt compelled to grab the wedding guests by the arm and tell his tale, so too R. C. was compelled to tell the tale of the holiness of God and the gift of the righteousness of Christ. That passion and drive propelled him, even into his late seventies as his body waned. R. C. put it this way: "I owe every human being I know to do everything I can to communicate the gospel to them."

There was also compassion. Vesta observed, "He liked people. He thought people were interesting, and he knew he could learn from them. I particularly appreciated that he could talk to a construction worker or the president of a Fortune 500 company, and he was comfortable doing both. But he remained himself. He didn't switch between two person-alities with regard to how he approached people."[9] Guy Rizzo, one of those golf club "heathen" that was led to Christ by R. C., knew R. C. for twenty-five years. He said that over all of those years, R. C. "never acted in a condescending way."[10] Those who worked at Ligonier or were able to work with R. C. on projects would express how kind the Lord was to give them that time with R. C.

Finally, in understanding the man in terms of the importance of family, his sense of humor, his passion, and his compassion, seeing his hobbies rounds out the picture. Sports, painting and drawing, reading biographies, watching classic movies and contemporary ones, music—listening and playing, piano and violin—and putting together puzzles. These were R. C.'s hobbies. Not to mention dieting. Any diet fad that came along could likely swoop up R. C. The Scarsdale Diet gave way to Atkins. There was "wheat belly." And probably one of R. C.'s all-time favorites: turkey bacon.

---

9 Vesta Sproul, in Dorotiak, "A Unique Perspective," 13.
10 Guy Rizzo, "Eulogy," R. C. Sproul memorial service, December 20, 2017, Sanford, Florida.

The hobby that most think of when they think of R. C., however, is sports. It actually might be incorrect to refer to sports as a hobby for R. C. Throughout the first eighteen years of his life, sports dominated. It was his beloved Pirates and Steelers in the black and gold. He never forgot watching his first baseball game. Pirates 5, Reds, 3. It was playing baseball in Mowry Park or hockey on the "ice rink" on the reservoir. It was all about sports. Golf started in seminary and did not end until November of 2017, fifty-five years on the golf course. Highlights include his hole-in-one, which was a hole-in-three. He teed up for a hole over a water hazard. He swung, and the ball ended up in the lake. Stroke one. He took the penalty and teed up again. Stroke two. From the tee, he swung, and the ball went on the green and into the cup. Stroke three. That is how you have a hole-in-one, which was a hole-in-three. R. C. said one of the best days of his life was in 1985 at the Gator Golf Day, a University of Florida event that pairs a foursome of golfers with a pro. That day, R. C. played with his longtime friend Wally Armstrong. R. C.'s team won, and R. C. outshot them all, even the pros. When R. C. golfed, he competed against the course, or so he would say.

Sports was in many ways more than a hobby. He transferred the grit and determination of the athlete to his work as a theologian. When he would speak, it was game time, and he was ready. He was the kind of player who "left it all on the field." So it was with his teaching and speaking.

Art was a hobby for a time. He enjoyed it, but he did not enjoy the cleanup. When he finally moved on from painting, Vesta said it was not because he lacked the time or inclination; it was because he lacked a sink.[11]

This discussion of his hobbies and personality points to R. C. as a real person. George Grant explained it well: "His down-to-earth, unpretentious and fervent character adorned his genius with peculiar grace."[12] Grant notes that was the first impression. He adds, "Over the

11 Stephen Nichols with Vesta Sproul, personal interview, October 29, 2018.
12 George Grant, "R. C. Sproul, 1939–2017," Grantian Florilegium blog, December 15, 2017.

thirty-five years that I knew him, that first impression has only been reinforced a hundredfold."[13]

This measure of the man also informs us of his method.

The Method

R. C. valued precision, clear communication, courage and conviction, and a populist approach. Anyone who ever drove R. C. knew he valued precision. He did not even need to look at the speedometer; he knew when someone was driving even a decimal point above the speed limit. Perhaps R. C. learned precision from his accountant father or his meticulous typist mother. He learned it from the lockstep precision of the elders coming forward for the Lord's Supper at Pleasant Hills. He did not learn theological precision there. That he learned from Gerstner, and from his past masters, Augustine, Aquinas, Calvin, Turretin, Edwards, Hodge, and Warfield. These were scientist theologians. They had to be precise. The opposite of precision is sloppiness. When it comes to the knowledge of God and His gospel, there simply is no room for sloppiness. Another opposite of precision is the more subtle "studied ambiguity" that R. C. fought against his whole life. Perhaps studied ambiguity was a far greater threat than blatant error. With the former, people could let their guard down, and subtle drips become waterfalls over time. R. C. valued precision.

He also valued clear communication. He took the complex and made it clear and understandable, without distortion. He made it compelling. He was persuasive.

He also valued conviction and courage. He had that note card on his desk that said: "To preach and teach what the Bible says is true, not what you want the Bible to say is true." That was the source of his courage. Like a prophet of old, or a Reformer of the sixteenth century, R. C. had a boldness because these were God's words, God's teachings. He proclaimed "that word above all earthly powers." John MacArthur, his

13 Grant, "R. C. Sproul, 1939–2017."

longtime foxhole companion, said, "The passion that motivated R. C. was his love of the gospel and his zeal for making sure the message is proclaimed without compromise or confusion."[14] Michael Horton said, "R. C. did not have much time for cowards in matters of great moment. The great movie 'Tombstone' was required viewing for his friends."[15] He was consistent in his courage and conviction. They say that you know what a great leader is going to say on a subject because he has a track record of dogged consistency. That was true of R. C. He held his convictions with integrity throughout his life, even if he found himself at the O.K. Corral.

Finally, he was a populist. He could lean over the lectern or the pulpit and, with his wide and warm smile, look you in the eye, even if you were in a crowd of thousands. He was looking at you, talking to you, teaching you. He could do the same through the video camera of a teaching series or over the radio of a *Renewing Your Mind* broadcast. He connected. This explains why so many felt that they lost a friend when they heard that R. C. died. They never met him, but they felt like they knew him. R. C. took his message to the people because that's what the Reformers did.

Andrew Pettegree makes this observation of Luther the Reformer:

> Luther was a cultured and purposeful theological writer. He wrote fine Latin, and his Latin works measured up well against his adversaries. But it was his German writings that redefined theological debate and reshaped its audience. The decision to make the case against indulgences with the 1518 *Sermon on Indulgence and Grace* was, as we have seen, momentous; and this proved to be only the first of several hundred original German compositions, many like this, short, terse, and phrased with a directness and clarity that was a revelation in itself. . . .

---

14 John MacArthur, "Comrades in Arms," *Tabletalk*, Special Issue, 2018, 52.

15 Michael Horton, "R. C. Sproul: In Memoriam," *White Horse Inn* blog, December 14, 2017, https://www.whitehorseinn.org/2017/12/r-c-sproul-in-memoriam/.

Luther called the German people to engage in serious questions of salvation and Christian responsibility, and they responded in huge numbers. In piquing their interest, the medium—Luther's choice of words and style, the accessibility of those ideas briefly put, the visual signals of pamphlets with an increasing design homogeneity—was in many respects as important as the message.[16]

Luther took the message to the people. He did not patronize them, but communicated to them clearly and free of technicalia. He knew they needed to hear truth well told. When R. C. admired Luther for being a populist Reformer, this is exactly what R. C. was admiring. These elements can also be found in R. C.'s own work. He too knew the power of words and phrases. He made serious ideas accessible to the people. He was an educated theological writer and could contest ideas in the academy. But he went straight to the people.

These truths of the doctrine of God and the doctrines of grace bring light out of darkness, life from death. His precision, clarity, conviction, and populist message were the method. The content can be seen in his contributions.

The Contributions

Depending on when you looked in on R. C.'s life, you might have a different answer as to his contribution to the church and the Christian tradition. If you were to look at 1978, you would say his biggest contribution was in the fight for inerrancy. If you were to look at 1994, or the Christology Statement of 2016, you would say that it was justification by faith alone. Others might say apologetics. Others might say he was one of the few Reformed people who found Thomas Aquinas rewarding. Others still would say no one else could talk about Aristotle's idea of cause in a sermon entitled "What Is the Gospel?" When others hear people say R. C.'s contribution was philosophy or inerrancy, they simply

16 Andrew Pettegree, *Brand Luther: 1517, Printing, and the Making of the Reformation* (New York: Penguin, 2015), 333–34.

do not understand. They would say that he reminded the church that God is holy. All of these reflect aspects of R. C.'s legacy.

His contributions include all that follows:

INERRANCY

R. C. planted the seed for the International Council on Biblical Inerrancy. He was ICBI's first president and a writer of significant ICBI material. Before and after the Chicago Statement on Biblical Inerrancy, R. C. never wavered on the doctrine of the uncompromising authority of Scripture expressed in the inspiration, inerrancy, and infallibility of Scripture.

CLASSICAL APOLOGETICS

In R. C.'s copy of volume 1 of Francis Turretin's *Institutes of Elenctic Theology*, he has written in:

> That He is
> What He is
> Who He is

To know "That He is" refers to Turretin's observation: "First we may know that he is (with respect to existence) against the atheist."[17] Belief in God is rational and demonstrable. As Turretin writes on the next page, "Nature proves the being of God."[18] Turretin learned it from Aquinas, who learned it from Aristotle. Aquinas and Turretin bequeathed it to Edwards, Edwards to Hodge and Warfield, Hodge and Warfield to Gerstner, and Gerstner to R. C. Natural theology was essential to R. C.'s apologetic. In his conclusion to *The Consequences of Ideas* he wrote:

> As I enter the twilight years of my life, I am convinced that . . . we need to reconstruct the classical synthesis by which natural theology

---

17 Francis Turretin, *Institutes of Elenctic Theology*, vol. 1, trans. Charles Musgrave Giger, ed. James T. Dennison Jr. (Phillipsburg, NJ: P&R, 1992), 169.

18 Turretin, *Institutes of Elenctic Theology*, 170.

bridges the special revelation of Scripture and the general revelation of nature. Such a reconstruction could end the war between science and theology. The thinking person could embrace nature without embracing naturalism. All of life, in its unity and diversity, could be lived *coram Deo*, before the face of God, under his authority and to his glory.[19]

Natural theology is roundly rejected by the presuppositionalists and by fideism. R. C. saw both as dangerous, not only for apologetics but also for the Reformed classical expression of the doctrine of God. He pushed against presuppositionalists for ceding far too much ground. R. C. was of the tough-minded camp of apologists. If someone said there were contradictions in the Bible, he would sit with them and resolve each and every one they could think of. Sometimes when they ran out of objections, he showed them alleged ones and then proceeded to resolve those.

THE HOLINESS AND SOVEREIGNTY OF GOD

R. C.'s two classics, published back-to-back—*The Holiness of God* (1985) and *Chosen by God* (1986)—could be seen as presenting the two attributes of holiness and sovereignty. On the one hand, they do. Both were eclipsed, and R. C. consistently through the decades of his ministry shone a spotlight on them. They are more than simply two attributes of God alongside a long list of others. For R. C., these were ways to express fundamentally in a palpable way the being of God. We can go back to Turretin, "What God is," with respect to His nature. More on that below. But these two books and these two reverberating themes throughout the works of R. C. are a distinct and necessary contribution. God is taken far too lightly. The book title by Edward Welch expresses this poignantly: *When People Are Big and God Is Small*.[20] Knowing God in His holiness and sovereignty is the corrective and rightly reverses the order.

---

19 R. C. Sproul, *The Consequences of Ideas: Understanding the Concepts That Shaped Our World* (Wheaton, IL: Crossway, 2000), 203.

20 Edward Welch, *When People Are Big and God Is Small: Overcoming Peer Pressure, Codependency, and the Fear of Man* (Phillipsburg, NJ: P&R, 1997).

JUSTIFICATION BY FAITH ALONE AND IMPUTATION

While R. C.'s key contributions of justification by faith alone and imputation are linked to the controversy surrounding "Evangelicals and Catholics Together" (ECT) in 1994, the emphasis on this doctrine may be seen across the decades of R. C.'s work. R. C. commented that ECT was "the most painful part of his whole career."[21] ECT caused division among friends, but to R. C. too much was at stake to compromise or yield.

In the opening monologue, "1517," of the CD *Glory to the Holy One*, R. C. recalls Luther's courageous stand for justification by faith alone and imputation. Then R. C. declares: "In every generation the gospel must be published anew with the same boldness, and the same clarity, and the same urgency that came forth in the 16th century Reformation." This issue with ECT had everything to do with the clarity of the gospel. R. C. saw ECT as promoting studied ambiguity, the old nemesis. When it comes to the gospel, ambiguity will not do. Only clarity will. Erwin Lutzer testified, "I cannot think of [R. C.] without bringing the righteousness of Christ to mind."[22]

While thinking about the impact of R. C. Sproul on his own life and ministry, John Piper connects the doctrines of justification and the doctrine of God:

> For me, it was this faithfulness to biblical texts, and this high view of God's sovereignty and holiness, that made R. C.'s fight for the imputation of Christ's righteousness so credible and compelling. The bigger and more central and more sovereign and more holy God is in our eyes, the more clearly we see our desperate need for justification by faith alone.[23]

All of these contributions arc back to what he so clearly said of himself, identifying as a Reformed classical theist. He believed theology is for life.

---

21 R. C. Sproul, in Joel Belz, "Sensible Teacher," *World* magazine, January 20, 2018, 4.
22 Erwin Lutzer, "In Loving Memory of R. C. Sproul: A Tribute," Moody Church Media, December 15, 2017.
23 John Piper, "An Unashamed Herald," *Tabletalk*, Special Issue, 2018, 64.

He believed theology is ultimately doxology. To know God is to worship God. He believed God is holy. We are sinful. Jesus Christ is our perfect sacrifice, who clothes us in His righteous robe. He believed all the above, and R. C. was passionate about all the above. That is the sum of his life's ambitions and work.

Hearkening back to his bachelor's thesis at Westminster College, R. C. entitled his "Right Now Counts Forever" column published in the August 2011 issue of *Tabletalk* as "The Unholy Pursuit of God in Moby Dick." He starts extolling the novel's place: "The Great American Novel was written more than a hundred and fifty years ago by Herman Melville. This novel, the one that has been unsurpassed by any other, is *Moby Dick*." R. C. declares the novel's greatness to be found in its "unparalleled theological symbolism." It is a great novel because it tells of the greatest epic, the story of God and man. R. C. believes that "Ahab's pursuit of the whale is not a righteous pursuit of God but natural man's futile attempt in his hatred of God to destroy the omnipotent deity." He then ends the article by contrasting the unholy pursuit of the Holy One and the holy pursuit—made possible only by "experiencing the sweetness of reconciling greatness." R. C.'s final paragraphs follow:

> I believe that the greatest chapter ever written in the English language is the chapter of Moby Dick titled "The Whiteness of the Whale." Here we gain an insight into the profound symbolism that Melville employs in his novel. . . . In this chapter Melville writes, "But not yet have we solved the incantation of this whiteness, and learned why it appeals with such power to the soul; and more strange and far more portentous—why, as we have seen, it is at once the most meaning symbol of spiritual things, nay, the very veil of the Christian's Deity; and yet should be as it is, the intensifying agent in things the most appalling to mankind. . . . Wonder ye then at the fiery hunt?"
>
> If the whale embodies everything that is symbolized by whiteness— that which is terrifying; that which is pure; that which is excellent; that which is horrible and ghastly; that which is mysterious and

incomprehensible—does he not embody those traits that are found in the fullness of the perfections in the being of God Himself?

Who can survive the pursuit of such a being if the pursuit is driven by hostility? Only those who have experienced the sweetness of reconciling grace can look at the overwhelming power, sovereignty, and immutability of a transcendent God and find there peace rather than a drive for vengeance.[24]

Moby Dick tells in fiction what Isaiah 6 and the story of Uzzah record in fact—inspired, inerrant, infallible, divinely revealed fact.

When R. C. wrote this piece for *Tabletalk*, it was forty years after his bachelor's thesis. From 1961—you could stretch back to 1957 and his first conversion and 1958 and his "second" conversion—until 2011, there was a dogged consistency to the theme that was central to R. C. He did not let up from 2011 through his death in 2017. From his very first reading of the Old Testament, in September, October, November, and December of 1957 he spoke of the "God who plays for keeps." That was the God he studied, that he longed to know, the God he proclaimed to his classmates, to his girlfriend, Vesta. It was the God he served, loved, and worshiped. In the months of September, October, November, and December of 2017, he was still studying and longing to know more of who God is, proclaiming who God is, and serving, loving, and worshiping God.

R. C. changed his mind on a few things over the course of his lifetime. He once joked that at one point or another, he held every possible eschatological view. He changed his mind on the meaning of "day" in Genesis 1. But on the doctrine of God he never shifted, never "rethought" his position, never capitulated. For almost sixty years he said one thing: it's all about the doctrine of God. And what one must understand here is that it was not just the doctrine of God—but it was the doctrine of God as taught and held in the historic orthodox Christian faith, which is also a synonym for the Reformed classical tradition. The issue here is "the Godness of God."

24 R. C. Sproul, "The Unholy Pursuit of God in *Moby Dick*," *Tabletalk*, August 2011.

Not the shallow, casual, low view of God—that will not do. And it is not simply a high view of God; this is the highest high view of God. Anselm started his *Proslogion* with the word *humuncio*, "Little man." He went on to call God "that which is greater than can be conceived." Conceive of great; God is greater still. When Augustine penned his magisterial *Confessions*, the very first word is *Magnus*, "Great are you God."

This gets to the heart of R. C.'s theology and the heart of his legacy and contribution. To see it, we need a contrast. That comes in the now famous sociological analysis of Christian Smith and Melinda Lundquist Denton's 2009 Oxford University Press book, *Soul Searching: The Religious and Spiritual Lives of America's Teenagers*. Sifting through reams of research, they concluded that the view of God of American teenagers could be summed up as "moralistic therapeutic deism," God being a cross between a "Divine Butler and a Cosmic Therapist." This is precisely the shallow view of God that led to Ahab's downfall. But it is not exclusive to the view of America's teenagers. It is shared by adults in America and elsewhere, inside the church and out. This is what R. C. was pushing against, fighting against, all those decades. R. C.'s teaching was the antidote to moralistic therapeutic deism—or any other view that falls short of the Bible's portrayal of its author—a consuming fire, a whirlwind, aflame in glory, blinding in purity and holiness. As John Piper observed, "This was R. C.'s goal: a heart that is stunned and humbled and captivated by the transcendent greatness and purity of God."[25]

Jared Wilson speaks of the influence of *The Holiness of God*:

> I read this seminal work for the first time while in college. Sproul sent me to Rudolf Otto, and I learned about the experience *mysterium tremendum*, which helped give shape to all my adolescent "fear and trembling." The book *The Holiness of God* seemed to hold the key to unlocking what made Sproul so blessedly different from even the most

25 John Piper, "An Unashamed Herald," 64.

well-spoken "celebrity preachers." He was obviously a man who walked in the graciously disturbing orbit of the true numinous.[26]

Wilson points us to a significant aspect of Sproul's legacy, that of his impact on the Young, Restless, and Reformed movement. Collin Hansen coined this term for a *Christianity Today* cover story, September 22, 2006, later developing the story into his book *Young, Restless, and Reformed: A Journalist's Journey with the New Calvinists*. Hansen's own journey involves R. C. He mentions how, while in college, "an older student took me to hear R. C. Sproul preach. I didn't go looking for Reformed theology. But Reformed theology found me."[27] Hansen speaks of Christian teenagers growing up learning about "buddy Jesus," needing to learn about "Father God." And they did from R. C. Matthew Barrett speaks of that constellation of people who fathered and mentored the Young, Restless, and Reformed: MacArthur, Mohler, Packer, Piper, and Sproul, adding, "It was Sproul that sat you down at the table to eat a theological feast." He continues, "Whether it was the holiness of God, the doctrines of grace, or *sola fide*, R. C. was proof that if we don't start thinking theologically, our Christianity will be nothing but a balloon full of hot air. And he was proof that it could be done not only in the academy but in the pews."[28] The Young, Restless, and Reformed movement was a testament to the long labors by R. C. and others. For decades, he faithfully planted the seeds of the doctrine of God and the doctrines of grace.

R. C. read the Old Testament and the New Testament. He was led by his faithful teachers to Augustine, to Aquinas, to Calvin, to Turretin, to Edwards. What he found in these Mount Everests of Christian history is that all of them "were intoxicated by the greatness of God." When he won the Jordon Award in 2007 for his lifetime of publishing, R. C. said, "I wanted to help people recover the giants of the past." He found them all to have a "common

---

26 Jared Wilson, "The Numinous and R. C. Sproul," The Gospel Coalition, December 15, 2017, https://www.thegospelcoalition.org/blogs/jared-c-wilson/numinous-r-c-sproul/.

27 Collin Hansen, *Young, Restless, and Reformed: A Journalist's Journey with the New Calvinists* (Wheaton, IL: Crossway, 2008), 25.

28 Matthew Barrett, "We Are Theologians Because of R. C. Sproul," *Credo* magazine, December 14, 2017, https://credomag.com/2017/12/we-are-theologians-because-of-r-c-sproul-matthew-barrett/.

substance," namely, "an overwhelming, passionate, soul commitment to the transcendent majesty of God. That was the message that captivated me. That is what I have wanted to communicate through my teaching and through my writing more than anything else."[29]

It was the message he found in the Reformers. Here's what Roland Bainton said of Luther, bringing together the wrath of God and the work of Christ:

> In the Lord of life, born in the squalor of a cow stall and dying as a malefactor under the desertion and derision of men, crying unto God and receiving for answer only the trembling of the earth and the blinding of the sun, even by God forsaken, and in that hour taking to himself and annihilating our iniquity, trampling down the hosts of hell and disclosing within the wrath of the All Terrible the love that will not let us go. No longer did Luther tremble at the rustling of a wind-blown leaf, and instead of calling upon St. Anne he declared himself able to laugh at thunder and jagged bolts from out the storm. This was what enabled him to utter such words as these: "Here I stand. I cannot do otherwise. God help me. Amen."[30]

Lest we forget the Genevan Reformer, at the 2009 Ligonier National Conference, a year which marked the five hundredth anniversary of Calvin's birth, R. C. remarked on Calvin's observation that we tend to keep our gaze on earth, on the horizontal. But what if we lifted our gaze heavenward?[31] That is what R. C. ultimately heralded: lift your gaze to heaven. Think about who God is. The chart below shows the streams of influence on R. C. The particular way he expressed the "Godness of God" was holiness. It was missing from the moralistic therapeutic deist

---

29 R. C. Sproul, video prepared for 2007 Jordon Lifetime Achievement Award from the Evangelical Christian Publishers Association (ECPA).

30 Roland Bainton, *Here I Stand: A Life of Martin Luther* (New York: Abingdon-Cokesbury Press, 1950), 386.

31 R. C. Sproul, "I Am The Lord, There Is No Other," 2009 Ligonier National Conference, Orlando, Florida.

culture. It was missing from many sermons. Holiness also was a brilliant stroke because it instantly led to sanctification. We are to be holy as God is holy. We who have come to the thrice-holy God, "Sanctus, Sanctus, Sanctus," are to pursue, full-throttled, sanctification. R. C. cared about what you know, but he wanted what you know to transform how you live. Ultimately, he wanted it to transform lives.

The holiness of God is the main story of R. C.'s story. It is the target to which every arrow of his life was sent.[32] The chart below offers some key expressions of the doctrine of God that R. C. learned, taught, and lived as he heralded the holiness of God.

The Godness of God

Biblical Foundation
  YHWH, I Am, The Lord
  Sanctus, sanctus, sanctus
  Hallowed be Thy name

Classical Reformed Tradition
  Aliquod primum principium, Self-necessary first principle
  Ens perfectissimus, Most perfect being
  In se est, Being in itself (aseity)
  Mysterium tremendum, Awe-inspiring transcendent mystery
  Tremendum, tremor; tremble

Jonathan Edwards
  The being with the most being

Herman Melville
  The whiteness of the whale (metaphorically)

Negro Spiritual
  Tremble, Tremble, Tremble

Rudolf Otto
  The numinous (purity and overpowering absolute might)

R. C. Sproul
  Holiness

---

32 When I first asked R. C., on March 10, 2013, if it was all right by him for me to write this biography, he agreed, then immediately said, "My love for the holiness of God began in college." It was clear to me that he wanted the holiness of God to be the main story of his story.

This theology, the knowledge of God, leads to doxology, the worship of God. R. C. said that he first learned that theology is doxology from Dr. G. C. Berkouwer. Berkouwer learned it from Aquinas. Theology, Aquinas said, is taught by God, teaches about God, and leads to God. We are led from the study of God to worship Him. The beauty, majesty, and splendor of God demands our worship. Psalm 27:4 declares:

> One thing have I asked of the LORD,
>   that will I seek after:
> that I may dwell in the house of the LORD
>   all the days of my life,
> to gaze upon the beauty of the LORD
>   and to inquire in his temple.

R. C. would want to make sure we do not miss the word *beauty*. He once said, "I am moved by beauty. I am moved by order, coherence, by excellence. I think God must be exquisitely beautiful."[33] We join the Seraph-throng and declare, "Holy, Holy, Holy." That is the singular contribution of R. C. Sproul that led him to manifold contributions on the battlefields of inerrancy in the 1970s, apologetics in the face of rampant secularism in the 1980s, and justification by faith alone and imputation in the 1990s. John MacArthur said, "Where there was a battle, R. C. was there."[34] He was there because he was, like his heroes, enraptured with the transcendent majesty of God.

The Books

As mentioned, in July of 2007 R. C. was awarded the Jordon Lifetime Achievement Award from the Evangelical Christian Publishers Association. James Dobson remarked how R. C.'s books kept "the flame of orthodoxy alive," adding that his writings reveal and promote a "commitment

---

33 R. C. Sproul, "Interview," *The Wittenburg Door*, vol. 79, June–July 1984, 13.
34 John MacArthur, "Eulogy."

to the historic Christian faith."[35] Joni Eareckson Tada spoke of how R. C. could make complicated theological issues not only understandable; he could make them come alive. Various Christian leaders spoke of the influence of his books, and, rather interestingly, they spoke of the influence of R. C.'s books on them personally.

Of his more than one hundred books, R. C. identified a handful that he hoped would prove useful for the church, by God's grace and will, for decades to come. There were his two classic texts, *The Holiness of God* (1985) and *Chosen by God* (1986). Additionally R. C. singled out *Not a Chance* (1994); *Classical Apologetics* (1984); *Truths We Confess* (published as three volumes in 2006 and 2007, and revised and published as a one-volume edition posthumously in 2019); *The Consequences of Ideas* (2000); and *Knowing Scripture* (1977). He mentioned this last one because it was about teaching people how to read the Bible, making its importance obvious.[36]

Vesta has a special place for his children's books. She explains why:

> R. C. would always say, "If you don't deeply understand what you're teaching, then you can't simplify it without distorting it." The more he thought about that, the more he thought he'd like to write children's books. Of course, having grandchildren was part of it. He also hoped that parents who read his children's books would understand the Bible better.[37]

Writing was a significant part of R. C.'s professional life from the time he published his first book, *The Symbol*, in 1973. He filled page after page of yellow pads that were then typed up by his secretary and sent off to a variety of publishers. Many of these manuscripts have wholly written chapters—without edits or cross outs or false starts. When Mrs.

---

35 James Dobson, Remarks on Awarding of ECPA Jordon Lifetime Achievement to R.C. Sproul, July 2007.

36 Stephen Nichols with R. C. and Vesta Sproul, personal interview, September 26, 2013.

37 Vesta Sproul, "A Unique Perspective," 15.

Buchman sent the manuscript for *One Holy Passion* to Bruce Nygren, R. C.'s editor at Thomas Nelson, she wrote in the cover letter, "This is a red letter day for me—sending you Dr. Sproul's manuscript for *One Holy Passion*. I hope everyone who reads it will benefit from it as much as I have in typing, reading, and re-reading it."[38]

Even after his death, R. C. has had, and will continue to have, books published, as there are teaching series and sermon material that will likely continue to make its way into book form. R. C.'s writing was simply an extension of his teaching. The goal of his teaching was that people would understand the Bible better and, consequently, have a better knowledge of who God is. That was the goal of all his books, that ultimately by reading them—whether the subject was theology, apologetics, biblical studies, or the Christian life—people would come away with a better and deeper understanding of God's Word and a more intense passion for it and a desire to obey it. Many people came to know R. C. through two primary ways: by listening to him on the *Renewing Your Mind* program or by reading one of his more than one hundred books. As they met R. C., R. C. wanted them to meet and to know God.

The Institutions

In addition to being known by his books, R. C. is known as the founder of Ligonier. Today Ligonier Ministries is an international teaching ministry (with boards of directors in the United States, Canada, and the United Kingdom), producing teaching materials in a variety of formats, in multiple languages, distributed through a variety of media. R. C. started Ligonier with a budget of $85,000 and a handful of staff in 1971. In 2021, Ligonier's fiftieth anniversary year, the staff totaled around 125 employees. R. C.'s specific contributions through Ligonier include teaching series and the long-form teaching episodes, *Tabletalk* magazine, the *Renewing Your Mind* radio broadcast, the *Reformation Study Bible*; and conferences.

---

38 Maureen Buchman to Bruce Nygren, July 17, 1986.

R. C. was a teacher, and at the heart of his work are the many, many teaching series he produced. Many of his books, but certainly not all, grow out of material either directly or indirectly from his teaching. His commentaries, taken from his Saint Andrew's sermon series, are a notable exception. The *Renewing Your Mind* episodes are teaching series. From the beginning, Ligonier employed new technologies to record and distribute the teaching series. Attention was given to quality. R. C. believed the form should reflect the content. He also believed that the form should not distract from the teaching. An emphasis was put on premium video and sound—after all, you needed to be able to hear the definite lines being thrown onto the chalkboard.

The other element of R. C.'s teaching is that, with minor exceptions here and there, he taught timeless truths. He avoided the "hot take" on the current issue. He believed that the timeless was the most timely, the classic the most urgent for the day. That means that much of his teaching will likely live on. Of course, the video is dated, especially the hair, but also the clothing styles. Remove that, and the content is fresh. This became a hallmark of Ligonier's teaching as a whole. Very rarely does Ligonier venture into the timely or take on a theological news reporting persona. R. C. believed that classic Reformed theology always has something significant to say to whatever situation one wakes up to. The teaching series were the heart and soul of R. C.'s productivity.

Tabletalk began as an eight-page monthly newsletter on May 7, 1977. It was actually four 11x17 sheets folded in half and center-stapled. Initially it was produced monthly; then from 1980 until 1988 it was published bi-monthly, though with much more content in each issue. In 1989 the format was changed, keeping articles and advertisements for Ligonier materials and conferences but adding daily devotionals, which ended with a brief application, referred to as "Coram Deo," how to live before God. Along the way *Tabletalk* transitioned to a smaller format and full-color glossy paper. It is not uncommon for *Tabletalk* readers to frame covers, as some have stunning artwork. Chief among them may very well be the commissioned artwork for the August 2011 edition: a painting of Moby Dick by Lisel Jane Ashlock. The artist painted a much larger edition that was installed behind R. C.'s desk in his office at Ligonier. R. C. kept up his "Right Now Counts Forever" column through the decades. His first column, in the very first volume, May 7, 1977, was "The Pepsi Generation." His last column was "The Problem of Forgiveness," published posthumously in the February 2018 issue.

Renewing Your Mind went on the air in 1994. The third time proved a charm for R. C. and radio broadcasts. His first broadcast had been launched back in western Pennsylvania from the Ligonier Valley Study Center. It was called "The R. C. Sproul Study Hour." The second was called "Ask R. C." It began airing in 1986. Today *Renewing Your Mind* is heard on terrestrial radio on stations across the United States and around the world, and it is heard on the Internet. Testimonials pour into Ligonier from all sorts of people and places as to the impact of *Renewing Your Mind*. Augustus Nicodemus Lopes was one of them. For a decade he served as chancellor of Mackenzie Presbyterian University in Sao Paulo, a university of over thirty-five thousand students. He lived sixteen miles away from the university and every day commuted on his Harley Davidson, listening to R. C. on the headphones inside his helmet: "Dr. Sproul was my companion on the motorcycle daily."[39]

R. C. was inducted into the National Religious Broadcasters (NRB) Hall of Fame in 2016. The next year, he spoke at one of the keynote sessions at Proclaim 17, the 2017 NRB International Media Convention, held in his hometown of Orlando, Florida. R. C. spoke on, of course, Luther and Scripture and justification, making a point that the uniqueness of the Reformers was in stressing as the essential teaching, *sola Scriptura* and *sola fide*, Scripture *alone* and justification by faith *alone*—R. C. put the emphasis on *alone*. R. C. was introduced by FamilyLife's Bob Lepine. In his introduction, Lepine recalled the first time

---

39 Augustus Nicodemus Lopes, "My Motorcycle Companion," *Tabletalk*, Special Issue, 2018, 49.

he heard R. C. on the radio teaching on the holiness of God. Then he noted how R. C. also taught the great themes of the Reformation, the event everyone was celebrating in 2017. Lepine noted by stressing these Reformation themes for over five decades of ministry, R. C. "almost singlehandedly reintroduced them to the church in our generation."[40] In 2018, a Spanish edition, with Jose (Pepe) Mendoza as the translator, began airing as *Renovando Tu Mente*, the flagship of Ligonier's Spanish language outreach.

R. C. would see the *Reformation Study Bible* as one of the key initiatives of Ligonier. It was first published as the *New Geneva Study Bible* in 1995. It was rereleased as the *Reformation Study Bible* in 2005. An entirely new edition was released in 2015. This new edition had significantly enlarged and rewritten book introductions and overhauled textual notes, with a significant number of additional notes added. The theological articles from the previous edition were replaced with all new material from R. C. There were also fourteen extensive articles in the back written by a constellation of Reformed scholars. There is also a hefty portion devoted to the creeds, confessions, and catechism of the ancient church and from the Reformation. It is over 2,500 pages in length. R. C. quarterbacked the project from start to finish.

R. C. liked to say that while the *RSB* is called the *Reformation Study Bible*, our hope for it is that it serves as a catalyst for Bible study Reformation. From his notebooks back in the 1960s and early 1970s, R. C. has many outlines and teaching notes for various Bible study courses. In many of them he starts off with this line: "It's not enough to <u>read</u> the Bible—we <u>must study</u> the Bible." The *RSB: Condensed Edition* was produced in 2017. As part of Ligonier's international outreach efforts, the German edition of the RSB was released in 2017, the Korean edition was released in 2017, and the Spanish Edition was released in 2020. Efforts are underway for Portuguese and Arabic editions.

---

40 Bob Lepine, "Introduction of R. C. Sproul," Proclaim 17, National Religious Broadcasters Convention, March 2, 2017, Orlando, Florida.

Having looked briefly at the teaching series, *Tabletalk*, *Renewing Your Mind*, and the *Reformation Study Bible*, we are left with conferences as the last specific contribution of R. C. to the church through his work at Ligonier Ministries. Conferences were part of Ligonier from the old study center days.

Conferences were also part of R. C.'s ministry even before he started Ligonier. On Labor Day weekend of 1965, R. C. spoke at the College Briefing Conference, held at the Ligonier Camp and Conference Center, only 12 miles away from the future site of the Ligonier Valley Study Center. The conference was held to reinforce students theologically and spiritually as they headed back to (mostly) secular colleges. R. C. met Tim Couch there. Later Couch would join the staff with R. C. at Ligonier. They were friends for life. It was already noted how significant R. C.'s teaching was at the Young Life conference in Saranac, New York. Conferences were more than just speaking to the gathered masses. They became like family reunions for R. C. and Vesta as they saw old friends and forged new relationships. R. C. also believed that concentrated times of trusted teaching could significantly equip and encourage believers, sending them back to their churches to serve. R. C. wanted the conferences to run smoothly and to ensure that the teaching and other platform times were free of distraction. Again, he believed the form should reflect the content. Much preparation happens behind the scenes at Ligonier leading up to and during a conference so that the "students," as R. C. wanted them to be called, could focus on the teaching.

R. C. also enjoyed the time with the various speakers who came to the conferences. Meals and times together were highlights for him, filled with much laughter and some teasing. One moment of much laughter happened when Sinclair Ferguson recalled a humorous moment from a past event when speakers had gathered one evening for dinner. While they ate, Ferguson recounted a time when he was rather tired when he went up to speak at a conference. In his fatigue he intertwined the stories of the parable of the good samaritan with the parable of the prodigal son.

Once he started entangling the details of the two, he couldn't stop. As Ferguson recalled that trainwreck of a sermon and horribly embarrassing moment, R. C. could not stop laughing, guffawing actually. He soon was in pain. Steven Lawson was present, and he called his brother, a doctor, who was able to come on the scene immediately. R. C. had laughed so hard he'd cracked a rib.

There was a lot of laughter. There was also a lot of praying and encouragement. Joni Eareckson Tada, a frequent speaker at Ligonier, recalls a time of R. C.'s kindness to her husband, Ken:

> When I was battling stage 3 cancer in 2010, R. C. and Vesta prayed earnestly for me and my husband. During my chemotherapy treatment, R. C. wanted to encourage Ken in the midst of his nonstop caregiving routines. Knowing Ken was an avid fly fisherman, R. C. sent my weary husband a G-Loomis Stream Dance 5 weight 10-foot rod. It was the best on the market. You should have seen Ken's eyes get wide with delight and amazement as he opened his gift. I will always treasure R. C.'s thoughtfulness with that precious gift. It was such a "guy thing" to do; he obviously knew what would brighten my husband's heart.[41]

The study cruises were another feature. R. C. loved being at the cruise destinations and walking in the footsteps of his heroes. He also enjoyed the times with people over meals and on the buses. R. C. reached tens of thousands through his books, broadcasts, and teaching series. On the tours and at the conferences he could see students face-to-face.

In addition to Ligonier, R. C. founded two other institutions: Saint Andrew's Chapel and Reformation Bible College. Saint Andrew's Chapel faithfully continues the work started by R. C. Sproul and that small group of families. The church has a variety of ministries serving the congregation and central Florida and beyond through missionary efforts. Reformation Bible College offers a bachelor of arts in theology, with majors in biblical

---

41 Joni Eareckson Tada, "A Sacrifice of Praise," *Tabletalk*, Special Issue, 2018, 67.

studies and history of Christian thought; an associate's degree in theology; a degree completion program; and the Foundation Year program leading to a certificate.

A Summer's Evening

R. C. could look out his office window at Ligonier and see Saint Andrew's Chapel to the left and Reformation Bible College to the right. He loved that. These were the institutions that God used R. C. to found—institutions that R. C. hoped would be faithful and, God willing, carry on in the service of the church, institutions that would proclaim, defend, and contend for the gospel. All three—Ligonier, Saint Andrew's, and RBC—encircle a pond. Central Florida is full of ponds and lakes. Many of them, even the large ones, are shallow, providing a perfect home for Florida's wild reptilian population and exotic birds. Centuries-old live oaks draped in Spanish moss cover the campus, as do magnolia trees and the palms that stretch into the sunny skies. Boxwood and podocarpus hedges and philodendrons, tis, and hibiscus complete the tropical setting.

Central Florida is flat and sunny, rather different from the rolling foothills of the Alleghenies of western Pennsylvania. There's snow to shovel up there. R. C. liked shoveling sunshine instead. He did joke, though, about the grass in Florida, saying that he had to spend money to grow down in central Florida what he used to kill up in western Pennsylvania. Whenever the Sprouls went north, they enjoyed stepping on real grass.

R. C. and Vesta had homes for brief times in different places. Boston, Bussum in the Netherlands, Philadelphia, Cincinnati. But his two main homes, the two places, were central Florida and western Pennsylvania. He did not miss western Pennsylvania winters. When it did get (relatively) cold in Florida, he would say, "If this keeps up, I'm moving to Florida." But it's hard to compete with those cool summer evenings in the Ligonier Valley.

Maples, oaks, tall pines, chestnuts, cedar, and scattered crab apple trees all stand guard around the study center. The cool breeze floats down from the tree-covered dome rising above Pine Lodge. There's a pond, a volley-ball net on a grass court, and a softball field. The summer sun makes its long descent over Stone House.

It's been a full day of lectures and teaching, conversations, and meals. After dinner, and as twilight sets, people file onto the softball field. J. Alec Motyer is there; he's been lecturing on Isaiah. An Irish biblical scholar, former vicar at St. Luke's, Hampstead, and Christ Church, Westbourne, he's the principal at Trinity College, Bristol. But this evening, he's wearing a crisp white T-shirt and is playing in the outfield on a hillside in western Pennsylvania. His mind is at work, not on a Hebrew phrase, but on how to transfer the skills of cricket to the game of softball. And there's a New Testament scholar there too. He could exegete with the best of them, but he's not much of a threat on the ball field. People watching wonder if he even knows whether a softball is stuffed or inflated. Ligonier staff and students round out the teams. Children watch for a moment, then find their own games to be far more interesting. It is the kind of evening you think will never end, and you hope it never will.

And R. C.'s playing shortstop. He's calling out nicknames: "Art the Dart, you missed that one!" He's teasing, kidding, with a mischievous, joker-sized grin, all the while making plays. Working, teaching, discipling, caring, loving, praying, playing, joking, laughing. Another day at Ligonier.

But he's on the ball field now. His eyes scan the spectators in their lawn chairs. He spots Vesta and gives her a wink.

Appendix 1

R. C. SPROUL'S FINAL
TWO SERMONS

"A Glorious Savior" and "A Great Salvation"

I pray with all my heart that God will awaken
each of us today to the sweetness, the loveliness,
the glory of the gospel declared by Christ.
R. C. SPROUL, NOVEMBER 26, 2017

DR. SPROUL STARTED A sermon series on Hebrews in the fall of 2017. He preached the third sermon of the series, on Hebrews 1:6–14, in mid-November. He preached the fourth sermon, on Hebrews 2:1–4, on November 26. It was his last sermon.

Hebrews 1:6–14 weaves together a number of Old Testament citations, drawn mostly from the book of Psalms. Noting how these texts point to the supremacy of Christ, R. C. then launched into a discussion of the eternality and immutability of the triune God. In this sermon, R. C. points to the glory of Christ in refulgent splendor.

In his last sermon, on Hebrews 2:1–4, R. C. turned from the person of Christ to the work of Christ. He presented salvation in all of its simplicity and beauty, and he used all of his characteristic sermonic drama to do so, even pulling in an extended illustration from his second favorite novel. He painted the picture of our dire circumstance as we stand under the wrath of God. There is no escape—except through salvation in Christ alone. R. C. called upon his hearers not to neglect this great salvation. In his final sentence, R. C. called for an awakening.

After he preached his last sermon on November 26, Vesta jokingly said to him, "You can die now, Sweetheart. That was the best sermon you ever preached." She would certainly want the reader to know that she and he joked like that quite often. It was Vesta's way of saying how that sermon, on Hebrews 2:1–4, encapsulated so much of what R. C. taught and lived over the course of his life and ministry. It was his final plea.

In front of the large oaken doors under a Gothic arch at the entrance to Saint Andrew's is a graveyard. R. C. always believed a church should have a graveyard. He thought it a strong object lesson for the congregation as they entered and left church. R. C. is buried in that graveyard. There is a place for Vesta next to him. On his stone the family had etched:

R. C. Sproul
Feb. 13, 1939
Dec. 14, 2017
He Was a Kind Man
Redeemed by a Kinder Savior

That is the message he proclaimed in life, the message of redemption by a kind—and glorious—Savior. That was the message proclaimed in these final two sermons.[1]

---

1 These sermons have been lightly edited for publication here with the consent of the Sproul family.

A Glorious Savior

And again, when he brings the firstborn into the world, he says,

"Let all God's angels worship him."

Of the angels he says,

"He makes his angels winds,
   and his ministers a flame of fire."

But of the Son he says,

"Your throne, O God, is forever and ever,
   the scepter of uprightness is the scepter of your kingdom.
You have loved righteousness and hated wickedness;
therefore God, your God, has anointed you
   with the oil of gladness beyond your companions."

And,

"You, Lord, laid the foundation of the earth in the beginning,
   and the heavens are the work of your hands;
they will perish, but you remain;
   they will all wear out like a garment,
like a robe you will roll them up,
   like a garment they will be changed.
But you are the same,
   and your years will have no end."

And to which of the angels has he ever said,

"Sit at my right hand
   until I make your enemies a footstool for your feet"?

Are they not all ministering spirits sent out to serve for the sake of those who are to inherit salvation? (Hebrews 1:6–14)

Let's pray: *Again, our Father and our God, we are overwhelmed by our own frailty and infirmity and inability to plumb the depths and riches of this, Your Word. We need help not only to preach it, but to hear it. We need the help of Your Holy Spirit, who is the Spirit of truth, that He may shed His light upon this text for our understanding. For we ask it in the name of Jesus. Amen.*

I love the Bible, all of it. But this particular passage is simply glorious. The basic message of Hebrews is the absolute supremacy of Christ, and that comes through so clearly in this text. Verse 6 declares, "And again, when he brings the firstborn into the world, he says, 'Let all God's angels worship him.'" This is most likely a reference to the nativity when the sky exploded with the glory of God and an entire army of angels were there in force. The heavenly host was there to greet the birth of the Savior. The angels were sent not only to announce His birth but to lead the worship of the Son of God. God does not call people to worship angels, but He calls angels to worship His Son. This first chapter of Hebrews presents a series of seven testimonies to the supremacy of Jesus over the angels, five of which are from the Psalms and two of which are from other parts of the Old Testament.

In verse 7, the author of Hebrews offers the first testimony by quoting Psalm 104: "He makes his angels winds, and his ministers a flame of fire." God uses the elemental forces and powers of creation as His messengers. He uses the wind. He uses fire to bear witness to Himself and to bring truth to His people. There are manifold ways in the Old Testament in which fire is used to display the presence of God. Moses sees a bush that is burning but is not consumed. That fire indicates the theophany, the very presence, of God. After God calls to Moses from the fire, Moses leads His people in the greatest act of redemption in the Old Testament, the exodus. Next Moses leads God's multitude through the wilderness, and he leads them by way of a pillar of cloud by day and a pillar of fire by night. Then, in a rather dramatic moment, God calls Moses to His holy mountain and tells Moses to consecrate the people and have them go through rituals of purification. None dare to touch that mountain lest they die. Then, behold, the mountain is filled with smoke and with fire. The mountain itself trembled as Moses went back up and the angels were said to mediate the law that is given to Moses. Throughout these epic moments, fire is God's messenger.

Later in the Old Testament we encounter the prophet Elijah, who had provoked the wrath of Jezebel. First Kings chapter 19 tells the story. This wicked queen sought out Elijah to destroy him. Elijah fled and took refuge, hiding in a cave. In that time of hiding, he was depressed and cried out, "O Lord, they have destroyed your temple. They've torn down your altars. They've broken the covenant." Then he succumbed to what has been called the "Elijah Syndrome." He saw himself as alone in his devotion to God, and he could not take any more. He went to the cave's entrance, stood there, and waited for God to speak. What happened next? First there came a mighty wind, but God wasn't in the wind. Then the Lord sent an earthquake. The Lord wasn't in the earthquake. Then God sent His messenger of fire, but God wasn't in the fire. Instead, God spoke on this occasion to His prophet, Elijah, in a still, small voice. He rebuked His prophet, declaring "I have reserved for myself seven thousand, Elijah, who haven't bowed the knee to Baal. Stop your nonsense, your crying and complaining and thinking that you alone are left." Elijah left his cave and returned to serving as God's prophet. When Elijah's work on earth was complete, God brought him to heaven on chariots of fire, driven by horses of fire, all riding upon a whirlwind (2 Kings 2:11). Wind and fire were God's messengers.

When God destroyed the earth with water during the days of Noah, He set His bow in the sky and made a covenant saying, "Every time you see the rainbow, remember that this is my sign that I've placed in the sky that I will never again destroy the earth with water." We almost doubted that promise a few weeks ago with the wind and the water that came to Central Florida. As mighty as the winds of Hurricane Irma and of the other hurricanes that have battered Florida were, those winds came and left. The winds ceased and, at last, the water receded.

There's another phenomenon of nature that we experience here in Central Florida. We're told by the experts that in Central Florida more lightning strikes hit the earth than in all the rest of the continental United States combined. Every time you see that flash of lightning in the sky, you might be reminded of this fire that God displays communicating His sovereignty, His majesty, His omnipotence. Rather than being fearful when the thunder roars and the lightning strikes, we should remember that our God is an all-consuming fire. All these elemental forces and powers of creation are God's messengers.

He goes on to say to Christ (who is higher than the wind, higher than the fire), "Your throne, O God" (Hebrews 1:8). God never addresses angels with the name of God, but He speaks here in anticipation of the enthronement of the messianic King. Christ is the subject of this verse. The author of Hebrews uses Psalm 45, which says of the Son, "Your throne, O God, is forever and ever, the scepter of uprightness is the scepter of your kingdom." In the ancient world, there were symbols of royalty and of monarchy. Some monarchs had gorgeous robes. Others wore crowns of gold. One of the standard symbols of royalty was the scepter, the staff that was held in the hand of the king. When anybody saw the king raise the scepter, they were to fall on their knees and bow before his authority and before his majesty. Now God speaks of the scepter of His King, the symbol of the kingdom of Christ. "Your scepter is a scepter of righteousness."

How many monarchs could boast a scepter of righteousness? The history of the kings of Israel in the Old Testament reads like a rogues' gallery of criminals. Through the centuries of history, the story of kings and queens and emperors is replete with tales of bloodshed and oppression and corruption. The scepter of the King of kings is one of righteousness. Why does He have this scepter? The psalmist gives a reason. The reason Jesus has this symbol, this scepter of righteousness, is because He has loved righteousness and hated wickedness. No ruler in the history of the world has ever had the affection for righteousness that our King Jesus displays. He loves righteousness and loathes evil and wickedness. "Therefore God, your God, has anointed you with the oil of gladness beyond your companions" (Hebrews 1:9). Many commentators believe that this is a reference to the moment of Christ's ascension to glory, the Shekinah glory, to heaven, where He would be anointed as king with the oil of gladness because God was so pleased and delighted to consecrate His Son, His only Son, as our king.

Continuing this series of testimonies, the author of Hebrews next employs Psalm 102, which celebrates God's work of creation: "You, Lord, laid the foundation of the earth in the beginning, and the heavens are the work of your hands; they will perish, but you remain" (Hebrews 1:10–11a). These incredible, astonishing works of nature that God has called into existence will not abide forever. All things that are created, all creatures great and small, go through a process of generation and decay. We are creatures who are born, who live, who change, who suffer deterioration as we age, and who gain infirmities. "They [heaven and earth] will perish but you remain; they will wear out like a garment." I have a pair of shoes that I've owned for thirty years, and I'm amazed every time I look at them. I rarely wear them, but I look at them and I say, "Wow. These things are still good." Most of my shoes have worn out, and even that pair that has lasted thirty years won't endure for eternity. Our clothes get old. They decay. They don't always fit us like they used to, and so we discard them. That's how God is describing the whole universe. It will wear out like our shoes and like our clothes.

We are now coming to my favorite part of this whole section, because this text talks about the eternal, infinite, immutable being of God. Everything wears out. But here's what we learn of the Son: "You are the same, and your years will have no end" (Hebrews 1:12).

I have been a student and professor of theology for many, many years. I love to study theology. I've read lots and lots of books about theology. I have to tell you one of the finest books I've read in my lifetime is one I just read a couple of months ago called *All That Is in God* by James Dolezal. While it is an academic book and for some it could be of a challenging nature to read, it plumbs the very depths of God's nature and character. Professor Dolezal addresses a crisis that very few people anticipated was coming in our day. That not only among evangelical scholars, but among respectable Reformed scholars, there's a negotiating of the immutability of God. They're saying that God is immutable in one sense, but that in the minute He created human beings, God began to be in a relationship with His people that requires that He change. They are saying that God is immutable and that He also changes. That is a contradiction. That is wrong. It is idolatry. Let me explain.

The fundamental, primordial sin of the human race, as the apostle Paul declares in the first chapter of Romans, is idolatry. What is idolatry? It is the exchange of the truth about God for a lie, exchanging the glory of God for a lie, serving and worshiping the creature rather than the Creator, worshiping creeping things, worshiping totem poles, worshiping the sun, worshiping some form of man-made statuary. When we think of idolatry, what do we think of? We think of that which is crude and crass such as tottering and wobbling statues, made by human hands, that people bow down to, talk to, and pray to. We look at that and say how foolish. Beloved, idolatry can become extremely sophisticated wherein our conceptions of God are slightly nuanced and diminished from the purity of His being. God, in His essence—and think about this for a second—is pure, absolute, unalterable *being*. To assert anything different is idolatry.

The ancient philosophers explored ultimate reality very closely and deeply. They came to the conclusion that the fundamental difference between ultimate reality and created reality is a difference between being and becoming. What does that mean? Becoming means change. Everything in this universe, as I've mentioned already, undergoes change. It is becoming. Even the Rock of Gibraltar, if you examine it carefully, microscopically, you will see that it is subject to minuscule elements of erosion. There's nothing in this whole universe that is created that is not changing. Everything is in a state of becoming. Now, what happens if you alter your concept of God and say there's a little bit of becoming in Him? Or what if you say there are slight ways in which God changes? This was the intrusion of process philosophy, which came into the academy and into the culture in the last century. This idea that God is becoming also infiltrated evangelical circles a few years ago through the view called open theism. In both process philosophy and open theism, God is given to change. But now, in this current moment, this errant thinking about God has penetrated even the Reformed community. The teaching is that God is just slightly changing, and it is not as blatant as either process philosophy or open theism. However, beloved, you add one scintilla of becoming to your concept of Almighty God, you have turned God into a creature. No matter how sophisticated that thinking is, it is ultimately idolatrous. It is an idolatry that cuts right to the heart of being a Christian. It gets right to the heart of why we are even gathered here for worship on this Lord's Day.

Why are we here this Sunday morning? We're supposed to be here in church because we want to worship God together. The reason we want to worship God is because He's worthy of our worship. He alone is worthy of our worship, because He alone is eternal. He alone is infinite. Everybody else, everything else, is finite. Everything else is dependent and derived and mutable, but God is from everlasting to everlasting. There's no shadow of turning in Him. We never have to wonder if even one element of His promises will ever fail. God is sure and certain. The boundless difference between me and a tree or the sun and God is not simply that I'm a human being and He's the supreme being or that He's a higher order of being. No, He is being, Pure Being. No becoming. No change. His clothes never wear out.

Aren't we glad that the righteous garments of our King are never subject to corruption and decay? Aren't we glad that the righteous robe that we wear, given to us by our Savior, will last forever? His cloak is given to us by the immutable, eternal God Himself. You wonder then why I get so excited about this passage? It puts chills up my spine. Nearly every day I stain the shirt I'm wearing. Vesta has a nickname for me: Spot. The clothes of our Savior are spotless. You will never have any need to roll them up and throw them away.

The author of Hebrews ends this series of testimonies with a citation from Psalm 110: "To which of the angels has he ever said, 'Sit at my right hand until I make your enemies a footstool for your feet'?" (Hebrews 1:13). We know that God doesn't have a right hand. God is a spirit. When the Scriptures speak of Christ seated at the Father's right hand, it is speaking of a place of prominence. Christ's invitation to sit at the Father's right hand is yet another declaration of Christ's supremacy over the angels. The angels are majestic beings that serve before the throne of God. The seraphim sing in the presence of God the *Trisagion*, "Holy, holy, holy is the Lord of hosts." The cherubim and the seraphim fall down before Him. Angels serve before the very throne of God. Jesus occupies the throne of God. Psalm 110 is quoted more times in the New Testament than any other passage from the Old Testament, and there's a reason for that—the psalmist is looking forward to the ultimate ascension of Christ and His session being seated at the right hand of God. No angel has ever heard those words from the lips of God: "Sit at my right hand until I make your enemies a footstool for your feet." Again, we see that Jesus is supreme. The author of Hebrews has laid before us this testimony of the absolute supremacy of Jesus, our Savior and our King.

Now we come to the final verse of chapter 1, the rhetorical question regarding angels, "Are they not all ministering spirits sent out to serve for the sake of those who are to inherit salvation?" (Hebrews 1:14). Angels don't just serve God. They didn't just minister to Christ. Angels minister to us and to our people.

Let's pray: *Thank you, Lord, for this incredible testimony, the superiority of Christ over the angels, for the immutability of You, our God, who is from everlasting to everlasting; who changes not under or from or by the influence of anything; and who is altogether worthy of our worship now and forever. Amen.*

A Great Salvation

> Therefore we must pay much closer attention to what we have heard, lest we drift away from it. For since the message declared by angels proved to be reliable, and every transgression or disobedience received a just retribution, how shall we escape if we neglect such a great salvation? It was declared at first by the Lord, and it was attested to us by those who heard, while God also bore witness by signs and wonders and various miracles and by gifts of the Holy Spirit distributed according to his will. (Hebrews 2:1–4)

Did you notice the "Therefore" that begins this text? What the author of Hebrews is getting at is the perfect marriage between doctrine and practice. If we believe the things that he has declared in the first chapter, that has radical implications for how we live our lives. He's beginning to show that now when he says, "Therefore we must pay much closer attention." There's a little grammatical problem in the words of that particular translation. The tension of these words is because it's not certain grammatically whether the author is using a comparative or a superlative. And so I would prefer that he would simply say that we therefore must pay the most possible attention to what we have heard, lest we drift away from it.

Think of that image of drifting. Some people go fishing in boats, and they don't set the anchor down. They allow the boat to move with the current, and they just drift. Where they end up can be somewhat problematic. The Scripture uses this kind of figurative language elsewhere when it talks about an anchor for our soul, which is the hope we have in Christ. Here he is saying, "Don't allow yourselves to drift aimlessly away from what you've heard." Again, he's speaking about this marvelous comparison that he's given in chapter 1 about the superiority of Jesus over the angels and over all created things. You've heard that. Don't drift away from it; instead pay the closest possible attention to it. Verse 2 says, "For since the message declared by angels . . ." The author is referring back again to the Old Testament and the idea hinted at in Deuteronomy 33 of the law being mediated by the angels. When Moses received the law from God, there were myriads and myriads of angels present on that occasion.

So he says, "For since the message declared by angels proved to be reliable, and every transgression or disobedience received a just retribution . . ." Again, the comparison continues. If the law that came from the angels was ignored by the people in the Old Testament and received a just retribution, a punishment, how much more responsible are we to that which has come to us directly from Christ? Now, beloved, the central theme of this chapter, or at least this portion of the chapter, is the theme of escape. When you think of escape, you think of some kind of deliverance from a dire and threatening life situation, like escaping from a kidnapper. Or you think of soldiers who are surrounded in battle and finding a way to retreat safely. That's an escape. But the most common idea with which we associate escape is imprisonment, not just from any jail, but from those prisons that are the most notoriously inescapable, such as the former condition of Alcatraz in this country, or Devil's Island, or perhaps the most dreadful of all French prisons, the Château d'If.

You remember the story; it's my second-favorite novel. Edmond Dantes is falsely accused and unjustly convicted of a crime. He is sent forth to the most dreaded prison, Château d'If. There he suffered for years in solitary confinement, until one day he met a coprisoner, an aged priest who had been there for decades and had spent much time trying to dig a tunnel to escape. But he didn't do his math correctly and ended up burrowing into Dantes's chamber. So the two met and had fellowship together. The old priest became Dantes's mentor and counselor, teacher of science and philosophy and theology. The priest also told Dantes about a map that led to a vast treasure, hidden under the waters in the sea. The old priest died in prison. Through an extraordinary series of circumstances, the death of the priest led to the possible escape of Edmond Dantes from Château d'If. Dantes found the vast treasure that financed the rest of his life and his nom de plume became the Count of Monte Cristo.

What an escape story that one is. But as dire and as dreadful as the circumstances were in the Château d'If, there's even a greater and more dreadful kind of captivity. The author of Hebrews speaks of an escape from this captivity when he asks the question, "How shall we escape if we neglect such a great salvation?" Beloved, this is a rhetorical question. The answer to the question is simple. How shall we escape if we neglect so great a salvation? The answer is, we can't. Alcatraz could possibly be escaped from, or Devil's Island, or even the Château d'If. But the one prison from which no one ever escapes is hell. There's no escape route. You can't dig under it. You can't climb over it. No guard can be bribed. The sentence cannot be ameliorated. So the author of Hebrews is saying, "Do you realize what we have heard from the Word of God Himself about a great salvation?" We use that word *salvation* all the time in the church. What does it mean?

When somebody says to me, "Are you saved?" the first question I want to say is, "Saved from what?" The idea of salvation suggests the idea of some kind of escape or deliverance from a dire circumstance. The Greek verb *sodzo* in the New Testament is used in a variety of ways. If you are saved from a threatening illness, as people were in the New Testament by the touch of Jesus, Jesus might comment, "Your faith has saved you." He's not talking about eternal salvation. He's speaking about their rescue from a dreadful disease. In the Old Testament it was used as the people of Israel went into battle and God intervened on their behalf and saved His people. He saved them from military defeat. That was rescue from a clear and present danger. This verb "to save" is used in all kinds of ways. In virtually every tense of the Greek verb, there is a sense in which you were saved, you were being saved, you have been saved, you are saved, you are being saved, and you will be saved. Salvation takes all these different tenses of the verb.

There's salvation in the general sense that has manifold applications. But when the Bible speaks about salvation in the ultimate sense, it's speaking of the ultimate escape from the ultimate dire human condition. What does it mean to be saved? It means, as the Scriptures tell us, to be rescued from the wrath that is to come. God's wrath, as we are told in Romans, is revealed to the whole world. But we're at ease in Zion. We're not afraid of His wrath because we've been told over and over again that God's not mad, that God's not angry. We don't need to worry about God. God's going to save everybody. All you need to get into heaven is to die. I wish that everybody who died went to heaven, but the Bible makes it abundantly clear that that's not the case, and that there awaits a judgment. The greatest calamity is to be sentenced to hell. The Château d'If is a luxury resort compared to hell.

The author raises this question: How do we escape? If we neglect that salvation, beloved, there's no escape. The question is this: to whom is the author of Hebrews speaking? He says, "How shall *we* escape if *we* neglect so great a salvation?" He's not talking about the run-of-the-mill pagan who goes through life, who not only neglects the gospel of salvation but is utterly disinterested in it and may be outwardly hostile to it. We have multitudes of people who live in this country and around the world who despise the gospel; they don't just neglect it. The author of Hebrews isn't talking about those people. He uses the word *we*. That's us. How shall we escape if we neglect so great a salvation? Again, the answer to the rhetorical question is we can't and we won't.

Did you pay attention to the beginning of the song that the girls' youth choir sang this morning? Let me refresh your memory about those words. Listen to what they sang: "O God, you are my God, and I long for you. My whole being desires you. Like a dry land, my soul thirsts for you. Let me see you in your sanctuary, and I will praise. And I will be satisfied as long as I live." When you listen to these words, do they sound like words that would come from somebody who neglects the gospel? What does it mean to be neglectful? To neglect something is to overlook it, take it lightly, certainly not to devote yourself steadfastly to it. Somebody asked me a question a couple of weeks ago. We were talking about different congregations, and I was telling them how much I love the congregation of Saint Andrew's. I said, "It's a fantastic congregation." And he said to me, "How many people do you think in that congregation are really Christians?" I said, "I don't know. I can't read the hearts of people. Only God can do that, but I know everybody that's a member of the church has made an outward profession of faith. So 100 percent of our people have professed the faith."

He then asked, "But how many do you think really mean it?" I responded, I don't know—70 percent, 80 percent. I may be seriously overestimating that, or I may be underestimating. One thing I know for sure is that not everybody in the congregation is a Christian. How do you know if you are? Can you sing the words of this song? "O God, you are my God, and I long for you. My whole being desires you." How can you be a Christian and neglect so great a salvation? Is the salvation not enough? Maybe you think it's all right. It's good, but really not great. Do you neglect it? I can't answer that question. If you neglect it and treat it lightly, it probably means that you've never been converted, that God has never quickened or awakened your soul from spiritual death. This salvation is incredible. It deserves our diligence, our energetic pursuit of it. Certainly it does not deserve neglect.

Perhaps the author of Hebrews had in mind what happened in the Old Testament, when the people had their greatest moment of salvation in the exodus. They were slaves. Pharaoh wouldn't give them any straw for their bricks, and they were brutally beaten and virtually imprisoned by Pharaoh. They cried and they groaned and they prayed. God heard the groans of His people, and He sent Moses to Pharaoh to say, "Let my people go!" God's people came out, multitudes of people fleeing from captivity. They got to Migdol, where in front of them was the sea and behind them were the chariots of Egypt. There was no escape. It seemed hopeless. Then the wind blew and dried up a pathway through the Red Sea, and Israel escaped.

But the chariots of Pharaoh did not escape. The horse and the rider were thrown into the sea. That was a great salvation. No sooner were God's people rescued from this tyranny, and they started complaining about the manna that God provided for them. "Oh, I wish we were back in Egypt. We might have been slaves, but we had garlic to eat, and leeks and onions." They betrayed their freedom. The author of Hebrews has in mind how the people of Israel in the Old Testament neglected and were ungrateful for their salvation. There were few who made it to the promised land. That is where we are right now. We've heard the Word of God. It's a message of good news—not just good news, but great news; not just great news, but the greatest of all possible news that those who believe in Christ will be saved from the wrath which is to come. How can you possibly neglect it in the first place? But that's not the question the author is asking when he says, "How can we possibly escape?"

His concern is how could we possibly neglect such a great salvation that "was declared at first by the Lord, and it was attested to us by those who heard, while God also bore witness by signs and wonders and various miracles and by gifts of the Holy Spirit distributed according to His will" (Hebrews 2:3–4). God doesn't ask us to believe in His gospel by taking a leap of faith into the darkness, hoping that Jesus will catch us. Nicodemus came to Jesus at night and he said, "Rabbi, we know that you are a teacher come from God, for no one can do these signs that you do unless God is with him" (John 3:2). Nicodemus's theology was sound. We don't try to prove the existence of God by miracles. There couldn't be miracles if you didn't first understand that God exists. The purpose of miracles is not to prove the existence of God. The purpose of miracles is to prove and attest to the truth of those who are declaring the gospel. God certified Moses by miracles. He certified Jesus by miracles. He certified His apostles by miracles and powers and signs and wonders, and even the spiritual gifts that were given to the church, to show the great salvation that God announced to the world. This is the good news.

Jesus declared it to us, not just the angels. If you neglect what Jesus says, and you neglect what God proves, then we're back to the theme. There is no escape. Beloved, if you come to church every Sunday, every single Sunday of your life, and go to Sunday school every week of your life, you may still be neglecting this great salvation. Is your heart in it? That's what I'm asking you. I can't answer that question for you. You know if you're neglecting your salvation. I don't have to tell it to you. I just have to tell you what the consequences are if you continue in that neglect. So I pray with all my heart that God will awaken each one of us today to the sweetness, the loveliness, the glory of the gospel declared by Christ.

Let's pray: *We thank you, O, Jesus, that you are for us the great escape. We're thankful that because of you and what you've done for us, we have nothing to fear from the wrath that is to come. But we pray, O God, that you would feed our souls, cause us to hunger and to thirst after you as the deer pants after the mountain stream. Ignite a flame in our hearts that we may not neglect you but pursue you with everything we have. For we ask you in Jesus's name. Amen.*

Appendix 2

R. C. SPROUL TIMELINE

February 13, 1939. Born to Robert Cecil and Mayre Ann (Yardis) Sproul in Pleasant Hills, Pennsylvania.

1945. Meets the love of his life, Vesta Ann Voorhis, while in the first grade and she in the second.

1957. Enters Westminster College, New Wilmington, Pennsylvania, on an athletic scholarship.

September 1957. Converted during his freshman year.

1958. Has "second" conversion to the holiness of God.

June 11, 1960. Marries Vesta Ann (Voorhis) Sproul.

1961. Receives bachelor of arts in philosophy.

1961–1964. Enters Pittsburgh Theological Seminary, Pittsburgh, Pennsylvania; studies under John Gerstner.

1964. Receives bachelor of divinity.

1964–1965. Begins doctoral studies under G. C. Berkouwer at the Free University, Amsterdam.

July 18, 1965. Ordained at Pleasant Hills Community Presbyterian Church (UPUSA), Pleasant Hills, Pennsylvania.

1965–1966. Teaches philosophy and theology at his alma mater Westminster College.

1966–1968. Teaches as assistant professor of theological studies at Gordon College, Wenham, Massachussetts.

1968–1969. Teaches as assistant professor of philosophical theology at Conwell School of Theology (Philadelphia); teaches adult Sunday school at Oreland Presbyterian Church, Oreland, Pennsylvania, sparking the vision for what would come to be the Ligonier Valley Study Center.

June 1969. Receives Drs, doctarandus degree, at Free University, Amsterdam.

1969–1971. Serves as associate pastor of evangelism, mission, and theology at College Hill Presbyterian Church (UPUSA), Cincinnati, Ohio.

Summer 1970. Speaks at Young Life conference on the holiness of God, during which he has a conversation with Dora Hillman of a possible study center in the Pittsburgh area.

August 1, 1971. Opens the Ligonier Valley Study Center in Stahlstown, Pennsylvania.

1973. Publishes first book, *The Symbol: An Exposition of the Apostles' Creed*.

1974. Produces first teaching series for videotape, How to Study the Bible; holds inerrancy conference and publishes the Ligonier Statement on Inerrancy.

1975. Moves ministerial credential to the Presbyterian Church in America (PCA).

1976. Receives honorary doctorate from Geneva College, Beaver Falls, Pennsylvania.

May 6, 1977. Ships first issue of *Tabletalk*, eight-page newsletter and "educational tool."

1978. Plays a lead role in the Chicago Statement on Biblical Inerrancy; serves as president of International Council on Biblical Inerrancy.

1980–1995. Serves as professor at Reformed Theological Seminary, Jackson, Mississippi, and at Orlando, Florida, campuses.

1984. Moves Ligonier Ministries to Orlando, Florida; publishes *Classical Apologetics*.

1985. Publishes *The Holiness of God*.

1986. Publishes *Chosen by God*.

1988. Hosts Ligonier's first annual national conference with the theme "Loving a Holy God."

1993. Receives honorary doctorate from Grove City College, Grove City, Pennsylvania.

1994. Contends against "Evangelicals and Catholics Together."

October 3, 1994. Airs first episode of daily radio program *Renewing Your Mind*.

1996. Publishes first children's book, *The King without a Shadow*.

July 20, 1997. Holds first service of Saint Andrew's Chapel in the Ligonier studios.

June 2007. Speaks against Federal Vision at the 35th General Assembly of the PCA.

July 2007. Receives Jordon Award for Lifetime Achievement from the Evangelical Christian Publishers' Association (ECPA).

2011. Founds Reformation Bible College, Sanford, Florida.

2011–2014. Serves as first president of Reformation Bible College.

2012. Receives honorary doctorate from Westminster Theological Seminary, Glenside, Pennsylvania.

2015. Releases first CD, *Glory to the Holy One*, in collaboration with Jeff Lippencott.

2016. Inducted into the National Religious Broadcasters Hall of Fame.

October 30, 2017. Speaks at Ligonier's "Reformation 500 Celebration."

November 26, 2017. Preaches last sermon at Saint Andrew's on Hebrews 2:1–4.

December 14, 2017. Dies in Altamonte Springs, Florida.

December 20, 2017. Memorial Service held at Saint Andrew's Chapel.

BOOKS BY R. C. SPROUL

1–2 Peter: An Expositional Commentary. Orlando, FL: Reformation
Trust, 2019.
Verse-by-verse commentary on the epistles of Peter. Previously pub-
lished 2011 as *1–2 Peter*, St. Andrew's Expositional Commentary
(Crossway).

Abortion: A Rational Look at an Emotional Issue. Orlando, FL: Reformation
Trust, 2010.
Provides well-considered and compassionate answers to the difficult
questions that attend termination of pregnancy; strives for a factual,
well-reasoned approach informed by careful biblical scholarship.
Previously published 1990 (NavPress).

Acts: An Expositional Commentary. Orlando, FL: Reformation Trust, 2019.
Explores important theological terms and themes and engages in
practical application. Previously published 2010 as *Acts*, St. Andrew's Expositional Commentary (Crossway).

Are We Together? A Protestant Analyzes Roman Catholicism. Orlando, FL:
Reformation Trust, 2012.
A stand for the cardinal doctrines of Protestantism in opposition to
the teaching of the Roman Catholic Church. The book is a result of
decades of study stretching back to R. C. Sproul's seminary courses.

Barber Who Wanted to Pray, The. Wheaton, IL: Crossway, 2011.

Based on a true story of a barber and his famous customer, Martin Luther. One of R. C.'s children's books, this teaches children to pray according to the Bible.

Basic Training. Grand Rapids, MI: Zondervan, 1982.

An overview of doctrine by offering an exposition of the Apostles' Creed. Previously published as *The Symbol* (1973) and later as *Renewing Your Mind* (1998) and as *What We Believe* (2015).

Before the Face of God: Book 1. Grand Rapids, MI: Baker, 1992.

Adapted from 1989 *Tabletalk* devotionals; covers the book of Romans verse by verse, with 233 daily studies and practical suggestions for living out faith.

Before the Face of God: Book 2. Grand Rapids, MI: Baker, 1993.

Adapted from 1990 *Tabletalk* devotionals; covers the book of Luke verse by verse, with 260 daily studies and practical suggestions; explores the life of Christ and His good news.

Before the Face of God: Book 3. Grand Rapids, MI: Baker, 1994.

Adapted from the 1991 *Tabletalk* devotionals; surveys the Old Testament, with over 250 daily studies and practical advice for Christian living; explores the history of God's people and God's work.

Before the Face of God: Book 4. Grand Rapids, MI: Baker, 1996.

Adapted from *Tabletalk* devotionals; covers the books of Ephesians, Hebrews, and James verse by verse.

Can I Trust the Bible? Sanford, FL: Reformation Trust, 2017.

Commentary on the Chicago Statement on Biblical Inerrancy. Includes the commentary as well as the text of the Chicago Statement. Previously published 2009; previously published 1980, 1996 as *Explaining Inerrancy: A Commentary* (ICBI).

Character of God, The. Ventura, CA: Regal, 2003.

The believer's quest to know God the Father is the basis of this study of God's biblically revealed attributes and characteristics.

Previously published 1995 (Servant) and 1987 as *One Holy Passion* (Thomas Nelson).

Choosing My Religion. Phillipsburg, NJ: P&R, 2005.

Targeted to teenagers, this short book seeks to answer whether there are many paths to God or only one. Previously published 1996 (Baker).

Chosen by God. Wheaton, IL: Tyndale, 1986.

The classical Reformed doctrine of God's electing grace discussed in its biblical and philosophical context.

Classical Apologetics. With Arthur Lindsley and John Gerstner. Grand Rapids, MI: Zondervan, 1984.

Defining apologetics as the rational defense of the Christian faith, this book offers a thorough presentation of the classical apologetics view and an extensive critique of the presuppositional apologetics view.

Consequences of Ideas, The: Understanding the Concepts That Shaped Our World. Wheaton, IL: Crossway, 2000.

An introduction to the ideas that have had lasting influence; offers an analysis of the history of philosophy from the pre-Socratic philosophers through Darwin, Freud, and Sartre. This books offers a summative treatment of much of R. C.'s teaching on and study of the history of philosophy.

Dark Side of Islam, The. Wheaton, IL: Crossway, 2015.

Interview with a former Muslim who explains little-known aspects of Islam. Previously published in 2003.

Defending Your Faith: An Introduction to Apologetics. Wheaton, IL: Crossway, 2003.

An introduction to apologetics, the science of defending the Christian faith. Builds off the material R. C. Sproul contributed to *Classical Apologetics.*

Discovering the God Who Is. Ventura, CA: Regal, 2008.

The believer's quest to know God the Father is the basis of this study of God's biblically revealed attributes and characteristics.

Previously published as *One Holy Passion* (1987) and as *The Character of God* (2003).

Discovering the Intimate Marriage. Minneapolis: Bethany Fellowship, 1975.

A Christian understanding of marriage with special emphasis on the meaning of intimacy.

Donkey Who Carried a King, The. Orlando, FL: Reformation Trust, 2012.

This children's book offers a unique perspective on the events of Jesus's Passion Week and calls all believers, both young and old, to follow in the footsteps of the Suffering Servant for the glory of God.

Doubt and Assurance. Edited by R. C. Sproul. Grand Rapids, MI: Baker, 1993.

Adapted from articles in *Tabletalk*; examines how doubts about the faith assail us and true assurance uplifts us. Contributors include Steve Brown, John Gerstner, Roger Nicole, Os Guinness, and others.

Effective Prayer. Wheaton, IL: Tyndale, 1984.

Short introduction to the biblical doctrine of prayer—its purpose, practice, and power.

Essential Truths of the Christian Faith. Wheaton, IL: Tyndale House, 1992.

More than one hundred key theological terms are defined here in brief expositions that simplify complex theological discussions. Sets the stage for in-depth theological study.

Ethics and the Christian. Wheaton, IL: Tyndale, 1983.

Short introduction to the subject of Christian ethics.

Everyone's a Theologian. Orlando, FL: Reformation Trust, 2014.

Surveys the basic truths of the Christian faith in nontechnical language.

Explaining Inerrancy. Orlando, FL: Ligonier, 1996.

R. C. Sproul's commentary on the Chicago Statement on Biblical Inerrancy. Includes the text of the Chicago Statement. Previously published as *Explaining Inerrancy: A Commentary* (1980).

Faith Alone: The Evangelical Doctrine of Justification. Grand Rapids, MI: Baker, 2016.

Explores the doctrine of justification by faith alone; R. C. Sproul's book-length response to "Evangelicals and Catholics Together" (1994). This book offers a summative treatment of R. C.'s teaching on Reformation theology and the *solas*. Previously published 1995.

Five Things Every Christian Needs to Grow, Revised and Expanded. Orlando, FL: Reformation Trust, 2008.

Identifies five of the crucial "nutrients" that promote spiritual growth: Bible study, prayer, worship, service, and stewardship. Previously published 2002 (W Publishing Group).

Following Christ. Wheaton, IL: Tyndale, 1991.

Provides answers from our one firm foundation, Jesus Christ. Previously published as four smaller books: *Who Is Jesus?*; *Effective Prayer*; *God's Will and The Christian*; and *Ethics and the Christian* (1983–1984).

Getting the Gospel Right: The Tie That Binds Evangelicals Together. Grand Rapids, MI: Baker, 1999.

R. C. Sproul's response to and commentary on the documents "The Gift of Salvation" (1998) and "The Gospel of Jesus Christ: An Evangelical Celebration" (1999).

Glory of Christ, The. Phillipsburg, NJ: P&R, 2003.

Though humbled as a man, the glory of Christ shone forth at strategic points in the life of Christ. From the angels' song of "glory to the newborn King" to the promise of His return on clouds of glory, Christ leaves us in awe and worship. Previously published 1990 (Tyndale).

God Is Holy and We're Not. Orlando, FL: Ligonier, 2014.

Abridged version of *The Holiness of God* created for outreach at the 2014 World Cup in Brazil.

God's Inerrant Word: An International Symposium on the Trustworthiness of Scripture. Edited by John Warwick Montgomery. Minneapolis: Bethany Fellowship, 1975.

The publication of papers presented at Ligonier's conference on inerrancy. R. C. Sproul served as convener of the conference and as contributor.

God's Love. Colorado Springs, CO: David C. Cook, 2012.

Explores the love of God, which finds its ultimate expression in His Son. Examines several paradoxes, such as a loving God and divine hate, and how love coexists with God's sovereignty.

God's Will and the Christian. Wheaton, IL: Tyndale, 1984.

Short book for those seeking to discover God's will, with a specific focus on personal choices such as career and marriage.

Gospel of God, The: An Exposition of Romans. Fearn, Ross-shire, Scotland: Christian Focus, 1999.

Full-length, verse-by-verse commentary on Paul's epistle to the church at Rome. Previously published 1994 as *Romans* (Christian Focus).

Grace Unknown: The Heart of Reformed Theology. Grand Rapids, MI: Baker, 1997.

Shows that the theology of the Protestant Reformers of the sixteenth century is simply an accurate, systematic summary of the teachings of the Bible.

Growing in Holiness: Understanding God's Role and Yours. Grand Rapids, MI: Baker, 2000.

Published posthumously, this book is comprised of lectures by R. C. Sproul on the doctrine of sanctification.

Holiness of God, The: Revised and Expanded. Wheaton, IL: Tyndale, 1998.

Explanation of what is perhaps the most important yet least understood attribute of God—holiness. Previously published 1985.

How Then Shall We Worship? Colorado Springs, CO: David C. Cook, 2013.

Examines the basic biblical principles of worship; calls the modern church away from shallowness to a reverence for the living God. Previously published as *A Taste of Heaven* (2006).

Hunger for Significance, The. Phillipsburg, NJ: P&R, 2001.

Explores the meaning and importance of human dignity. Previously published 1983, 1991 as *In Search of Dignity* (Regal).

If There's a God, Why Are There Atheists?: Why Atheists Believe in Unbelief. Fearn, Ross-shire, Scotland: Christian Focus, 2018.

Analysis of why men reject the God of the Bible in favor of lesser deities. Previously published 1997 (Ligonier); previously published 1974, 1988 as *The Psychology of Atheism* (Bethany Fellowship).

In the Presence of God. Nashville, TN: Word, 1999.

Devotional readings based on fifteen attributes of God.

In Search of Dignity. Ventura, CA: Regal, 1983.

Explores the meaning and importance of dignity in the life of everyone.

Intimate Marriage, The. Phillipsburg, NJ: P&R, 2003.

A Christian understanding of marriage with special emphasis on the meaning of intimacy. Previously published 1975, 1986 as *Discovering the Intimate Marriage* (Tyndale).

Invisible Hand, The: Do All Things Really Work for Good? Phillipsburg, NJ: P&R, 2003.

Examines the doctrine of providence; demonstrates that Christians can put their complete trust in God, who works all things for the good of those who love Him. Previously published 1996 (Word).

John: An Expositional Commentary. Orlando, FL: Reformation Trust, 2019.

Verse-by-verse commentary on the Gospel of John. Previously published 2009.

Johnny Come Home. Ventura, CA: Regal, 1984.

Novel featuring two men who choose dramatically different roads in their lives. Won the Angel Award for 1984.

King without a Shadow, The. Phillipsburg, NJ: P&R, 2001.

Children's book highlighting, through a simple story of a boy and his dog, the holiness of God. R. C. Sproul's first children's book. Previously published 1996 (Chariot).

Knight's Map, The. Orlando, FL: Reformation Trust, 2016.

Allegorical tale that teaches the reliability and trustworthiness of the Bible by telling the story of a brave knight's quest to find the Pearl of Great Price, guided by an ancient map.

Knowing Scripture. Expanded ed. Downers Grove, IL: InterVarsity Press, 2016.

A basic guide to hermeneutics, the art and science of interpretation. Previously published 1978.

Last Days according to Jesus, The. Grand Rapids, MI: Baker, 2015.

Response to the skeptic's charge of error in Christ's prophecies. Previously published 1998.

Legacy of Luther, The. Coedited by Stephen J. Nichols. Orlando, FL: Reformation Trust, 2016.

Overview of the life, thought, and legacy of the great Reformer, commemorating the five hundredth anniversary of the posting of the Ninety-Five Theses and featuring contributions from a distinguished group of scholars and pastors.

Lifeviews. Grand Rapids, MI: Revell, 1986.

A guide for understanding the prevailing attitudes and ideas that shape our culture.

Lightlings, The. Orlando, FL: Reformation Trust, 2006.

An allegorical tale for children that captures the essence of the biblical story of redemption. A race of tiny beings known as lightlings are a picture of humanity as they pass through all the stages of the biblical drama.

Loved by God. Nashville, TN: W Publishing Group, 2001.

A study of the many aspects of God's love for His people.

Making a Difference: Impacting Society as a Christian. Grand Rapids, MI: Baker, 2019.

Previously published as *Lifeviews* (1986).

Mark: An Expositional Commentary. Orlando, FL: Reformation Trust, 2019.

A verse-by-verse expositional commentary on the Gospel of Mark. Previously published 2011 as *Mark*, St. Andrew's Expositional Commentary (Crossway).

Matthew: An Expositional Commentary. Orlando, FL: Reformation Trust, 2019.

A verse-by-verse expositional commentary on the Gospel of Matthew. Previously published 2013 as *Matthew*, St. Andrew's Expositional Commentary (Crossway).

Mighty Christ: Touching Glory. Fearn, Ross-shire, Scotland: Christian Focus, 1995.

An introductory-level explanation of what the Bible teaches concerning the person and work of Jesus Christ.

Moses and the Burning Bush. Orlando, FL: Reformation Trust, 2018.

Adapted from the teaching series of the same name; presents the doctrine of God from the perspective of Moses's encounter.

Mystery of the Holy Spirit, The. Twenty-fifth anniversary ed. Orlando, FL: Reformation Trust, 2015.

Focuses on the hidden and unseen regenerating work of the Holy Spirit in the life of the believer. Previously published 1990 (Tyndale); previously published 2009 (Christian Focus).

New Geneva Study Bible. Nashville, TN: Thomas Nelson, 1995.

First Reformed study Bible since the original Geneva Bible of 1560; provides study aids including textual notes, chapter introductions, theological sidebars. R. C. Sproul served as general editor of the project and wrote the notes for the book of James.

Not A Chance: God, Science, and the Revolt against Reason. Grand Rapids, MI: Baker, 2014.

Exposes the chance theory of the universe's origin as a logical absurdity and a scientific impossibility. Helps defend reasonable faith against unreasonable alternatives. Previously published 1994 (Baker).

Now, That's a Good Question. Wheaton, IL: Tyndale, 1996.

Adapted from transcripts of the *Ask R. C.* radio programs, provides succinct answers to more than three hundred common questions.

Objections Answered. Ventura, CA: Gospel Light-Regal, 1978.

Response to common objections to Christianity, which were collected by Evangelism Explosion. Also published as *Reason to Believe* (1978).

One Holy Passion: The Consuming Thirst to Know God. Nashville, TN: Thomas Nelson, 1987.

The believer's quest to know God the Father is the basis of this study on God's biblically revealed attributes and characteristics.

Pleasing God. Colorado Springs, CO: David C. Cook, 2012.

An in-depth look at God's plan and pathway for spiritual maturity. The book's call to live the Christian life is built on the premise that knowing God leads us to obeying and desiring to please God. Previously published 1988 (Tyndale).

Prayer of the Lord, The. Orlando, FL: Reformation Trust, 2009.

Shows that the model prayer Jesus gave to His disciples is a treasure trove of principles for an often-neglected and misunderstood spiritual discipline; shows to whom believers are to pray, then explains how we are to pray and what we should ask in prayer.

Priest with Dirty Clothes, The. Orlando, FL: Reformation Trust, 2011.

R. C. Sproul's second children's book tells the story of a mud-covered priest who can only find cleansing from the Great Prince. The book teaches the doctrine of imputation in a way a child can understand. Previously published 1997 (Tommy Nelson).

Prince's Poison Cup, The. Orlando, FL: Reformation Trust, 2008.

Part of a series of books designed to present biblical truths to children. This work focuses on the atonement, showing that Jesus had to endure the curse of sin in order to redeem His people from their spiritual death.

Promises of God, The. Colorado Springs, CO: David C. Cook, 2013.

Explores the meaning of covenant and looks at the specific covenants in the Old and New Testaments, showing how God fulfills His plan of redemption in and through His people.

Psychology of Atheism, The. Minneapolis: Bethany Fellowship, 1974.

Analysis of why men reject the God of the Bible in favor of lesser deities.

Purpose of God, The: An Exposition of Ephesians. Fearn, Ross-shire, Scotland: Christian Focus, 2002.

Verse-by-verse commentary of the issues raised by Paul as he dealt with the Ephesian church. Explores the powerful message of God's sovereign choice and the importance of the church to the believer. Previously published 1994 as *Ephesians* (Christian Focus).

Race of Faith, The. Orlando, FL: Reformation Trust, 2016.

Adaptation of the teaching series Basic Training created for outreach at the 2016 Summer Olympics in Rio de Janeiro.

Reason to Believe. Grand Rapids, MI: Zondervan, 2016.

Response to common objections to Christianity. Previously published 1982; previously published 1978 as *Objections Answered* (Regal).

Reformation Study Bible (ESV). Orlando, FL: Ligonier, 2015.

This first Reformed Study Bible since the original Geneva Bible of 1560 provides study aids including textual notes, chapter introductions, theological sidebars, and more. Dr. Sproul served as general editor of the project and wrote the notes for the book of James. Previously published 2005.

Reformation Study Bible (NKJV). Orlando, FL: Ligonier, 2016.
Updated, revised, and expanded edition of the *Reformation Study Bible* in the New King James Version. Previously published 1998 (Thomas Nelson) and 1995 as the *New Geneva Study Bible* (Thomas Nelson).

Renewing Your Mind. Grand Rapids, MI: Baker, 1998.
Exposition of the Apostles' Creed. Previously published as *The Symbol* (1973) and as *Basic Training* (1982).

Right Now Counts Forever. 4 vols. Orlando, FL: Reformation Trust, 2021.
These four volumes reproduce R. C. Sproul's *Tabletalk* columns spanning forty-one years, from 1977 until 2018.

Romans: An Expositional Commentary. Orlando, FL: Reformation Trust, 2019.
R. C. Sproul's sixty sermons on Romans, which he preached from 2005 to 2007 at Saint Andrew's. Previously published 2009 as *Romans*, St. Andrew's Expositional Commentary (Crossway).

Running the Race. Grand Rapids, MI: Baker, 2003.
Designed to help recent graduates face the issues they will soon encounter. Currently out of print.

Saved from What? Wheaton, IL: Crossway, 2002.
Explains the great salvation provided through the life, death, and resurrection of Christ for all who believe. Asks what we are saved from, saved for, and saved by.

Scripture Alone: The Evangelical Doctrine. Phillipsburg, NJ: P&R, 2005.
A statement of the Protestant doctrine of Scripture consisting of R. C. Sproul's most important articles on the subject as well as his commentary on the Chicago Statement on Biblical Inerrancy.

Soli Deo Gloria: Essays in Reformed Theology. Edited by R. C. Sproul. Phillipsburg, NJ: Presbyterian & Reformed, 1976.
Festschrift for John H. Gerstner. Includes articles by Sproul, Cornelius Van Til, J. I. Packer, John Murray, John Warwick Montgomery, Roger Nicole, and others.

Soul's Quest for God, The. Phillipsburg, NJ: P&R, 2003.

Draws from biblical portraits and church history to trace the beginning of the quest in regeneration to its fulfillment in heaven. Previously published 1993 (Tyndale).

Stronger than Steel: The Wayne Alderson Story. San Francisco, CA: Harper & Row, 1980.

Story of the life and work of Wayne Alderson, the man who defused a potentially explosive strike at a Pennsylvania steel foundry, thereby providing a model for future peaceful negotiations between workers and management.

Surprised by Suffering. Twenty-fifth-anniversary ed. Orlando, FL: Reformation Trust, 2014.

The sovereign work of God in the life of suffering believers is considered in this compassionate look at the problem of pain. Previously published 1989 (Tyndale) and 2009 (Reformation Trust).

Symbol, The: An Exposition of the Apostles' Creed. Phillipsburg, NJ: Presbyterian & Reformed, 1973.

R. C.'s first book, offering a discussion of doctrine by way of exposition of the Apostles' Creed. Designated by *Christianity Today* as one of the significant books published that year.

Taste of Heaven, A. Orlando, FL: Reformation Trust, 2006.

Examines the key components of prayer, praise, and sacrifices that God gave to His people in the Old Testament and shows how biblical principles can guide today's worshipers.

Thy Brother's Keeper. Dallas: Word, 1992.

Novel featuring two men who choose dramatically different roads in their lives. Won the 1984 Angel Award. Previously published as *Johnny Come Home* (1984; 1988).

Truth of the Cross, The. Orlando, FL: Reformation Trust, 2007.

A comprehensive introduction to the atonement of Christ.

Truths We Confess: A Layman's Guide to the Westminster Confession of Faith. Vol. 1, *The Triune God.* Phillipsburg, NJ: P&R, 2006.

Covers chapters 1–8 of the Westminster Confession of Faith; brings readers to a deeper knowledge of and greater love for the doctrines of grace set forth in God's Word. Includes Holy Scripture, God and the Trinity, his decree, creation, providence, the fall into sin, God's covenant, and Christ the Mediator.

Truths We Confess: A Layman's Guide to the Westminster Confession of Faith. Vol. 2, *Salvation and the Christian Life.* Phillipsburg, NJ: P&R, 2007.

Covers chapters 9–22 of the Westminster Confession of Faith; explains the doctrines of free will, effectual calling, justification, adoption, sanctification, faith, repentance, good works, perseverance, assurance, God's law, Christian liberty, the Sabbath, and oaths.

Truths We Confess: A Layman's Guide to the Westminster Confession of Faith. Vol. 3, *The State, the Family, the Church, and Last Times.* Phillipsburg, NJ: P&R, 2007.

Covers chapters 23–33 of the Westminster Confession of Faith; treats the civil magistrate, marriage and divorce, the church and communion of the saints, baptism and the Lord's Supper, church government, and the final judgment and afterlife. Also included are indexes to the three volumes.

Truths We Confess: A Systematic Exposition of the Westminster Confession of Faith. Revised ed. Orlando, FL: Reformation Trust, 2019.

A one-volume revision of the three-volume Truths We Confess: A Layman's Guide to the Westminster Confession of Faith, published 2006–2007.

Ultimate Issues. Phillipsburg, NJ: P&R, 2005.

Addresses the tough issues facing young adults. Previously published 1996 (Baker).

Unexpected Jesus, The. Revised edition. Fearn, Ross-shire, Scotland: Christian Focus, 2011.

An introductory-level explanation of what the Bible teaches concerning the person and work of Jesus Christ. Previously published

2005; previously published as *Mighty Christ: Touching Glory* (1995).

Unseen Realities: Heaven, Hell, Angels and Demons. Fearn, Ross-shire, Scotland: Christian Focus, 2011.

Biblical perspective on heaven, hell, angels, and demons and how all four realities impact everyday lives.

Walk with God, A: An Exposition of Luke. Fearn, Ross-shire, Scotland: Christian Focus, 1999.

Devotional studies of Christ based on the book of Luke.

What Is Reformed Theology? Grand Rapids, MI: Baker, 2005.

Shows that the theology of the Protestant Reformers of the sixteenth century is simply an accurate, systematic summary of the teachings of the Bible. Previously published 1997 as *Grace Unknown* (Baker).

What We Believe. Grand Rapids, MI: Baker, 2015.

Previously published as *The Symbol* (1973); as *Basic Training* (1982); and as *Renewing Your Mind* (1998).

What's in the Bible: The Story of God through Time and Eternity. With Robert Wolgemuth. Nashville, TN: Word, 2001.

Shows how the stirring stories of the Bible fit together into a cohesive narrative, helping the layperson to read through the entire Bible with greater satisfaction.

When Worlds Collide. Wheaton, IL: Crossway, 2002.

Addresses the presence of God in the midst of tragedy and explores how God has providentially worked in history concerning the issues of suffering, war, and peace.

Who Is Jesus? Orlando, FL: Reformation Trust, 2017.

Short examination of what the Bible teaches about the person of Jesus Christ. This new edition contains content excerpted from *Everyone's a Theologian*. Previously published 1983 (Tyndale); previously published 1991 as part of *Following Christ* (1991); previously published 2009 (Reformation Trust).

Willing to Believe: Understanding the Role of the Human Will in Salvation.
Grand Rapids, MI: Baker, 2018.

Argues for a return to the biblical doctrine of God's sovereignty over salvation, giving historical, biblical, and logical reasons for rejecting the "free will" position commonly held today. Previously published 1997 (Baker).

Work of Christ, The. Colorado Springs, CO: David C. Cook, 2018.

Explains the theological significance of the crucial events in Jesus's life and ministry from His birth and baptism to His ascension and second coming. Previously published 2012.

CRUCIAL QUESTIONS BOOKLET SERIES TITLES BY R. C. SPROUL

Are People Basically Good?

Are These the Last Days?

Can I Be Sure I'm Saved?

Can I Have Joy in My Life?

Can I Know God's Will?

Can I Lose My Salvation?

Can I Trust the Bible?

Does God Control Everything?

Does God Exist?

Does Prayer Change Things?

How Can I Be Blessed?

How Can I Be Right with God?

How Can I Develop a Christian Conscience?

How Does God's Law Apply to Me?

How Should I Live in This World?

How Should I Think about Money?

What Can I Do with My Guilt?
What Can We Know about God?
What Do Jesus' Parables Mean?
What Does It Mean to Be Born Again?
What Is Baptism?
What Is Faith?
What Is Predestination?
What Is Repentance?
What Is the Church?
What Is the Great Commission?
What Is the Lord's Supper?
What Is the Relationship between Church and State?
What Is the Trinity?
Who Is Jesus?
Who Is the Holy Spirit?
Why Should I Join a Church?

Appendix 5

LIGONIER NATIONAL CONFERENCE THEMES AND R. C. SPROUL LECTURE TITLES

Conference Date	Conference Title and Sproul Lectures
1988	Loving a Holy God
1989	Only Holy Passion
1994	The Christian and Society: War of Worlds "Who Is Our Commander?" "What Is Our Charge?"
1995	Defending the Faith in a Faithless World "A Reason to Believe" "A Reason for Being" "A Reason for Humility"
1996	The Sovereignty of God "Let There Be: God's Sovereignty over Nothing" "Unless the Father Draws: God's Sovereignty over the Soul"

Conference Date	Conference Title and Sproul Lectures
1997	Essential Truths of the Christian Faith "Infant Baptism" "The Covenant" "Soli Deo Gloria"
1998	Amazing Love "God Is Love" "Amazing Love"
1999	The End? Finding Hope in the Millennial Maze "The Intermediate State, Heaven, and Hell"
2000	Upsetting the World "Christ Crucified" "Upsetting the World" "The Heavenly Feast"
2001	Holiness "The Father as Prophet, Priest, and King" "A Holy Vision" "Worshiping a Holy God"
2002	War on the Word "A Bruised Reed" "This Means War!" "The Covenant"
2003	The Power and the Glory "The Glory of God" "The Glory of God through Man" "Beholding His Glory"
2004	A Portrait of God "Before the Beginning: The Aseity of God" "Yesterday, Today, and Tomorrow: The Immutability of God"
2005	5 Keys to Spiritual Growth "How to Study the Bible" "How to Be a Good Steward"
2006	Bought with a Price "Challenges to Intimate Marriage" "One, Holy, Catholic, and Apostolic Church" "The Church's Destiny"

Conference Date	Conference Title and Sproul Lectures
2007	Contending for the Truth "The Task for Apologetics" "The Resurrection of Christ"
2008	Evangelism according to Jesus "Sola Fide" "Counted Righteous in Christ"
2009	The Holiness of God "I Am the Lord, There Is No Other" "A Consuming Fire"
2010	Tough Questions Christians Face "What Is Evil and Where Did It Come From?" "Can We Enjoy Heaven Knowing of Loved Ones in Hell?"
2011	Light and Heat: A Passion for the Holiness of God "Defending the Faith" "Clothed in Righteousness"
2012	The Christian Mind "Have You Lost Your Mind?" "Love the Lord Your God with All Your Mind"
2013	No Compromise "The Articles on Which the Church Stands or Falls" "No Compromise, No Surrender"
2014	Overcoming the World "The End and Purpose of the World"
2015	After Darkness, Light "Holy, Holy, Holy"
2016	The Gospel "The Word Made Flesh: The Ligonier Statement on Christology" "The Transforming Power of the Gospel"
2017	The Next 500 Years (Unable to speak due to illness)

Appendix 6

REPRESENTATIVE TEACHING SERIES BY R. C. SPROUL

Title	Year
Holiness of God	1975
Titles of Jesus	1975
Understanding Ethics	1975
Themes from Ephesians	1978
Themes in Apologetics	1980
Doctrine of Sin	1980
Contemporary Theology	1980
Economics	1983
Developing Christian Character	1983
Themes from Genesis	1983
Themes from Romans	1985
Christian Worldview	1985
God We Worship	1985
Basic Training	1985
Silencing the Devil	1985

Title	Year
Making Tough Moral Decisions	1985
Classical Apologetics	1985
Chosen by God	1985
Themes from Hebrews	1986
Themes from James	1986
Holy Spirit	1986
Building a Christian Conscience	1986
Your Christ Is Too Small	1986
Choosing My Religion	1987
Objections Answered	1987
Holiness of God	1987
Questions Answered	1987
Great Men and Women of the Bible	1987
Born Again	1988
Surprised by Suffering	1988
Pleasing God	1989
Cross of Christ	1989
Shattered Image	1989
Intimate Marriage	1990
Authority of Scripture	1990
Majesty of Christ	1990
Hath God Said?	1990
Abortion	1990
Handout Apologetics	1990
Providence of God	1990
Blueprint for Thinking	1992
Battle for Our Minds	1992
Communion of Saints	1992
Ultimate Issues	1994
Face to Face with Jesus	1995
Classic Collection	1996

Title	Year
Creation or Chaos?	1996
What Is Reformed Theology?	1997
Dust to Glory	1997
Consequences of Ideas	1998
Last Days According to Jesus	1998
Dealing with Difficult Problems	1999
Willing to Believe	1999
Foundations: A Systematic Theology	1999
Prayer	1999
Psalm 51	2000
Fear and Trembling	2000
Just War	2001
Preachers and Preaching	2001
Kingdom Feast	2001
When Worlds Collide	2001
Defending Your Faith	2001
Loved by God	2001
Mystery of the Trinity	2002
God Alone	2002
The Cross and the Crescent	2002
Angels and Demons	2002
Knowing Christ: The I Am Sayings of Jesus	2002
Assurance of Salvation	2002
Promise Keeper	2003
Recovering the Beauty of the Arts	2003
What Did Jesus Do?: Understanding the Work of Christ	2010
Luther and the Reformation	2011
Moses and the Burning Bush	2011
Parables of Jesus	2012
Justified by Faith Alone	2015

Appendix 7

SELECTED SERMON SERIES TITLES PREACHED BY R. C. SPROUL AT SAINT ANDREW'S CHAPEL

Series Title	Number of Sermons
The Gospel of Mark	62
The Gospel of Matthew	129
The Book of Romans	59
1st & 2nd Peter	34
1st & 2nd Samuel	68
Gospel of John	57
The Book of Acts	63
Names of God	6
Philippians	?
Luke	113
Ephesians	19
Galatians	?
Hebrews 1:1–2:4	4

A NOTE ON THE SOURCES

ONE COULD ALMOST WRITE a biography of Dr. R. C. Sproul based on the personal stories he tells in his more than one hundred books. I have drawn from that material. Additionally, I had interview sessions with him devoted exclusively to the biography. These took place in his home in Sanford on the following dates in 2017: March 24, April 7, May 12, May 26, June 23, September 8, October 13, and October 20. I was also able to interview Dr. Sproul on books that influenced him for the *Open Book* podcast, which aired in 2018. They were all recorded in 2017 on the following dates: January 13 (three episodes), June 30 (three episodes), and October 13 (four episodes). I also interviewed Vesta Sproul for the biography on the following dates in 2018: May 1, September 5, September 19, and October 29. Vesta has graciously provided photographs, letters, and memorabilia. Additionally, I spent many moments with the Sprouls at Ligonier events, conferences, and tours, and shared with them many lunches and dinners. I have files full of conference programs, paper menus from banquets, napkins, a plethora of hotel notepads—all with scribbled notes of anecdotes R. C. shared and stories he told. These are cherished memories all.

I also drew from the early issues of *Tabletalk*, replete with details about the life and times of the people and the place of the Ligonier Valley Study Center. Having grown up 20 miles from the study center, I speak the language, even the dialect, of western Pennsylvania.

I had access to Dr. Sproul's personal library, retracing his steps through the sources that influenced him and (enjoying) reading his marginalia. I also had access to people who knew him for decades and knew him best. I had access to his personal notebooks from the 1960s and early 1970s. I endeavored to listen to not quite everything he ever said, but a lot of it. I also used material from the memoirs sessions Ligonier Ministries recorded, ten in all, from 2010 through 2015.

I am grateful to Vesta, Sherrie Sproul Dorotiak, Maureen Buchman, and Chris Larson for providing both information and their personal memories. One other source was R. C.'s longtime friend Archie Parrish. I interviewed Archie in his home in Atlanta on July 11, 2019. Archie joined his friend and the heavenly throng three months later. At the end of our time together, Archie, ever the prayer warrior, asked if he could pray for the book. I offer his prayer here for this book now that it is published and also for you, the reader and friend of R. C.:

Father,

Turning backward and reflecting over some of your magnificent deeds through your Servant R. C. Sproul is a bittersweet experience. It's sweet because of so many incredible things You allowed us to do together, and things You allowed me to watch him do. It's personally a little bitter, because he's not here. But I wouldn't have him come back from glory for anything.

You make it very clear to us that our minds can't begin to imagine what life in glory is all about. But we know that it is glorious; it's with You. And we know that is what he is experiencing right now. I pray that as Stephen works on this book, You'll guide his hand, his mind, every phrase, every word.

Use this book as a tool to inspire others to be daring, to move ahead, to trust You, to do things through them they cannot do on their own. We live in desperate times. We need a fresh outpouring of Your Holy Spirit and awakening. Use this as a tool for that, for Christ's sake.

Amen

Archie Parrish, July 11, 2019

GENERAL INDEX

SCRIPTURE INDEX